T0325323

SHOWDOWN IN DESIRE

SHOWDOWN IN DESIRE

the black panthers take a stand in new orleans

by Orissa Arend

The University of Arkansas Press
Fayetteville
2009

ISBN-10: 1-55728-896-8
ISBN-13: 978-1-55728-896-7

13   12   11   10   09   5   4   3   2   1

Designed by Liz Lester

☉ The paper used in this publication meets the minimum requirements of the American National Standard for Permanence of Paper for Printed Library Materials Z39.48-1984.

LIBRARY OF CONGRESS CATALOGING-IN-PUBLICATION DATA

Arend, Orissa.
    Showdown in Desire : The Black Panthers take a stand in New Orleans / by Orissa Arend.
        p.   cm.
    Includes bibliographical references and index.
    ISBN 978-1-55728-896-7 (cloth : alk. paper)
    1. African Americans—Civil rights—Louisiana—New Orleans—History—20th century. 2. African Americans—Crimes against—Louisiana—New Orleans—History—20th century. 3. African Americans—Louisiana—New Orleans—Social conditions—20th century. 4. Black Panther Party—History. 5. Violence—Louisiana—New Orleans—History—20th century. 6. Police-community relations—Louisiana—New Orleans—History—20th century. 7. Public housing—Louisiana—New Orleans—History—20th century. 8. New Orleans (La.)—Race relations—History—20th century. I. Title.
    F379.N59N42   2009
    323.1196'073'076335—dc22
                                            2008046794

This book is dedicated to the former
residents of Desire and the Black Panthers
who risked their lives for them.

CONTENTS

PART III:
PRISONERS AND THOSE WHO LOVE THEM

PART IV:
MAKING SENSE OF IT

CONTENTS

FOREWORD

Bayou Revolutionaries:
The Meaning of the New Orleans Black Panther Story

The Black Panther Party, cofounded by Huey P. Newton and Bobby Seale in October 1966, still remains one of the most indelible icons embodying both the promise and challenge of radical grassroots politics during the turbulent 1960s. During its relatively short sixteen-year existence (1966–82), the Black Panther Party (BPP) gained both national prominence and international stature. Its revolutionary bravado, community service, and uncompromising leadership of African Americans came to serve as a model for other oppressed groups who wished to engage in their own struggles for political empowerment, a model emulated not only by oppressed groups within the United States but also by their counterparts abroad. Indeed, the historian Clayborne Carson maintains that "more than any other group of the 1960s, the Black Panther Party inspired discontented urban African Americans to liberate themselves from oppressive conditions."[1]

Despite the significant role assigned to the Black Panther Party within domestic and international struggles for political empowerment, the party's legacy is arguably shrouded, still hotly contested and debated among scholars and political observers. Although many scholars might concede the BPP's preeminence within the realm of American radicalism, consensus regarding the party's specific legacy remains elusive.

So, it is with some irony that as we recently observed the fortieth anniversary of the founding of the Black Panther Party in 2006, we have come to witness a renaissance in an organization that has been both praised as a prototype for successful grassroots community organizing and maligned as the epitome of well-intentioned, but ultimately misguided, leftist guerilla politics gone amuck. The rebirth of interest in the Black Panther Party has manifested itself in an explosion of new publications. Interestingly enough, this rebirth is not relegated to the hallowed halls of academia but extends beyond, to include the works of former party members and others who were more intimately associated with the Black Panther Party in which they attempt to reflect on and to capture the meaning of their experiences.

Within academia, a sampling of the myriad scholarly books that have appeared on the Black Panther Party since 2002 include Judson L. Jeffries's *Huey P. Newton: The Radical Theorist;* Jeffery Ogbar's *Black Power: Radical Politics and African American Identity;* Curtis Austin's *Up Against the Wall: Violence in the Making and Unmaking of the Black Panthers;* and Andrew Witt's *The Black Panthers in the Midwest.*[2] These texts and other recent scholarly works on the Panthers have been critical in properly situating the Black Panther Party within the larger theoretical context of black politics and American radicalism. Equally important, however, are the research and recollections of party members and other activists who were more closely involved with the Black Panther Party.

A diverse array of recent biographies, memoirs, anthologies, and photographical accounts mark this genre of publications. A brief survey of these works includes Mumia Abu-Jamal's *We Want Freedom: A Life in the Black Panther Party;* Jasmine Guy's *Afeni Shakur: Evolution of a Revolutionary;* Evans D. Hopkins's *Life after Life: A Story of Rage and Redemption;* Florence Forbes's *Will You Die with Me? My Life and the Black Panther Party;* Elbert "Big Man" Howard's *Panther on the Prowl;* Stephen Shames's *The Black Panther Photographs;* and the edited collections *Black Panther: The Revolutionary Art of Emory Douglas,* edited by Sam Durant; *The Huey P. Newton Reader,* edited by David Hilliard and David Weise; and *Target Zero: A Life in Writing Eldridge Cleaver,* edited by Kathleen Cleaver.[3]

It is within this latter category that Orissa Arend's intriguing study of the New Orleans Black Panther Party belongs. Arend's *Showdown in Desire: The Black Panthers Take a Stand in New Orleans* is unique among the recent proliferation of Black Panther Party literature, providing a much needed in-depth case study of the dynamic of political repression and its impact on a southern BPP chapter.

Arend's study addresses at least one glaring bias in the existing literature on the Black Panther Party by focusing on a southern BPP chapter—highlighting an important yet understudied region within Panther scholarship. Undoubtedly, previous work on the Black Panther Party has been uneven in terms of the coverage given to chapters in the larger urban centers of the North, West, and Midwest, relative to Panther chapters in southern and smaller cities. For example, in *Bitter Grain: The Black Panther Story,* Michael Newton devotes a mere two pages to Panther activism in the Crescent City.[4] The Black Panther Party, while often perceived as a peculiarly urban and northern phenomenon, actually made extensive inroads in the southern battleground of the 1960s civil rights struggle. Louisiana was one of many southern states with Panther chapters. There were also chapters in Georgia (Atlanta); Kentucky (Louisville); Maryland (Baltimore); Mississippi (Cleveland); North Carolina (High Point and Winston-Salem); Tennessee (Chattanooga, Memphis, and Nashville); Texas (Dallas and Houston); and Virginia (Richmond).

Arend's study convincingly demonstrates the critical role of the BPP chapter in New Orleans grassroots organizing. By contrast, some existing studies of New Orleans politics have tended to underplay the Panthers' significance. For example, Adam Fairclough, in his seminal study of the black freedom struggle in Louisiana, *Race and Democracy: The Civil Rights Struggle in Louisiana, 1915–1972,* reduces the BPP presence in New Orleans to infantile leftism when he writes, "The Panthers thrived on violent contributions because such clashes provided martyrs, confirmed their revolutionary credentials, and proved that America was evolving into a fascist state."[5] Indeed, Fairclough's portrayal of the New Orleans BPP chapter suffers from an acute case of "Panther mythology"—a set of falsehoods and misperceptions that tend to minimize the historical significance of the party. Fortunately, Arend begins to challenge and debunk the "Panther mythology" through her impressive and well-documented research.

Arend's case study is further distinguished by her evidence, particularly her unprecedented access to firsthand accounts of those who operated within the local levels of repression in New Orleans. Arend makes extensive use of oral histories to excavate the story of the New Orleans Black Panther Party from the footnotes of African American and Southern history. Her study is anchored by a litany of impressive interviews of the key participants involved in the confrontations between the Panthers and New Orleans city officials. Her interviews with both the leaders and rank-and-file members of the New Orleans BPP give voice not only to former New Orleans Panthers but to community activists as well, all of who share their recollections, reflections, and introspections on their efforts to organize in a Deep South city. Yet it is Arend's extraordinary access to prominent officials and law enforcement authorities that differentiates her research from other case studies on the BPP. Arend's study, heretofore, is one of the few recent works on the BPP that uses primary interviews with key public officials, such as the mayor and the police chief, who were critical decision makers in Panther-police confrontations.

Moreover, Arend's research is noteworthy in that it contains the testimonies of police officers who infiltrated and posed as members of the New Orleans Black Panther Party. While a few accounts of party members who turned out to be police and/or FBI informants exist, the memoirs and interviews of police agent provocateurs have been relatively absent in the Black Panther Party literature. One early exception is the memoirs of Earl Anthony, an early national captain of the BPP turned informant, who details his fascinating personal BPP odyssey in *Picking up the Gun,* one of the first books published on the Black Panther Party, in 1970. [6] A second example can be found in the work of the late Henry Hampton, producer of the award-winning documentary *Eyes on the Prize,* who shares a compelling interview with William O'Neal, the chief of security of the Chicago BPP chapter, who also served as a FBI informant. O'Neal gives a haunting account of his role in perhaps the most egregious act of repression lodged against the BPP: the December 4, 1969, Chicago police raid of a party office that led to the deaths of Mark Clark and Fred Hampton, and the wounding of several other Chicago panthers.

Given the heavy infiltration of the Black Panther Party by the police and FBI agents, it is important to gain access to credible data in order to document as accurately and as systematically as possible the full panoply of political repression. Arend achieves this, for example, with her insightful and extensive interviews with Larry Preston Williams and Israel Fields, two black undercover New Orleans Police

Department officers who infiltrated the New Orleans chapter, and provides a chilling, up-close account of the dynamic of local repression. She skillfully integrates archival materials, participants' memoirs, and secondary sources with numerous interviews to reconstruct a compelling narrative of the New Orleans Black Panther Party. While Arend specifically focuses on the distinctive culture of the "Big Easy," in many respects her narrative of Panther activism in New Orleans serves as a microcosm of BPP dynamics nationwide, providing a detailed glimpse of some of the successes and challenges facing other Panther chapters. In closing, Arend offers an intriguing approach to the Panther Party, one that will undoubtedly serve as a model to influence scholars and other activists interested in gaining a fuller understanding of the dynamic of political repression and its impact on the Black Panther Party.

CHARLES E. JONES PhD
Editor, *Black Panther Party Reconsidered*
Georgia State University

INTRODUCTION

New Orleans, Louisiana: the Crescent City; birthplace of jazz, gumbo, and the French Quarter; home to one of the most notoriously brutal and racist police departments in the United States; and home of one the largest chapters of the Black Panther Party (BPP). By the time BPP leadership authorized the opening of a National Committee to Combat Fascism office in this river city, the BPP had spread from Oakland, California, all the way to the East Coast, where it had chapters from Hartford, Connecticut, and New York City down through Philadelphia, Washington D.C., Baltimore, and Winston-Salem, North Carolina. Its growth spurt coincided with the operation of free breakfast programs, free health clinics, free busing to prison programs, sickle-cell anemia testing centers, and a plethora of voter registration programs. Along with this growth came a local, national, and federal response that was ruthless in its efforts to discredit and destroy the organization. The group in New Orleans, like most chapters, took a valiant stance against this repression and wrote yet another chapter in the long, bloody struggle for black liberation.

By the time Huey Newton and Bobby Seale appeared on the stage of history in October of 1966, black Americans and their allies had dismantled the legalities of segregation, secured a constitutional right to vote, and demonstrated their willingness to fight oppression beyond the confines of nonviolence. The urban rebellions in Los Angeles, Detroit, Harlem, Chicago, and a host of other cities helped to usher in a new wave of consciousness among those unwilling to allow the status quo to remain constant. This new wave of under-standing manifested itself in the nationwide movement popularly called Black Power. Not quite as significant a departure from the civil rights movement as many historians have been apt to conclude, this newly named movement simply elevated blacks' willingness to see themselves as one group and to demand their freedom and dignity by any means necessary. When the Panthers emerged as one of the many Bay Area groups vying for leadership in this phase of the black struggle, they helped to begin a process that changed the tenor of race relations in the United States forever.

Insisting that blacks, like whites and others, deserved to be treated with dignity and accorded all their rights, the Panthers set out to make this demand a reality. Having concluded that black communities in cities and towns across the nation were colonial outposts kept in check by occupying police forces, the Panthers picked up arms to expel these agents of their oppression. This bold move led them down a revolutionary road of change that would leave many of them incarcerated, dead, or too demoralized to continue their fight. Before it became clear that this move might not have been the best and only alternative to their dilemma, the BPP was able to create cadres of willing soldiers from coast to coast who believed it was their duty to bring about complete liberation of blacks and other poor people. In the process, this small but significant group raised the ire of a determined federal government and found out the hard way that revolution in a nation of laws was illegal. The subsequent trials, killings, shootouts, and standoffs became central features in the lore of the group, leaving its community service programs to be portrayed as almost a footnote to its short but storied lifetime. Despite the fact that the BPP helped change many social policies in America by creating programs that addressed the needs of the people, these outbursts of violence have been what made headlines and evening news shows, and therefore, this aspect of the party is what most people think of when they hear of or read about the organization.

This book is an excellent start in the process of making sense of the group's complicated career and tragic demise. The New Orleans chapter epitomized all that was good about the Black Panthers and all that was wrong about black life in urban America. The intransigence of racism in this southern city, as in all the locales where the party established chapters, made the BPP necessary, and a select group of courageous would-be revolutionaries stepped on the scene to play their parts in a drama that continues to unfold even in the twenty-first century.

Like its forebears on the West Coast, the BPP affiliate in New Orleans faced immediate opposition after it formed. Doing needful things like stopping the violence in tough areas like the Desire and Magnolia housing projects, protecting the elderly from attackers, preventing home break-ins, and feeding the hungry made this organization a clear threat to established authority. Despite knowing it would be more than just an uphill battle against the forces of the status quo, newly minted BPP members like Malik Rahim, his wife Barbara, and Althea Francois took up the mantle of the struggle Malcolm X had fought so hard to advance and carried it to what they believed was the next level. Forced to act by an unforgiving economy, the threat of an entire life of poverty, an inability to find meaningful employment, and a host of other factors that spelled social disaster, people like these put their lives on the line to ensure a bright future for their children and the children of millions of others who were at risk of being used and forgotten by the captains of industry and the majority of middle-class America.

This set of circumstances led to strained relations between the BPP and those it saw as the perpetrators of the wrongs it had delineated in its Ten Point Platform and Program, which called for land, bread, peace, justice, fair trials, and an end to police brutality and murder of blacks, among other things. These strained relations manifested themselves in a violent exchange that left many Panthers dead or seriously wounded and others serving long prison sentences. Eventually, a concerted campaign to annihilate the organization crept into the federal government's planned response to the party. While this annihilation took years to accomplish, in the short run, it wreaked havoc on party members and those who were kin to and cared about them.

Under its revamped counterintelligence plan to handle extremists and those who favored a more just and favorable America, the FBI used a program called COINTELPRO to discredit and dismantle the party. When character assassination and the threat of violent reprisal failed to prevent the Panthers from carrying out their long-awaited revolution, the government, with the help of local and state police officials and organizations, opted for sterner stuff. In acts that resembled the violence in the jungles of Vietnam half a world away, police agencies attacked, arrested, imprisoned, shot, and tortured those it deemed responsible for enemy activity.

Having killed members of the group in Los Angeles and Oakland before the organization turned two years old, the feds proved to be fast learners and found ingenious ways to cause chaos, confusion, and catastrophe in the party. Infiltrating informants, spies, and agent provocateurs into the organization, local, state, and federal agencies succeeded in their efforts to divert the party's attention away from organizing and serving the needs of the people, to defending themselves in court and avoiding arrest for spurious charges. Two particularly egregious examples will serve to illuminate this activity and its results.

The party in Chicago, like its counterpart in Los Angeles, was particularly keen on succeeding in representing the needs and desires of the people. Its spokesperson in the Windy City, Fred Hampton, was exceedingly eloquent in describing the organization's reason for being, its programs, and the reasons why all oppressed people should join it in its fight against what it called fascist America. Hampton, who helped to organize breakfast programs and liberation schools, and who distributed the party's paper, the *Black Panther Newspaper,* widely, almost immediately became a target for neutralization. Following his movements and arresting him at seemingly every turn, the Chicago Police Department and the Illinois State's Attorney's office turned up the heat on the organization and determined to make it pay for its temerity in challenging the status quo. When these tactics failed to silence the young warrior, a plan came about that made Hampton a target for outright murder. Subsequently, William O'Neal, the party's chief of security and Hampton's personal body guard, a black man, made good on his promise to help federal agents silence the organization.

He made sure that Hampton's attempts to politicize and solidify Chicago's many youth gangs did not come to fruition by starting quarrels, rumors, and in some cases, shootouts. He then provided his handlers with a list of individuals who stayed in the house with Hampton, the number and types of weapons stored in the edifice, and a detailed floor plan of where the Panther chairman and others slept. Because there had been a series of shootouts between the Panthers and the police in this midwest city that resulted in the deaths of two police officers, three Panthers, and a number of wounded on both sides, the police used these clashes as justification to get rid of the Panther leader once and for all.

At the appointed time, on December 4, 1969, a contingent of local, state, and federal police officials approached Hampton's West Side apartment and prepared to raid the place. By 4:00 a.m., they were in place and ready to attack. Bursting through the front and back doors at the same time and shooting as they entered, the fourteen raiders sprayed automatic and semiautomatic gunfire throughout the entire apartment. One Panther, Mark Clark, the defense captain of the Peoria chapter, was killed instantly when the raiding officers burst through the front door. The shotgun he held discharged after he was fatally wounded, and that explosion wound up being the only shot the Panthers fired. In less than ten minutes, the raid ended, and a half dozen Panthers were suffering from bullet wounds. The main quarry, Fred Hampton, lay dead, bleeding in a pool of blood that streamed from his arms and the two gunshot wounds that came as a result of one officer firing his .45 automatic from pistol point-blank range into the back of his head. The other Panthers, whether or not they were wounded, were then beaten by the police officers, dragged into Chicago's icy streets, and arrested for assault and attempted murder. Hampton's fiancée, Deborah Johnson, now known as Akua Njeri, was eight and a half months pregnant with Hampton's son, Fred Hampton Jr. She too was among those manhandled and arrested. These killings eventually led to the demise of the Illinois chapter of the party. Although there was a resurgence of Panther activity in the Windy City in the mid-1970s, the party never again enjoyed the popularity and success it had seen under the austere leadership of Hampton.

Less than a week after this not-so-veiled assassination, the authorities turned their attention to sunny Los Angeles, where the party had been leading the fight for black freedom since early in 1967. Led by defense minister Alprentice "Bunchy" Carter and chairman John Huggins, the BPP in L.A. had developed a penchant for tough talk and then for supporting this verbiage with actions. Like in Chicago, the L.A. police and Panthers had gun clashes on numerous occasions, and nearly a half dozen local Panthers had been killed by the police by the end of 1969. This time, however, police officials were able to use members from a rival organization to do their bidding. US, a cultural nationalist organization run by the New Jersey–born Ron Karenga, had been in a running feud with the BPP over the appointment of a director for a newly established black studies program at UCLA. Each group supported a different candidate.

On December 8, 1969, they met on the campus at Campbell Hall, where the Black Student Union (BSU) would be housed, to debate and discuss the merits of each group's choice.

After a heated argument, the meeting broke up with no decision having been made on who would hold the well-paying academic position. Unfortunately, an argument between US members and Panthers ensued, and the end result was one US member with a shoulder wound and Bunchy Carter and John Huggins dead of multiple gunshot wounds. The US members somehow managed to get away and to avoid apprehension. The shooters eventually turned themselves in, were tried and sentenced, and eventually escaped from prison. Again, the party in Los Angeles, having lost two of its most valuable leaders, headed toward an era of decline and eventually hit rock bottom because of further police repression. This further repression included a four-hour gun battle that started after the police tried to force their way into Panther headquarters and were met with gunfire. Elmer "Geronimo" Pratt, who was born in Morgan City, Louisiana, and who subsequently took the places of John Huggins and Bunchy Carter, was instrumental in outfitting the L.A. headquarters with steel-plated roofing that withstood several dynamite charges the LAPD dropped from helicopters, sand-bagging the office to protect it from gunfire and tear gas, and training local Panthers in the art of self-defense and counterattack. Because of his contributions to the struggle and because of his abilities, the federal government's COINTELPRO program finally made Pratt a prime target, and through manipulation of evidence, the creation of division within the party's infrastructure, and a relentless pursuit of his comrades in arms, succeeded in taking the Vietnam vet off the streets of Los Angeles.

Framed for killing a Santa Monica teacher and wounding her husband, Pratt, who had actually been at a party central committee meeting in Oakland at the time of this dastardly crime, was sentenced to life imprisonment by a local court. Like many other Panthers held as political prisoners in jails throughout the United States, Pratt spent some twenty-seven years behind bars. The attorney Johnnie Cochran succeeded in proving that the Panther had been framed by a government conspiracy to destroy the legitimately constituted party. Before all this happened, however, Pratt was instrumental in setting up chapters, fortifying offices, and training Panthers across the country in guerrilla tactics and political organizing. One of the places where his mark was indelibly made was in the city of New Orleans, not far from where he had been raised in the bayous of Morgan City.

It was Pratt's idea to send operatives from Los Angeles, New York City, and Connecticut to the Crescent City to establish a chapter. Because he knew the city and the people of the Pelican State quite well, Pratt was successful in directing individuals to this Deep South city with little notice from the authorities. By the time the group had firmly established itself in the black community of New Orleans, it would take more than a notion to get rid of it.

Gaining notoriety seemingly overnight, the Panther chapter in New Orleans, operating under the guise of the National Committee to Combat Fascism, signed up forty to sixty members in its first year of operation. While most of these were high school and college students, their cohorts of the same age were not in school. A good number of them hailed from the working class, and a significant minority had served in the armed forces, some of them having been in Vietnam and Korea. This mix of young and old, male and female, professional and layman, laid the groundwork for an organization that was effective in changing the nature of the people's relationship with the power structure.

Their success of course meant trouble for the mostly young revolutionaries. As soon as the opportunity presented itself, police officials infiltrated two spies into the Panther organization. As had the spies in other locales, these individuals passed along information that they hoped would prove useful in getting rid of the Panthers. Because the New Orleans group had watched with apprehension as others around the country were rounded up, jailed, and murdered, it made preparations to defend itself against the same type of onslaught. With these thoughts in mind, it ensconced itself deep in the black community, where poverty was real and police brutality existed as part of the normal order of things. The Panthers' presence, however, meant that the time for change had come.

Rallying around the party like bees to honey, many New Orleans residents immediately saw the usefulness of an organization that had as one of its goals the feeding of children and the protection of the elderly. They also welcomed this courageous group of men and women who seemed not to be afraid of the hard-core policemen who had previously used brutality to keep residents in their prescribed social "place." Once they discovered that identifying with the mother continent of Africa and learning the history of black people in America was part of the group's method of serving the community, many residents saw little reason to hesitate to join and/or to support the party.

The bayou Panthers needed all the support they could muster, because by the time they had made their presence known, there was a police plan in place to rid this increasingly black city of the Panther "menace." The supporters the Panthers had eventually numbered in the thousands. As had happened in other areas of the country, the New Orleans Panthers had solicited and received the support of very wealthy and influential whites. Not only did groups like the Students for a Democratic Society and the mostly white Peace and Freedom Party support the BPP, but individuals like Marlon Brando and the famous composer Leonard Bernstein gave millions and raised thousands for the Panther cause as well. In New Orleans it would be the Tulane Liberation Front (that school's version of SDS) and personalities like Jane Fonda that came to the group's aid. Most important, however, the residents in and surrounding the Desire Housing Project were crucial to the Panthers' survival.

Placing themselves between Panther headquarters and a contingent of federal, local, and state police numbering into the hundreds, these residents demonstrated to the power structure that the Panthers' demands were their demands. At one point preventing the authorities' use of an improvised tank designed to batter and to blow the Panthers from their dwelling, these individuals succeeded in showing the Panthers that their dedication, love, and sacrifice had not been in vain. Despite this show of solidarity, however, the authorities stopped at nothing to rid the city of these so-called revolutionaries bent on securing the peoples' human rights.

The New Orleans chapter of the Panther story, therefore, reads very much like that of the chapters in other large American cities. The biggest difference, however, is that the New Orleans Panthers, for the most part, have lived to tell their own stories—and their one-time adversaries, with 20/20 hindsight, have reached out to explain their version of what transpired. Even though more than a dozen New Orleans Panthers spent time in jail in the aftermath of a serious shootout that left no one dead but dozens of community members arrested, they were all acquitted of the charges and came home to continue organizing.

This book is a welcome addition to the slowly burgeoning collection of studies being written on the Black Panther Party. Unlike many of them, however, it traces the history of the Crescent City Panthers through the words of those on both sides of the issue. It shows not only how the party was seen through the eyes of its members but also provides a glimpse into the mindset and thinking of the authorities charged with containing, controlling, and ultimately destroying the organization. Through Arend's adept use of interviews with key figures in the mayor's office, the police department, and high- and low-ranking members of the party, a wonderful picture of chaos, change, growth, disappointment, and triumph emerges as it concerns the brief lifespan of one of the most effective and well-known organizations of the Black Power movement. The powerful testimonies, coupled with primary documents like newspapers and city records, give this study a unique place in the pantheon of Panther scholarship. It demonstrates that due diligence and patience can yield amazingly positive results in researching an organization whose members have been basically silent for nearly forty years.

Indeed, Arend's work is the first of its kind that has led to a process where healing and reconciliation became the goal of both sides. As city officials and former Panthers looked back on their city's history, they came together and, with the clarity of hindsight, began to try to understand each other's motivations. These efforts culminated in a public forum where grievances were aired, unknown stories were told, and forgiveness was freely offered from both the antagonists and protagonists of a story that has still yet to be fully told. This story is even more valuable because it shows that people, with all their various hang-ups and shortcomings, are essentially good and interested in the welfare of their fellow men. Despite the racism and violence that ran rampant through this Gulf Coast enclave, each side came to see that their lives were so intertwined that only by working together could they hope to make the dramatic changes that activists so vehemently demanded during the tumultuous 1960s and early 1970s.

The year 2006 marked forty years since the BPP opened an office in a North Oakland storefront. They celebrated this landmark event by putting on photo exhibits, hosting forums, and reminding people of the many contributions the BPP made to the civil rights struggle and to America in general. These events culminated in October 2006 with a conference and grand reunion that featured Panthers (and their children) from all over the country and throughout the world, who put on workshops in an attempt to make sense of their powerful legacy.

The New Orleans legacy mirrors the Black Panther legacy in other areas of the country. Their liberation schools, free health services, free breakfast programs, and political education classes have been picked up by local, state, and federal government agencies, and their unceasing demand for freedom and justice for all has been picked up by younger activists seeking to finish the work of their forebears. When Hurricane Katrina devastated the lives, hopes, and dreams of hundreds of thousands of New Orleans's residents, former Panthers and their allies once again showed that their trial by fire during the 1960s had instilled in them the desire to lend aid and comfort to any and all people willing to accept it. Former Panther Malik Rahim's multiracial Common Ground Collective has led the way in showing New Orleans and the rest of the world that all power truly rests in the hands of the people—if only the people would demonstrate the inclination to access and exercise it. Having set up shelters, clinics, food programs, and counseling services in this hurricane-ravaged city, this interracial group of warriors is intent on defeating the multifaceted threat of racism, poverty, government neglect, and discrimination against the most vulnerable section of America's minorities. Arend's study is an excellent start for those seeking the deep roots of community activism, antiracism, and a commitment to freedom by any means necessary on the part of those individuals who came of age and matured in a city and an era that to this day has yet to be adequately explained.

CURTIS J. AUSTIN
Author, *Up Against the Wall: Violence in the Making and Unmaking of the Black Panther Party*

PREFACE

How I Got Hooked on Desire

Two days before Thanksgiving in 2002, I was shopping for dessert for the family meal. Instead of the crowded isles of my favorite uptown family-owned grocery store, I was in the home of Robert King Wilkerson (most people call him King) buying Freelines, a praline-like confection that King learned to cook and trade during his almost three-decades-long residence in solitary confinement at Louisiana's Angola State Penitentiary. I was looking for dessert, but I got a lot more than I came for.

Many consider King to have been a political prisoner in one of the nation's most notoriously brutal institutions. "When I left Angola I said I was free of Angola," King told me, gesturing toward the Freelines, "but Angola will never be free of me. I would be a thorn in its side."[1]

King was in his sixties when I met him—solidly muscular, scarred and tattooed, clear-eyed, miraculously open, even innocent. After all those years of being locked up, he turned to making and selling Freelines on the outside, because it was hard to make a living organizing for the rights of prisoners. For him, making Freelines was an act of gratitude for his freedom, sweet like the candy. He also made them to call attention to the plight of his comrades who are still locked up.

King and his two closest prison comrades, Albert Woodfox and Herman Wallace, were incarcerated in the late 1960s for various crimes. In 1970 they were recaptured after a jailbreak and sent to Orleans Parish Prison where they encountered the New Orleans Black Panthers and adopted the Panther Ten Point Program as a way of life.[2]

Woodfox, Wallace, and Wilkerson (King) received lengthy prison sentences and were sent to Angola, where they organized one of the first Black Panther chapters behind bars. Soon after their arrival, they were labeled as troublemakers and placed in solitary confinement. All three were accused of prison murders in the early 1970s. Woodfox and Wallace remain incarcerated as of this writing.

By the 1990s the three had become an international cause célèbre known as the Angola Three. They all credited the Panther principles as the foundation upon which their lives and sanity have remained intact.

Around the time of King's release in 2001, I read about him in the *Times-Picayune,* New Orleans' daily newspaper. A picture covering most of the page showed a man with a round face and broad nose, penetrating eyes, and a slightly bemused half-smile. He was wearing a fedora rimmed in fabric printed with something that looked like license plates. Behind him was a "Free the Angola Three Now" poster picturing a black panther lunging head-on. A picture of Black Panther cofounder Huey Newton seated in a fan-backed rattan chair and holding a rifle hung next to it. King leaned on the mantle of a brick fireplace displaying African fabric and works of art.[3]

At first glance, the article seemed to be one of those "interesting kitchens in New Orleans" pieces. After having perfected the recipe during his long stint in solitary, cooking with smuggled ingredients and using cold-drink cans and toilet paper for a stove, on the outside, King began making Freelines in his tastefully decorated home, the article told me. But the subtext of the article, I discovered as I read further, was revolution. I stopped at every coffee shop on my rounds that day to collect extra copies of the paper so I could point out these distinctly New Orleans ironies to my friends.

A year or so later, a mutual friend offered to introduce me to King and asked if I could interview him about the Freelines for my general opinion column in the *Louisiana Weekly*. King graciously consented. I became a regular customer for his Freelines, and we became friends. When I stopped by his place on that day approaching Thanksgiving 2002, I finally had the chance to meet his partner, Marion Brown. While King bagged the candy, Marion reminisced about her introduction in 1970 to the Black Panther Party when she was nineteen and a freshman at Tulane University. I had heard that King was a Panther, but before meeting Marion, I hadn't given the Black Panthers more than a passing thought.

Marion told me that what appealed to her about the party was that "Panthers talked about standing up for yourself in defense of the community, not aggression, but asserting your manhood or womanhood and acting out of pride instead of just being beaten down."[4] As she spoke, I realized I had my tape recorder with me, even though I had only come for candy. I was so struck by the power of her words that I risked rudeness and asked if I could record her story. So began this book—with the purchase of a confection born of captivity called Freelines and the unexpected musings of a new acquaintance whose life was shaped by her involvement with the Black Panther Party.

Within a week, King and Marion arranged a conversation between the three of us and another former Panther, Malik Rahim. Several of their Panther friends initially agreed to be interviewed and then changed their minds. The Panther saga has been so sensationalized, and otherwise distorted, that it is no wonder so many distrust the media, especially when it is represented by a white woman like me, with no personal connection to the story.

I used the interviews as a basis for my regular column in the *Louisiana Weekly,* a black-owned paper established in New Orleans in 1925. The appearance of the interviews in the *Weekly* seemed to trigger a rapid series of serendipitous events. After only a few columns had run, I met Moon Landrieu by chance while both of us were campaigning on behalf of his daughter Mary Landrieu in a U. S. Senate race. Maurice "Moon" Landrieu had been mayor of New Orleans in 1970 when the Panthers came to town. I introduced myself and asked if I could interview him about the Panthers. He invited me to his house, which was the same house in the same working-class neighborhood where he, his wife, and their nine children had lived in 1970 when Mary was a child.

About this time, my next-door neighbor William Barnwell, who had moved back to New Orleans after a few years in Boston, asked me to read his memoirs. The manuscript began with a firsthand description of the Black Panther–police showdown in the Desire Housing Project in New Orleans. Upon reading it, I realized that I knew two of the priests who had mediated between the Panthers and the city administration in an urgent attempt to avoid bloodshed. Barnwell was one: Father Jerome LeDoux was the other. I attend his church, St. Augustine Catholic Church, in Tremé.

Eager to find more who remembered those days, I looked in the phone book and made a cold call to the former police chief Clarence Giarrusso. I had been told he was in his eighties and in poor health, so I didn't expect to get an interview. But after I spoke to him and his wife several times on the phone, he also invited me to his house so we could talk face to face.

After the eighth Panther column appeared in the *Weekly,* I got an e-mail from Bob Tucker, who told me that he had been Mayor Landrieu's young black special assistant in 1970 and offered to provide me with several little-known aspects of the Panther story. He set up interviews with Cecil Carter, Henry Faggen, Charles Elloie, and Don Hubbard, all of whom were integral to the story.

Though I tried repeatedly to get their parts of the story, I wrote the first draft of this manuscript with no firsthand knowledge of the rank-and-file police point of view. Undercover cops Melvin Howard and Israel Fields seemed not to want to talk to me. But in 2005 the filmmaker Royce Osborn introduced me to Larry Preston Williams, an African American who, at the age of twenty-two, had worked in the NOPD Intelligence Unit when the Panthers arrived in New Orleans. It was his job to find ways to infiltrate the Black Panther Party, the Republic of New Africa, the Ku Klux Klan, and the American Nazi Party. Williams agreed to an interview and convinced Fields to speak to me in some detail.

I could hardly ignore these and the other fortuitous circumstances that propelled me into the telling of this story, although I am keenly aware of the irony of having the Panther story entrusted to me. I am a contemporary of the Panthers, but I'm white; I've led a privileged and sheltered life. I'm a pacifist who has been inundated with the violent stereotypes attributed to the Panthers.

In 1970, I was twenty-four, living in New Orleans, newly married, teaching school, dealing with the loss of an eye, and afraid of dying from the melanoma that had taken it. In fact, I was blind to much of what occurred beyond my limited world. I was completely unaware of the Panthers and of the drama that was unfolding all around me.

I have preserved the story of the Piety Street shootout, the subsequent negotiations between the Panthers and church leaders and city officials, and the standoff in Desire in the exact words of key participants for several reasons. First, these participants, to a person, are great storytellers. As I recorded their stories, I felt transported to that other place and time, and I hope to share that experience with my readers. I was amazed at the detail and vividness of these accounts, which stood as witness not just to narrative abilities but also to the depth of the impressions left on these historical actors by their participation in the events.

A second reason for leaving these oral histories intact is that the nuances of how they are told, what is remembered, and what associations each storyteller brings to each event preserve an historical truth that I fear would be lost through analysis or summary. Moreover, the stories together, each so different in rendition, form a complete whole. They complement rather than contradict each other. That is something I didn't expect from Malik Rahim, the Panther; Larry Preston Williams, the black policeman; Moon Landrieu, the mayor; Henry Faggen, the Desire resident; Robert Glass, the white lawyer; Jerome LeDoux, the black priest; and William Barnwell, the white priest.

My third reason for presenting what I hope is a faithful rendition of memories is the way the stories came to me, almost unsought. I did not go looking for them. I'm not a historian. They came to me serendipitously through a series of seemingly chance encounters and relationships, both old and new, as I went about my ordinary business of work and play in New Orleans—writing my newspaper column, making groceries (as we say here), going to church, campaigning. Because of the help I received in gathering and writing these stories, both human and, to my way of thinking, divine, I see them less as research notes than as a sacred trust handed to me so that I might pass them on. Therefore, I have steadfastly refused to abbreviate, censor, or interpret what strikes me as the kernel of the spoken narratives. In so doing, I acknowledge that I am asking a lot of the reader: to share the experience with me and to form his or her own conclusions.

I am confident that this will happen because a Panther booklet that

I hastily put together containing some of the oral histories has been reprinted (4,000 copies to date), pirated and sold, and used as a text book at two colleges in the Midwest. It has mysteriously appeared for sale in an upscale New York men's boutique, grabbed the attention of Panther scholars, and been made into a docudrama and performed publicly in New Orleans. It inspired high school students to make video shorts. An AmeriCorps mediator whom I was supervising even tattooed a part of the cover onto the back of his neck.

I can only assume that what generated such enthusiasm were the exact words of the participants and not my very much removed telling of a story that happened almost four decades ago. So I ask my reader to carefully attend to the telling of this story in its myriad forms so that its meaning may emerge and provide insights about how to deal with persistent racial challenges going forward.

The conditions the Panthers struggled against have not improved in thirty-eight years; they have gotten worse, many former Panthers believe. Hurricane Katrina ripped the pretense off of an ongoing systemic war waged against poor people, most of whom in New Orleans are black. It put that war on fast-forward, providing all manner of "justifications" for eliminating most of public housing, privatizing much of education, and leaving those with limited means few options for health care. Drug wars and attendant murders were quick to return after the storm, while the police, the mayor, the district attorney, and the judges all blamed each other for incompetence. Malik Rahim noted before the storm that the escalating violence in the black community is prophetic as well as genocidal: "African Americans are like a canary in a coal miner's cave. They predict our fate. They are a sign of things to come."[5]

The Panthers' struggle was aborted both here and elsewhere in the mid 1970s. Referring to the Black Panther Party, Robert King Wilkerson told me, "If this revolutionary baby would have been given a chance to gestate, I think that it would have initiated change, so we wouldn't be feeling what we're feeling now."

This book is partly an exploration of that thesis. I love New Orleans. I have told this story so that readers can relive and reexamine the tensions and possibilities that were so dramatically collapsed into a three-month period on Piety Street and in the Desire Housing Project.

The story that I have cobbled together came to me thirty-three years after the events had occurred. In most places, unrecorded history gets hazy or differently remembered. People move away. But in New Orleans, for my informants, the Panther story remained vivid. More than once, the same conversation was repeated to me word for word by different people. An amazing number of the original participants are still here or have come back.

In New Orleans the past is never really behind us. It permeates the present in mysterious ways. My hope is that the lessons from this powerful story, which, oddly, has never been told, will rise to instruct us. This is not the whole story. Indeed, several of my sources have stressed that they carry secrets about these events that they will take with them to their graves.

But it is my hope that the people in the story, all these years wiser and as determined as ever, will step forward to show us the way to the solution of some of our current problems.

PART I
Bullets and Breakfast on Piety Street

1 Desire and the Panthers

When Donald Guyton crawled on his belly through the Piety Street house beneath the tear gas and bullet holes, he didn't foresee the mild September evening thirty-three years hence when he would again come face to face with the people responsible for those bullets and that tear gas. Guyton, who was in charge of security for the fledgling Black Panther chapter in New Orleans in 1970, was trying to assess the carnage. The shooting had stopped, and his fellow Panther Charles Scott had instructed Guyton to go room to room and shout back who was injured and who was dead. Guyton dreaded what he might find in the next room. But he had come back from Vietnam skilled as a warrior. He was totally focused on his assignment.

The shootout on Piety Street between the Black Panthers and the New Orleans police was actually a thirty-minute war. It occurred on September 15, 1970, the seventh anniversary of the bombing of the Sixteenth Street Church in Birmingham that killed four little black girls. There was a growing feeling among young black men and women that the dominant strain of pacifism in the civil rights movement was not an effective strategy against the terrorism of white supremacy. The Panthers offered Guyton, and many like him, a real alternative.

Years later, Guyton would become a Muslim and change his name to Malik Rahim. From his perspective in 2003, he would be able to connect Birmingham, Piety, Vietnam, and many other events and ponder an overarching explanation for them all. But on that September day in 1970, all he could do was defend, count, and report. His mind didn't

3

wander from the immediate task, And yet, even on his belly, as he wiped the sweat from his brow with a gritty forearm, he sensed the presence of four little guardian angels, the children murdered that day seven years ago in Birmingham.

The tensions leading to the shootout on Piety Street had been building for months. During the summer before it happened, Donald and his wife Barbara went to their friend Puchimo's house every day for Panther meetings. Those were the early days of the party in New Orleans, and Puchimo's house was one of the gathering places. Donald, the oldest of the prospective Panthers, was only twenty-two. Even though he had been halfway around the world, his encounter with the Panthers in his hometown awakened him to new ideas and new possibilities. Thirty-three years later he would reflect, "It was the first time I ever talked to a brother who had no fear,"[1]

That brother was nineteen-year-old Steve Green, the founder of the Louisiana chapter of the Black Panther Party, who had come to New Orleans in May from Compton, California. When Donald and Barbara wanted to join the party, Steve had tried to discourage them. They had two children, and Panthers had to be ready on a daily basis to put their lives on the line for their principles. "Too dangerous," Steve had told them.

But Donald and Barbara prevailed, and by the fall of 1970 they were members of the National Committee to Combat Fascism (NCCF), an organizing bureau for the Black Panther Party. Headquartered on Piety Street, the Panthers were just outside of the largest, poorest housing development in New Orleans.

The twenty-three-million-dollar project had opened to tenants on May 21, 1956, with 388 four-bedroom apartments and 968 three-bedroom apartments. It was built for large, poor black families. The project, located on the outskirts of New Orleans in a cypress swamp and dumping ground, was named Desire. The *Times-Picayune,* one of New Orleans' daily newspapers, would later call it a "disaster from its inception . . . a mind-numbing series of careless decisions that amounted to a blueprint for disaster."[2] It wasn't designed for people to live in; it was designed, rather, to warehouse the city's poorest residents, according to Ed Arceneaux, a former Desire manager and housing management specialist with the federal Department of Housing and Urban Development.

Developers had been under orders to build the project to minimum standards at minimum cost. Twice the size of its neighboring project, Florida, which was built for white tenants, Desire was made up of a series of two-story, bricked-over-barracks-type buildings clustered around courtyards. It was the only project built without cement beneath its floors and steps. As the buildings sat on soggy soil, the ground beneath the first 262 buildings began subsiding immediately, causing foundations, then pipes, to break and crumble. Porches fell away from their buildings. Sidewalks cracked. Gas, water, and sewer lines twisted and ruptured—all before the first tenant settled in.

Residents, desperate as they were for housing, were not naïve about what was being built for them. A tenants' association report made public on April 9, 1956, six weeks before Desire opened, stated, "It is our conclusion that this project is a waste of public money, that it is undesirable for many reasons and finally that it is unsafe for human habitation." The report concluded, "A proper investigation, we feel, will reveal the Desire project as a real scandal and a blight on public housing in New Orleans."[3]

When residents finally did move in, they lacked privacy, because they were forced to share poorly maintained hallways, porches, and courtyards. A further adjustment for the tenants that arrived to fill Desire's first 508 units in the summer of 1956 was that they found themselves removed from the city they had grown up in—its employment opportunities, stores, churches, and bus routes. Even emergency vehicles couldn't readily come and go. There were not enough schools, so children had to go in shifts. There were no playgrounds. In 1989, Larry Jones, the executive director of the Housing Authority of New Orleans (HANO) blamed racism for the problems. He told the *Times-Picayune* that the aim in building the Desire project had been quantity, not quality, and so housing officials had constructed an unwieldy giant: "This was for poor black people. I just think that the commitment was not there . . . They just felt like poor people don't deserve a whole lot."[4]

In the late 1950s, when previously all-white projects opened their doors to black people, the residents of Desire began moving out, deciding that any move would be a move up. In 1965 Hurricane Betsy put Desire under six feet of water, making grim conditions worse. And yet poverty forced other families to move in and stay there. By 1970, 10,594 residents, 8,312 (75 percent) of them under the age of twenty-one, were crowded into an area twelve blocks long and three blocks wide.[5]

On a typical summer day, women sat on their porches fanning the tepid air and exchanging news and banter while barefoot children jumped rope and played ball in the dirt. Broken glass, old shoes, and the remains of drug deals and hastily eaten meals littered the trampled weeds between the apartments, but the porches and courtyards offered a welcome alternative to the dank living quarters reeking of sewage. Holes in the walls and broken pipes accommodated a sizeable population of audacious rats.

However, the city administration did not become concerned about the plight of the people in Desire until the Black Panthers, demanding attention and advocating revolutionary action, established a headquarters on Piety Street half a block from the project. At the same time, the Panthers were setting up services to provide some relief and to point out that simple and humane remedies to the problems facing the residents could be provided, if not by the city, then by young revolutionaries who felt they were under siege.

When the city finally did take notice, Robert H. (Bob) Tucker Jr. was a young, idealistic black special assistant to Mayor Moon Landrieu. In August of 1970 the mayor sent Tucker to Desire to investigate and write a report. Tucker spent seventy-two hours "living" in the home of Desire resident Henry Faggen. Describing Desire as "one of the most explosive areas of the city," Tucker wrote, "Life in any multi-family structure for the low income family is a very difficult proposition, to say the least. The Desire housing project is a classic study of the worst."[6]

He reported that children swam in clogged sewers for lack of recreation facilities; families were afraid to leave their homes at night because of high rates of assault, robbery, muggings, and rape; piles of garbage went uncollected for days, even weeks. Desire was isolated, Tucker found, culturally and geographically from the rest of the city. Located in the Ninth Ward, downriver from the city, it was bordered by railroad tracks, the Mississippi River, the Industrial Canal, and a corridor of industrial plants.[7] But it had nonetheless spawned community leaders, entrepreneurs, and social activists.

Desire Community Center leaders told the *States-Item:*

> We are fighting against the top . . . to acquire operational funds, against ignorant powers . . . against public leaders who are all too often ignorant of the misery and frustration that cause addicts to revert to drug-dependence behavior . . . We are fighting against the bottom—the crummy building we live in, reeking with the smell of urine, the dirty floors and broken windows, the backyard that's littered with garbage; the millions of cockroaches crawling over us when we are asleep, sharing our coffee when we are awake; the huge flies and tiny mosquitoes that come through our window, left open in summer heat so that we can breathe "fresh pollution."[8]

Tucker reported that 61 percent of the families in Desire lived on less than three thousand dollars a year. Food-stamp recipients were held up in broad daylight by junkies and vagrants. He told the *Times-Picayune* that a major source of irritation in the community was a local food store that failed to meet health standards and that inflated prices on days when welfare checks arrived in residents' mailboxes. This store, owned by a black man named Clarence Broussard, would soon become an even larger source of irritation.

As reported in the *Times-Picayune* just days before the shootout that put Guyton on his belly in the Piety Street house, Tucker had proposed an eleven-point program to Mayor Landrieu to help alleviate some of the conditions. Included in the program were suggestions that the New Orleans Public Service return regular bus service to the area after midnight; that the Board of Health rigidly inspect the grocery store in question; that the Housing Authority of New Orleans and the City Sanitation Department provide more jobs for neighborhood residents, particularly ex-addicts; and that clogged sewers be cleaned.[9]

Tucker was not the only person making public statements about the conditions in Desire. Walter Rogers, a white activist who lived in the Lower Ninth Ward, circulated a flier fifteen days after the shootout.

He was a member of Local 406 Operating Engineers and the AFL-CIO, and he was a construction worker. He was seventy and his wife Elizabeth was seventy-eight when the Panthers moved into the neighborhood. Rogers, who had been one of the construction workers who laid the sewer pipes in Desire, had some insight about the problems with the project's sewers:

> I saw those faults, which I don't think can ever be mended, without tearing down the unhappy brick houses. It's in the sewers. These were laid about 12 feet deep. The rule is, to fill with shell above the sewer pipe, to cushion the pressure from buildings and pavement above. Pittman [the contractor] ignored this rule; apparently the inspectors did too. He crammed in huge stumps and cement lumps (less costly than shell), then ran bulldozers over it. When the cracked pipes began to show leaks, the scandal broke. A walk through Desire today shows sewers still leaking, and after [Hurricane] Betsy, 1965, we saw sewage flowing up through the pavement on Louisa [Street], where it stood for days before the city acted.[10]

Broken pipes weren't the worst damage Desire sustained as a result of Hurricane Betsy. Rogers, whose house had flooded during the hurricane, claimed, "Most workers believe, and there is evidence, that U.S. Engineers actually blew up Industrial Canal levees to make [the Lower Ninth Ward] a spillway, thus saving wealth and industry upstream."[11]

Citing the broken promises of urban renewal between 1965 and 1970, Rogers went on to say, "At last into this hellhole of poverty came the Panthers like a fresh wind, to start doing what Government should have done hundreds of years ago. Free breakfasts, free clothing, donations from merchants (like the churches get); self-respect, self-discipline, community responsibility and authority, the asserting of self-defense against attacks by cops, goons, dogs, and spies."[12]

Rogers had his own theory about what really threatened the established authorities: "What scares the cops and their kennel-owners is not just the bottles, rocks and fire-bombs of angry poor folk. Nor the free breakfasts, clinics, [and distribution of] clothes the Panthers have begun and the people carry on. What the Powers fear is THE TRUTH. The Panthers have seen the truth; millions more see it clearer daily:

That NONE OF THE ILLS CREATED BY CAPITALISM WILL EVER BE CURED BY CAPITALISM."[13]

The conditions in Desire, the arrival of the Panthers, and the subsequent shootout captured the imagination of the national press. In an article called "Death in Desire," *Time Magazine* stated, "The streetcar no longer runs on Desire Street, but New Orleans does have a housing project there named Desire. It is torn by frustrations and passions— as brutal as anything in Tennessee Williams' play. It is also as dirty, crime-ridden and crowded as any black ghetto in the North . . . Alarmed by the report of one of his black appointees [Bob Tucker], who described the area as 'potentially explosive,' Mayor Moon Landrieu was scheduled to make a tour of it last week. The slum erupted before he got there."[14]

The reality of the housing development stood in stark contrast to its evocative street names. Piety intersects Pleasure, Humanity, and Desire, streets named by an eighteenth-century Creole who first developed that part of town. In this Catholic city, the names of the landowners' daughters, Piety and Desiree, morphed into a primary human emotion and its superego counterpart, desire and piety.

According to *Webster's Dictionary,* the term *piety* means "fidelity to natural obligations, faithfulness to that which one is bound by a pledge, a duty, or by a sense of what is right or appropriate." In many ways, Piety was the right street for the Panthers. That duty, pledge, sense of what is right, was the Panthers' commitment to self-determination for black people. And Piety intersected Desire. Desire was a fitting name also, because in this housing development, there was a pervasive feeling, angrier than hopelessness, born of a longing that could never be fulfilled.

But the Panthers hadn't begun their operations in New Orleans on Piety Street. In May of 1970 a caller identifying himself as "Steve" had informed Bill Rouselle, deputy director of the city's Human Relations Committee, that he had just arrived from the West Coast to set up a Black Panther headquarters. Rouselle said "Steve" asked him for help in opening a free breakfast program for black children. Help never came.[15]

The Panthers' first, brief home was adjacent to the St. Thomas Housing Development. St. Thomas was like Desire in that it also had a large concentration of poor African Americans. Located between downtown and the posh Garden District, it was, however, much more a part of the city. Until the 1960s the residents of St. Thomas had been all white. The building that housed the Panther headquarters at 2353 St. Thomas Street was owned by Criminal District Court judge Bernard J. Bagert. The Panthers' public education classes held in the house attracted crowds of young people from all over town, up to 150 according to police intelligence.

Police chief Joseph I. "Joe" Giarrusso was worried. He was at the end of his tenure, and he was "old school," as one of his officers would describe him. Some would say that he was brutal in his intolerance of threats to police authority. And according to information from the FBI director J. Edgar Hoover, those threats loomed large. Hoover issued a report during the summer of 1970 calling the Black Panther Party "the most dangerous and violence prone of all extremist groups."[16]

That summer, Chief Giarrusso sent several memos to newly elected Mayor Landrieu to present "intelligence information on certain activists in the New Orleans area." He stated, "The organization of greatest concern and considered most dangerous was the BLACK PANTHER PARTY." He quoted Hoover as saying, "Extremist all-negro, hate-type organizations such as the Black Panther Party, continue to fan the flames of riot and revolution . . . Many of these groups, whose leaders preach violence and hatred of the white race, have been involved in shootouts with local police. Many attacks on police by black extremists are unprovoked and nothing more than planned ambushes."[17]

In June, Judge Bagert started eviction proceedings against the Panthers living and working in the St. Thomas Street house. According to the alternative newspaper *NOLA Express,* Judge Bagert was a slum landlord who evicted the Panthers from their first headquarters because he didn't like what they stood for.[18] Judge Bagert told the *Times-Picayune:* "I'm only glad I don't live in the project . . . We ought to take a bulldozer [to the buildings] and start over."[19]

After the June eviction of the Panthers from the St. Thomas property, Panthers from all over the city met to talk about what to do next. They decided in mid-July to move into a house near Desire on Piety Street, because Desire was the largest and poorest housing development.

On July 30, Chief Giarrusso sent another memo, informing the mayor of the Panthers' move. Hammering away at his point, he wrote, "As I have stated in previous memos to you concerning this organization, it is considered the most dangerous of black militant organizations and its activities are of great concern to this department."[20]

High on the list of activities of concern to Giarrusso was the Panthers' breakfast program for children. Barbara Guyton, married to Donald at the time, was the breakfast coordinator. In a flier she wrote and distributed, and that eventually became part of Mayor Landrieu's personal papers (now housed in the New Orleans Public Library), she stated:

> All children in grammar schools, and growing young adults in junior high schools, can receive a full hot breakfast, free of charge. The fact that the Black Panther Party, in implementing this program, has fed over 100,000 children over the past year, is reason enough for the continuance of the free breakfast program.
>
> Because we realize that our children cannot receive an effective education on empty stomachs, we're asking for your full support in seeing to it that the children begin their school day on full stomachs.[21]

Chief Giarrusso, however, was wary of this "effective education" and concerned about what the children were being fed. In an August 20 memo to Mayor Landrieu he said, "The breakfast program is used, primarily, to reach young children with their hate philosophy. This tactic may be more dangerous than the attacks on law enforcement. It is easy to see the far-reaching effects of continually propagandizing children with a hate philosophy that poisons the mind against all established authority, and especially the white race."[22]

Less than three weeks after the Panthers' move to Piety Street, police received a report of fighting in the block. When they arrived, they were jeered by a gathering crowd. Believing that the incident was purposely staged by the Panthers, the New Orleans Police Department quit patrolling Desire. Except for two black patrolmen, Raymond Reed and Joseph Orticke, all of them stayed on the periphery. Reed, who had grown up in Desire, was accused by the Panthers of being overly tough in handling suspects in the project. Both officers were singled out by Panthers as "Uncle Toms."[23]

In November the *Black Panther Newspaper,* published by the Panthers' central office in Oakland, would report some additional police presence. Well aware of the power of language to shape perception, the Panthers across the nation called the police "pigs," a term that at once ridiculed the police and helped to remove their association with terror:

> The pigs moved into the house directly behind us. They also occupied a two story house a block away behind our house and placed informers in a house across the street. On Piety Street itself, the pigs moved into a house one block away and made many raids on the community from that position. The black bootlicking pig capitalist [Clarence] Broussard, who owns most of the rat infested houses (including the house the NCCF rented) [and the grocery store mentioned in Tucker's report] on the block, filed a criminal trespassing complaint against the members of the NCCF and the pigs gave until Friday to move.[24]

Chief Giarrusso was indeed keeping a watchful eye. He reported to Landrieu that a Harold Joseph Holmes had been sent to New Orleans from Des Moines, Iowa, to organize a Panther chapter. His report continued:

> Information has just been received from a very reliable source which indicates that Holmes' superiors are not satisfied with his lack of militancy and he is being recalled and will be replaced by one George Lloyd. This could indicate a stepped-up program which would parallel [P]anther activities in other parts of the nation. My Intelligence Division has information indicating that these people now have in their possession at least three hand guns, two of which are 357 Magnums, a very powerful weapon, four shotguns, and several boxes of shotgun cartridges. These shotgun cartridges are of the 00 buckshot "slug variety." This type of ammunition is seldom used for sporting purposes and is considered offensive in nature. In addition to

these weapons, they have a 22 caliber rifle that is equipped with a scope.

One room of the new headquarters building located at 3544 Piety Street has been sandbagged up to window level, partially barricading the building. This situation should be of a great deal of concern to the entire community. The Police Department is attempting to maintain sources of information in an effort to determine the path to be followed by this group. You will be advised of all future developments immediately.[25]

I quote Joe Giarrusso at length to give the reader a taste of the detailed, repetitive, alarming memos that he issued frequently that summer of 1970. He seemed obsessed with the Panthers and his duty to report the danger he thought they posed. For their part, the Panthers were adept at fueling those fears with their violent rhetoric.

But as Larry Preston Williams, a young black man charged by the NOPD with infiltrating hate groups, will point out, the Panthers didn't hate white people, they hated the oppressor. Joe Giarrusso, unlike his brother Clarence, who would follow him as police chief, could not distinguish between the two.

Later that September, Donald Guyton was filling sandbags and making other security precautions. Hurricane Felice was hovering in the Gulf, so many all over town were probably filling their own sandbags in case this turned out to be another Betsy. Hurricanes have a way of prompting New Orleanians to contemplate their own mortality most Septembers. Like Mardi Gras, hurricane preparation is a communal, equalizing rite. The Catholic community offers flowers, statues, and candles to Our Lady of Prompt Succor. The Voodoo community offers Barbancourt Rum, daggers, spicy black beans, and unfiltered cigarettes to Ezili Danto, Our Lady's Voodoo counterpart. The ceremonies often overlap, and both ladies are believed to have intervened historically on New Orleans' behalf when hurricanes have threatened.

A sandbag doesn't always stop a bullet or a wall of water, but in times of emergency it gives people who live below sea level in New Orleans something concrete to do. Many in New Orleans believe that such communal rites as sandbagging make it less likely that during manmade disasters, we will kill each other.

Meanwhile, Steve Green had left town, allegedly to take care of business elsewhere. Barbara Guyton's breakfast program was drawing one hundred or more children every day.[26] Landrieu and Tucker were planning their site visit to Desire, scheduled for September 15, to take a closer look at its problems. Tucker would be making a site visit that day without Landrieu; but it was not the scheduled one. Giarrusso was redoubling efforts at garnering intelligence. He wanted the city administration to give its full attention to his assertion of the need for a high alert, because he would be leaving his post in a few weeks, handing it over to his brother.

The battle lines were being drawn.

2 The Panther,
the "Mayor of Desire," and
the Mayor's Special Assistant

Donald Guyton's and Henry Faggen's families had known each other since Guyton was a child. The Faggens were one of the first families to move into the Desire Housing Project. Bob Tucker and Henry Faggen had come to know each other through Tucker's research for his study of Desire. All three men would be pivotal in the looming confrontation between the Panthers and city officials. Their personal histories prepared them for their roles.

MALIK RAHIM

By the time the Panthers were headquartered on Piety Street, Donald Guyton (later known as Malik Rahim) had become a regular at their meetings. His history helped shape the fledgling chapter; and the people in the chapter honed a few of his rough edges in return.

In 2003 Malik Rahim, Marion Brown, and Robert King Wilkerson sat with me in Marion's and King's comfortable living room, which looks like a scene from a revolutionary good housekeeping magazine with brick and textured walls, earth tones, and African art. A ceramic panther crouches by the fireplace and posters of Malcolm X and Huey Newton adorn the walls. I was there for my follow-up visit after having come by for the Thanksgiving Freelines. King and Marion had arranged for an expanded interview to include Malik.

When I met him, Malik was a large, muscular man with long, graying dreadlocks. His demeanor, at once gentle and forceful, easily dissolved into infectious laughter, especially when he was with King, whom he had known since they were youngsters. All three were world-class storytellers. Malik settled into a chair in front of the window that looked out onto the porch as he remembered growing up on what New Orleanians call "the West Bank."

When he was seventeen years old, he signed up for the military. It was 1965 and the military was the only way Malik knew to get out of the community located across the Mississippi River from New Orleans proper called Algiers, where he had lived all his life. In the mid-1960s Algiers was fairly isolated, and Malik didn't watch the news. He didn't know the United States was fighting a war in Vietnam. When he heard at boot camp that Malcolm X had been killed, he didn't know who Malcolm was.

After boot camp, Malik was shipped off to Vietnam. But when he got there, he decided he didn't want to fight. "In order to kill people, you had to think of the Vietcong as 'gooks.' The soldiers who called Vietcong 'gooks' also called black people 'niggers.'"[1]

One of the many lessons he learned in Vietnam was that the racism that he had experienced at home in New Orleans was a worldwide problem. Malik got to leave Algiers. He got to fight in a war that was raging before he even heard about it. "After that," he told me, "I've always watched the news."

After Vietnam, he worked odd jobs in California. He couldn't get hired at the post office, as had some of his veteran friends, even with his honorable discharge. He suspected it had something to do with the posters of Che Guevara he kept in his locker while he was in the military. So he decided to come back to New Orleans to do pipeline construction and apply for his seaman's papers. There were Panthers in New Orleans, a friend told him when he arrived. On Canal Street, he met Alton Edwards selling the Panther newspaper.

Once Malik started going to meetings, he imbibed most of the Panther principles. They respected everyone—black and white and all colors—but Rahim had come back from Vietnam with a hatred for white people. "The Panthers had to re-educate me on that."

Malik was the first Vietnam veteran to join the Black Panther Party in New Orleans. The majority of the members in New Orleans had come from public housing, according to him. "Mayor Moon Landrieu complained about outside agitators. But I looked around and couldn't find them. The New Orleans Panthers could have used some outside help." Even Steve Green—or "Steve from the West Coast," as the media would call him—had grown up in New Orleans.

Malik recalled the work of the Panthers that drew him and many others into the party. With little outside help, the New Orleans Panthers set up a breakfast program that served hundreds of children —the first of its kind in the area. They established free sickle-cell screening, conducted classes on self-determination, and organized and carried out clean-up projects. They dealt effectively with crime in Desire, "making it clear to drug dealers on the corner that they had to move on. We didn't necessarily try to stop the dealing, but we insisted that it couldn't be carried on around children." Panthers escorted senior citizens to shop or cash their checks on payday; and they guarded people's houses when they were out of town.

Malik's theory is that the authorities wanted the deplorable conditions in Desire to continue because federal funds were awarded, in the early 1970s, based on poverty and high crime rates. But the Panthers had decided "it was time we stopped destroying ourselves."

As he spoke, the setting sun began to come through the living room window at an angle that produced a halo backlight to Malik's dreads. "New Orleans is a city based on tribalism," he said. "But, for a time, under Panther leadership in the Desire, rivalries between residents of different housing developments were set aside. People came together for the good of the most oppressed."

HENRY FAGGEN

Henry Faggen, who lived in Desire, set himself apart from the young revolutionaries who had moved into the development in 1970. He was an established community leader with some civil rights experience under his belt, including involvement with the Congress of Racial Equality (CORE) in Chicago. During his seven years there, he worked for a Veterans Administration hospital. A veteran himself, he filed suit to integrate its tuberculosis ward. Lean and handsome, with dark black skin and a fiery intensity, he cast an imposing presence in Desire and was fondly christened its "mayor."

I recorded Faggen's story in 2003 at the Hubbard Mansion, a bed and breakfast owned by Don and Rose Hubbard on St. Charles, New Orleans' grandest avenue.[2] Don Hubbard and Bob Tucker had become very successful businessmen in the years following the Panther encounter, while Faggen had remained on the margins financially. But as always happens in New Orleans, they would run into each other from time to time.

When Bob decided to convene a group interview at the Hubbard Mansion to fill out what he had read of the Panther story in my *Louisiana Weekly* column, he and Don had no trouble finding Faggen. These three, and several others who will enter the story later, seemed as comfortable together in the plush red drawing room as they had been thirty-three years ago working as a team out of Faggen's humble Desire abode.

Well into his seventies in 2003, Faggen was still lean and handsome, with ebony skin and eyes that intermittently teased and charmed. He had a way of telling a story that was open, expansive, and completely without guile. He took his listeners with him, making it easy to see things from his point of view.

When Faggen was six years old, he moved to New Orleans from a plantation on Bayou Goula in Plaquemines Parish, where his family labored. The serflike conditions in rural Louisiana were just one step above slavery. Leander Perez, the arch-segregationist who ruled Plaquemines Parish with an iron hand for most of the twentieth century, was said to have even segregated his black and white cows.

"My family came with chickens and boxes tied onto their caravan like the Beverly Hillbillies," Faggen recalled.

After his years in the army and in Chicago, Faggen came back to New Orleans in the early 1950s and landed a job as one of the first black bus drivers. He was assigned only night hours. Once he had to abandon his bus because, in what was probably a racist attack, someone shot out the windows. "You were a nigger bus driver on the street and you was the double nigger bus driver at the station. We were just paying our dues to the [white-run] union and not getting anything." So Faggen organized the black bus drivers. That "really sparked something. We realized we don't have to take this."

In October of 1956 Faggen and his wife moved into the new

Desire housing development and started a family. They would eventually have fourteen children and sixty-eight grandchildren. "Desire was such a beautiful place," Faggen remembered. It had only three families and the furthest street back was Abundance. What a change the next fourteen years would bring.

According to Faggen, Desire in the 1950s was a "live, vibrant community . . . It was manicured to the nines." He recalled the Miss Desire Beauty Contest and all the groups that worked for the betterment of Desire. But "It just got out of control because of the density. Single mothers trying to raise men. And I'm a firm believer; a woman can't raise a man. I just don't believe that. It takes two to tango and we didn't have two in Desire."

The Housing Authority designed it that way, according to Faggen. A woman couldn't get any assistance if there was a man around. "They'd come in your house, look in your closet, under your bed. And if any man clothes were there, you were cut out."

"A bunch of years came along and density got thick. Things started happening. Of course drugs came in. Then the Panthers came in." Faggen noted that every black project had a black police unit. When black police were put into black neighborhoods, "they thought that in order to sustain themselves with some dignity, they had to be brutal. That was the attitude they came in with."

Desire, which had been built for African Americans, was right across the canal from Florida, a white project where university students lived. Black policemen couldn't arrest white people; they could only detain them, Faggen told me. So the two projects had very different relationships with their respective police.

By the time the Panthers moved into Desire in 1970, Faggen was known as the "Mayor of Desire." "Everyone in Desire knew him, but more importantly, they respected him. So he had the ability to move in between all these groups," said Tucker.

The Panthers didn't invent community concern in Desire, Faggen emphasized as he told his story. They brought some of it with them, but some of it was already in place. "There were plenty of militant groups—Deacons for Defense, Sons of Desire, Ujima, Lower Ninth Ward Crusaders, and Thugs United . . . The Panthers were not the movement. *We* were the movement. This town was on fire with black culture, nationalism, independence, Free Southern Theater . . . But them kids [Panthers] was marching by their drumbeat—black people sticking together, economic development, lovin' each other, we're here to help you, we gonna feed you. Over half of the households in Desire were females. You see, that impressed them ladies. Somebody takin' care of their children, givin' them breakfast."

Faggen was a bridge between the Panthers and the city administration. He could see both sides, but his allegiance was with neither. He was solidly rooted in his community, Desire, and wholeheartedly committed to the protection and support of the rising aspirations of its people.

In 1970, tensions between the Panthers and the city administration came to a head, with the people of Desire caught in between. When the tensions erupted into a full-scale showdown, Faggen found himself at its vortex.

BOB TUCKER

The interview at the Hubbard Mansion—a mini-reunion as much as anything—was Bob's brilliant idea. Bob hatches ideas at a rate I never dreamed possible before getting to know him. He follows through on most of these himself, but he generously delegates many to others to complete and then patiently supports his recipients until he can revel in their success. Maybe that's why he always seems to be in a good mood and why his energy is so infectious. I can't even sit still when I'm talking to him on the phone. His mental agility also seems to be good for his health. He stays compact, muscular, not restless, but constantly on the move.

Bob Tucker always had a sense of his place in history. "Dear Mom and Dad," he wrote from Clark College in Atlanta in 1960. "By the time this letter reaches you the news of what I am about to tell you will have spread all over the nation, and probably the world." The letter goes on to lay out the strategy that he and 150 fellow students would use to confront the racist power structure in Atlanta with coordinated sit-down strikes. "I personally could find no better cause to die for than this," Tucker informed his parents.

He told them not to worry, though, because his group had three hundred dollars in bond money, and before he went to bed he declared that he would pray, study, and figure out whom he could borrow lunch money from. He said Martin Luther King's brother would be marching with them. Tucker did end up, the next day, going to jail; but he was quickly processed and released.

In 1968 he was still protesting. He helped organize the Memorial March for King to the steps of the New Orleans City Hall during the Schiro administration. There were many groups represented, Tucker recalled: Catholic nuns, Baptist ministers, the Republic of New Africa, a whole spectrum of the African American community and their white friends. There were many disagreements. "We argued for hours over whose method was the best method for liberation. I knew we were making progress when we finally began arguing over the mule." There was much discussion about what kind of mule should pull the symbolic casket. "Somebody said they had a mule they could talk to. So it was settled."

"We had ten non-negotiable demands, any nine of which we were probably ready to negotiate if any one would listen to us. We had to leave them on the door of City Hall, kind of like the Edict of Wurms thing." As the procession approached City Hall, only one city councilman, Moon Landrieu, was there. He stood on the sidelines and watched.

When Landrieu was elected mayor in 1970, he asked Tucker, a brilliant and aspiring young organizer, to be his special assistant. Tucker welcomed the opportunity to be one of the first influential blacks in city government, but he made it clear that he intended to have a real voice in the administration and not just be a "spook by the door."

3
Remembering and Forgetting
What Really Happened

The Panther, Malik Rahim, and the city official, Bob Tucker, were poised against each other in 1970 in a life-and-death struggle. Henry Faggen stood firmly in between. Thirty-three years later, they would be together again, telling the story at a public forum. The forum was another of Bob's brilliant ideas. Many who attended had been in Desire in 1970 and had tried to forget the traumatic events. Other attendees were young and astounded that they had never heard the story, not even from relatives who had grown up in Desire. Bob characterized the Panther story as a page missing from New Orleans history books—and not just books, but even people's recollections. He wondered if it was a page deliberately torn out. Several of the panelists agreed to participate even though they believed that nobody cared about these events anymore.

But a strange curiosity attracted so many people that a crowd had to be turned away. I took that as a sign that the forum organizing committee had unleashed something important to the communal psyche of New Orleans, something heretofore repressed. As a psychotherapist, I am intrigued by memory. It just did not make sense to me that dramatic events remembered by consummate storytellers in a city that lives as much on memory as anything else would have been "forgotten."

By the time of the forum I had met and interviewed enough Panthers, attorneys, city officials, and Desire residents to put together a good story. So I acted on another of Bob's brilliant ideas and published a Panther booklet consisting of the interviews I had collected and incorporated into my newspaper column. But I was missing an important piece of the story. I had spoken to the police chief, but I had given up on interviewing any of the undercover cops. When I went to the second district headquarters to look for Melvin Howard, who thought he was passing as a Panther on Piety Street, he came down to meet me but said that he wanted to put that history behind him. Israel Fields, who also infiltrated the party, set up two interviews with me and then failed to show up.

I didn't even hear about Larry Preston Williams until two years after the forum.

In September, October, and November of 1970 there was so much action and so many perspectives on the action that, after hearing the stories, I spent months trying to get clear about what had happened when. To aid that process, I immersed myself in the news accounts of the day, which were rich and varied, both locally and nationally. On the national level, in addition to the *New York Times* and *Time Magazine*, the *Black Panther Newspaper* came out weekly and devoted much coverage to the New Orleans events. Locally, we had two competing dailies, the *Times-Picayune* and the *States-Item,* as well as a true underground newspaper, the *NOLA Express,* and an established black weekly, the *Louisiana Weekly.* Coverage of the events varied widely, as did editorial opinion. News accounts provided some of the small details that helped organize and bring these stories to life for me. For that reason, I have quoted these sources in some detail.

I spent weeks with the special collections in the Howard-Tilton Memorial Library at Tulane University studying the meticulously collected clippings files on the Panthers. Reading the emotionally charged reporting of the events as they happened transported me to a transformative time in my own life. I felt like I was filling in some huge blanks about how society had been changing around me at a time when I, at the age of twenty-four, had been consumed by my narrower personal drama. My research was the closest I could get to going back and reliving it. I'd walk home from the library (through the campus where I had been a student in the late 1960s) and want to pull on bell-bottoms or a miniskirt in my closet when no one was looking. I was torn between the sadness of lost possibilities and an excited urgency to tell a story whose lessons might still be completely applicable.

But in a cruel trick of fate, even those poignant documents in the Louisiana Collection are now relegated only to memory. When I went back in 2007, two years after Hurricane Katrina, to find out how to reference those vertical files for my end notes, the keeper of the files told me they had been frozen. When I had conducted research there earlier, he had guarded his temple/archive with a consuming fastidiousness. Try as I might, at no time did I cheerfully arrive to do my research without being chastised for some inadvertent infraction of rule or ritual about how to enter, formulate a request, extract the information, or leave. Even the copy machine, with its rules (about how and when one could use it) and its voracious appetite for small coins, was impossible for me to master without assistance. Our relationship, based on my fawning dependence and his steadfast commitment to my continued correction, had evolved, before the storm, into a grudging respect.

"Frozen?" I queried in 2007, assuming that this was a euphemism for "somehow placed beyond my reach." "Yes," he said glumly. "They flooded with Katrina and we put them in a block of ice. If we ever get insurance money, we'll thaw them out and see if there is anything left." I looked, maybe for the first time, compassionately at the librarian and thought to myself that that was one of the saddest things I'd ever heard.

This only increased my determination to publish the newspaper accounts, many of which will now be hard to find, word for word.

Since it took me so long to sort out in my own mind what really happened, I'll go ahead and lay it out as I understand it here:

The outing of two undercover police officers at the Panther headquarters on Piety Street a few blocks from the Desire Housing Project precipitated a shootout with police on September 15, 1970, one that resulted, miraculously, in no deaths on either side. Twelve Panthers were arrested on attempted murder charges. In the volatile aftermath of the shootout, a young man was killed by police outside of a grocery store that police claimed he was trying to firebomb. Evidence suggests that he was merely an innocent bystander.

Despite the destruction of their headquarters and the mass arrests, the Panthers—mostly the women—carried on the survival programs, including the free breakfast for children, and kept the office functioning, moving it into the Desire project proper at the invitation of Desire residents on October 25. The twelve Panthers were held in Orleans Parish Prison for eleven months until they were acquitted. Their experience there and their meeting of Woodfox, Wallace, and Wilkerson, who would start a Panther chapter at Angola State Penitentiary, forms a revealing side story.

On November 19 the police again assailed the Panther headquarters, purportedly in an attempt to evict them. Chief Clarence Giarrusso sent in 250 armed white cops backed by a tank and helicopters. Surely, there would have been an easier way to execute a trespass warrant. Again, miraculously, no one was killed and no shots were fired, except for one accidentally, according to one account. That was because Desire residents, many of them children, surrounded the Panther apartment to protect the Panthers and stayed there until the chief called his men back to their busses and left.

A few days later, the actress Jane Fonda came to town to support the Panthers. But her visit ended in a debacle as twenty-five people were arrested when they tried to leave town to go the People's Revolutionary Constitutional Convention in Washington D.C. in cars she had rented for them. That was November 25.

The next day, Thanksgiving, at 1:30 in the morning, police disguised themselves as priests and postal workers and raided the Panther Desire headquarters, shooting Panther Betty Powell in the shoulder as she tried to slam the door on them. They arrested all six Panthers inside and charged them with attempted murder and violation of the Federal Firearms Act. All were eventually acquitted.

I provide a summary of these potentially violent events as an anchor upon which to hang the oral histories and press accounts that will appear in the following chapters. The events themselves do not represent the essence of what the Panthers were about, but, like any trauma in a personal or collective narrative, they are remembered vividly. When they are spoken about, they elicit projections, insights, emotions, and rationales that help to illuminate the courageous bid for self-determination that the Black Panthers made in New Orleans.

Since it was the outing of the undercover cops that set this sequence in motion, I will begin with an insider's story of why one black person took this job with police intelligence and how he did his work. I quote the firsthand account of Larry Preston Williams at length because his thought processes exemplify the philosophical dilemma facing many black men at that time and highlight the peculiarly humorous New Orleans ways in which those conundrums played out. His account is also a case study of race relations both inside the police force as it began to open its ranks to black people and beyond in police-citizen interactions.

4 The Nuts and Bolts of Infiltration

Larry Preston Williams Sr., an African American, joined the New Orleans Police Department (NOPD) when he was nineteen years old. The NOPD was only about 15 percent black in the late 1960s, but Williams's draft number was ten, and he didn't want to fight in Vietnam. He wanted to finish college instead, and he saw joining the NOPD as a means to an end.

Williams was born in Detroit. His family moved to New Orleans when he was small, and it was there that he was raised and educated. In 1970, when he was twenty-two, Williams was assigned to NOPD's Intelligence Unit. It was the job of his division to find people to infiltrate the Black Panther Party, the Republic of New Africa, the Ku Klux Klan, and the American Nazi Party and then to collect and evaluate the information from those diverse infiltrators. He loved the assignment, which was a welcome change from the routine police work in "the District."[1]

I met Williams in 2005 through the filmmaker Royce Osborn, who is the videographer for the New Orleans Black Panther story. He had encountered Williams, who is now a private detective, in connection with another documentary.

After an initial phone conversation, Osborn and I set up an interview with Williams at an ornate Chinese restaurant in the east of New Orleans. I approached this interview with some apprehension. During the last three years, I had gotten to know my sources well. Introducing another one, someone I didn't know and didn't yet trust, was an unsettling prospect. However, it was important to me to have the perspective of a police insider for the story, so I set out for the interview with two tape recorders, both of which I carefully checked, and resolved to stay open to whatever I would learn.

Amid the red and black dragons and masks that decorated the restaurant, Osborn and I peppered Williams with questions, which he graciously answered in lavish detail. The six-foot-four Williams, who was in his fifties when I interviewed him, was charming and articulate. Figuring that as a detective and former undercover cop, he would know more about recording equipment than I did, I gave the best of the tape recorders to him to set up.

The three of us had an interesting and revealing two-hour conversation. I rode home on a high of new understanding about how police intelligence really works, about the erroneous perceptions of white leaders at the time, and about some, often funny, realities that fly in the face of stereotypes about extremist organizations. Above all, Williams's loyalties and sympathies, and the fact that he had so freely shared them, came as a surprise. But when I sat down to transcribe my tape, nothing was there. I fast-forwarded to several other places: no words, only the whir of the wheels of this machine I was cursing. I lost my appetite for dinner and went to bed physically sick.

The next morning, I called Royce and King for confession and solace. Royce said, "Don't worry, just do the interview over again."

King said, "What did you expect from an undercover cop?"

Fortunately, Royce's proposal, which I considered a long shot, was right on target, and Williams generously consented to have lunch again the very next day. This time, I made sure the microphone was on.

Williams described the police academy as "difficult racially." The training instructor used the "n" word. All six of the black recruits in Williams's class threatened to leave, but their superiors talked them out of it. "I hit the District in March of 1969. I worked with some good, decent white officers. But I noticed that white police officers were over-all *terrible* at dealing with black males. Black males had hostility against police officers . . . I mean, sometimes you'd get on a scene of a crime and for no reason you'd find black males being hostile to police officers because it was fashionable and politically correct at the time if you were African American to be hostile to a police officer. If they were hostile to a white officer," continued Williams, "they were more hostile to me."

If there was a confrontation between black and white citizens, the black person in the confrontation would talk to Williams and the white person would talk to the white officer. "You'd get two different versions. Every now and then, I'd be at odds with the white officer as to what to do, and I'd notice that the white officer would sometimes just discount the black person's version; and I would sometimes discount the white person's version. I noticed that there was definitely a difference in how white officers related to black people and black officers related to white people. I see that it can't work to have a majority white police force that's patrolling a black area. Too many frictions."

In fact Williams later filed a Title VII race discrimination suit with some other people in the police department, "not because I wanted anything personally, but because having a community that was 50 percent black with a predominantly white police department was bad enough. But when you consider all of the serious crime and all of the serious enforcement activities and arrests and investigations that go on in the black community, even the most well-intended white officer was at a disadvantage."

Williams remembered investigations in which a black person would tell him he could come in the house, but the white officer couldn't. "It seemed to me that if black people had their options, they would rather deal with black cops than white cops. I noticed most people would prefer to deal with female cops of either race than white males."

The Intelligence Unit was different—about equally divided between black and white. "We were all friends. We ate together—dined together. We would go to each other's homes. It was just the opposite of the District.

"My commander, Sergeant Fredrick O'Sullivan, was restrained. There were certain things he just wouldn't do. When you have this secret organization, the Red Squad [referring to the Intelligence Unit], there's a lot of nasty things you can do and get away with it because it's secret. But Sgt. O'Sullivan came from that school of thought that you don't mistreat people if you don't have to. That's why it was nice to work for him. I liked working for him."

When asked if he had any inner conflict about managing the infiltration of the Black Panther Party, Williams responded: "The only conflict I had was my views of radicals, because I always considered myself to be as far to the left as I could get. So my conflict was managing the infiltration of groups that I wouldn't say I identified with—but groups that I had admiration for. Having that assignment was very, very interesting."

The police department's guide on whom to infiltrate was the U. S. Attorney General's list of subversives who were considered dangerous. "If they were on the list, we watched them." Williams said he was, and is, a nonviolent person. He didn't like the threat of violence. "If the Panthers hadn't threatened violence," he said, "I wouldn't have taken the job to infiltrate." He saw the potential for violence in a community, Desire, that he thought didn't "deserve to be in the cross-fires, literally. If something had happened between the Panthers and the police department, a lot of innocent people would have been killed. That bothered me.

"But an organization that was sensitive to police brutality, wanted to feed kids, wanted to get drug dealers out of the neighborhood—had I not been a cop—was an organization that I would have supported. I don't think I would have joined, but I could have supported [it], because in theory they were good ideas. In concept. Very good ideas. So of course there was no conflict there. It was a matter of violence."

Williams was a little chagrined to learn that although the rhetoric of the Panthers was violent, the New Orleans chapter did not perpetrate acts of violence. He had a similar disappointment with the Klan. Of the Panthers, he says, "The police department probably became convinced that these people posed a danger to the police department, and of course the police department would try to convince people that they posed a direct threat to the community, especially the white community. But there was nothing that I saw or heard from infiltrators to convince me that these people disliked white people because they were white. There were particular white people that they thought were oppressive. There were cops, black and white, that they thought were the arms of an oppressive society that they would resist. But just hating people because of the color of their skin—I never got that from the Panthers."

Regarding their program, Williams noted, "As a group I thought this chapter was pretty devoted to doing things for the Desire area.

I thought generally their stated goals were good. I thought they went about them fairly efficiently given the resources that they had. I thought they were sincere. I thought they were good people." He added, "The only problem I had with them was that they seemed to have an intense dislike for most police officers. It wasn't individual. They just didn't like police officers."

Williams compared the organizations he was assigned to infiltrate in this way: "The Panthers were easy to infiltrate because they did a lot of recruiting. The Klan was easy to infiltrate because they were idiots. They had no standards. The Republic of New Africa was a little more difficult because they were Afrocentric. If a person came and he didn't seem to know a lot about Africa, or if he was not politically conscious and politically astute, he might have a problem. So the people we chose to infiltrate those organizations needed to be just a little more well-read, a little more intellectual, a little more philosophical than, let's say, the Panthers.

"The toughest one to infiltrate was the Nazi Party. They tended to have above-average intelligence. Some of them were very educated. They were a close-knit group and they were violent. They were not easy. I was never able to get anyone in."

Williams contrasted the various organizational philosophies: "The Panthers were revolutionaries, whereas the Republic of New Africa were separatists. The Republic of New Africa believed that the black man should have his own piece of land that he should occupy and leave the rest to whites. The Panthers were a little different. They wanted to take over communities by force if necessary— remove policemen and white businessmen from the community. They were more revolutionary, more in your face, more likely to discuss being prepared for when there's a race war."

Williams noted that he heard Panther-like rhetoric from the Klan and the Nazi Party. But the latter two groups hated and wanted to remove people because of the color of their skin, whereas "the Black Panther Party had a dislike for people they thought were oppressive to others. That's a big distinction," stated Williams. "Of course the Klan was not at all revolutionary. They were more oppressive. They were just idiots. The Panthers were a little smarter, a little more politically aware."

As an example of how unique to New Orleans the local Klan was, Williams told this story: "I went to interview a Klan member who lived right outside the Quarter. Sergeant O'Sullivan got a kick out of sending black detectives to interview people who were thought to be Klansmen. We'd go to the home. We'd introduce ourselves. Surprisingly, most of them would talk to black officers. Sometimes they wouldn't invite you in, but they'd come out and talk. (I'm in plain clothes. I identify myself. 'We understand you were at a Klan meeting the other night. We'd like to know if you would tell us what went on.')

"Most of the time they wouldn't. These were not scary guys. They were just regular white guys who spewed a lot of hate. But this particular guy—he lived in what they call a slave quarter, which is a little house behind a double. I knocked on the door and when I went inside—it was summertime—he was sitting on the side of the bed getting his shoulders massaged by a black transvestite."

Williams laughed. "You know right then that there's something wrong with that picture. I mean, this is the Klan! He's using the 'n' word. He has two black detectives. He has a black transvestite massaging him. He has a black female prostitute and a white female prostitute all in the same house. And this guy's in the Klan! It was 'niggers this and niggers that' and 'the white man can't get anything.' I get ready to leave and he asks me to loan him a dollar."

Williams pointed out that Klansmen would live in mixed neighborhoods. That's how New Orleans is. "Black people knew they were Klansmen and seemed to accept the fact . . . Weird. Of course this is not a town where you can really have an active Klan chapter. They couldn't get enough people. I don't think they ever had more than seven or eight people, of which one was a cop, another was an informant. They never got anywhere. Never did anything."

Williams said that theoretically, they were dangerous, but "that's only in theory. When you looked at them, they were much different from the Mississippi Klan or the Alabama Klan, or the Georgia Klan or the North Louisiana Klan. These guys were nice. They were as nice a guys as you can find hating black people. Just to sit down and talk to them—they were just decent guys."

Of black and white people generally in New Orleans, Williams said, "I'm not saying that they had always liked each other. But in this town, you know how to coexist, so you didn't have that hostility. The Klan people were not really hostile. The Black Panther Party people were not hostile. They Nazis were hostile. And the Republic of New Africa was a little more hostile. But generally, the homegrown Klansmen and the homegrown Panthers were just not hostile people. A big disappointment."

Williams may have noticed some of my initial interviewer bias resurfacing at this juncture. Any good detective probably could have read the accusing question on my face: "Why would you be disappointed when people aren't hostile?"

In any case, he launched into an explanation: "I'm glad that no one got hurt, but I'm looking to infiltrate a group that was doing something worthy of infiltration. You felt like you were wasting your time. I mean you've got Klansmen who go out to bash black people and they'd get a flat tire and have no spare! Or they'd go out to harass someone and end up talking to the person and then drive away. They just couldn't raise themselves to that level of consistent hate." A Klansman would decry interracial marriages and then introduce Williams to a biracial grandson.

But according to Williams, the extremists from out of town were another story. Herman Bell was a New York Panther who was wanted for the killing of two police officers—one black and one white—who had been beat cops in a housing development in New York City. Said Williams: "Herman was the shooter or one of the shooters. He leaves New York City. He comes down to New Orleans and is captured in New Orleans. It becomes a movie. *He* was violent. But he wasn't from here. This stupid bastard, when he comes to town, he starts sleeping with one of our informers, who turns him in. He gets to town. He forms a relationship two or three days later, and we call New York and they come down and book him. He's still in jail in upstate New York.

"Here's the irony. He came here with a very, very violent guy. I found the violent guy first. He came from another place in order to get Herman situated, to assist Herman. He was supposed to be one of the most violent Panthers in America. I forget his name. My source was on the lookout for him. When I finally tracked him down, they were in the car together. I told her to bring him to a certain place, and we had a marked unit stop him. The marked unit took him out of the car and he started crying. He didn't have a place to sleep. So I brought him home and he slept on my couch. Go figure. I mean, he cried like a baby. The next morning I brought him to police headquarters and bought him a sandwich. That was the last I saw of him.

"Within a few days they catch Herman. The other guy came here to help Herman and ended up ratting him out. The really violent guy was not hard core, not serious; would fold once you got him on the side."

When I asked Williams how he had recruited people to infiltrate these organizations, he told me that there were officers who worked at Central Lockup (where people who are arrested are taken and detained after they are booked until they are either bonded or denied bail). At that time, NOPD managed Central Lockup, whereas today it is managed by the sheriff's office. "We'd tell them the kind of people we were looking for. So if a guy came in with a large Afro and combat boots and a field jacket, we'd go visit him in lockup and we'd tell him, 'You know, we can make these charges go away but we want you to hang around with the Panthers or the Republic of New Africa or some particular person. Or if there was a redneck American, we'd say, 'In consideration of making these charges go away, I'd like you to hang around these guys. If he or she would agree, we'd ask the District Attorney not to process the charge until we told him to do so. And once that person proved himself, if we had the budget, we would pay him or her because we got better results when we paid someone than when we motivated them with fear and intimidation."

When I asked how the infiltrator would prove him or herself, Williams informed me, "They would attend meetings and we would always have somebody in there to check their reports and see if they coincided with [those of] a trusted agent or police officer. We always tried to have a police officer in there, because if something happened we would need somebody with some credibility. Many of our non-police undercover agents had criminal records and would present credibility problems [as witnesses].

"Interestingly enough, back in those days, many African American people thought that we only went against the Black Panther Party. But the Black Panther Party was very public. So our activities against the party were more likely to become known throughout the community." Williams claimed that they were just as tough on the Klan. But because the Klan was more secretive, operations against the Klan very seldom became public. "We'd go to their jobs. We'd knock in their neighborhoods. Same things that the Panthers were complaining about."

Williams loved being in the Intelligence Unit. He found it exciting, everything he expected and more. "The challenge was to get information from the groups. I found that I could get more information from the groups if I infiltrated them with women rather than men. Men didn't suspect women of being undercover agents. Women could form confidential relationships. Women always know things that the guys didn't know, saw things that the guys didn't know. They could go places where the guys would be suspicious. They could ask questions that wouldn't arouse suspicion, whereas if a guy asked the same question, there would have been suspicions." Williams told me he had a female in the Panthers and one in the Klan, both of whom worked out well.

"All you need is one female. And she doesn't need to be intimate with anybody. What's important is the role that she plays. She's always in there. She's supposed to take care of the house, and so she sees everybody who comes in. She feeds people. She has all the telephone numbers. She makes all the telephone calls. She has a list of people to call if something happens. I mean, it's just great. *One woman!*"

Williams knew the Panthers quite well, but they didn't know him, because his knowledge of them was indirect. "There was a guy who would talk to me, Harold 'Poison' Holms. I thought Harold was a witty little guy, because every time he would see me he walked up behind me and asked me, 'Larry,' how do you like livin' in Babylon?' And he'd walk off and laugh. I thought he was kind of funny. There was another guy I liked to talk to—Marshall Kellen. He would talk about how oppressive things were. Betty Powell would never talk to me. Neither would Leah Hodges. But for the most part, you could have a dialogue if you chose to. But I usually wasn't that close to them. My role was, I'd take pictures if they were on the demonstration line. Sometimes we'd do surveillance at their places. We'd sit out on the street and take photos of people who would go in and out. I learned a lot about them, but never directly."

The direct action for Williams happened on Piety Street. He was involved in the Piety headquarters shootout on September 15, 1970, and on November 19 he was again directly involved when the huge contingent of New Orleans cops tried to flush the Panthers out of their Desire headquarters. And he was right in the middle of the action yet again a week later when the police donned their disguises, shot, and tricked their way into the Panther apartment early Thanksgiving morning and made their final Panther arrests.

The police chief Williams worked for took direction from a mayor who considered himself an ally of the black community. Mayor Landrieu agonized about the decisions he had to make that determined strategy. Some of the strategy he left to the police chief, Clarence Giarrusso. Williams helped carry out that strategy, but he considered it fundamentally "white," that is, lacking in consideration of realities that were obvious to him from a black person's point of view, and therefore flawed.

What follows is a bit of the city's political history as well as the personal histories of Mayor Landrieu and Chief Giarrusso. These histories informed their decisions and strategies. Everything was changing, and these two capable leaders represented a clear break from the past. But would that be enough to prevent a race war?

5 Moving the System

In 1970 the consciousness of Malik Rahim and many other black New Orleanians was changing. So was the city administration. Newly elected Mayor Moon Landrieu shocked the city by bringing African Americans into top leadership positions in City Hall. Cecil Carter was named deputy director of the Human Relations office. Robert Tucker was appointed the mayor's executive assistant. Don Hubbard was tapped as director of the Total Community Action neighborhood center in the Desire Housing Project and, later, director of the Division of Youth Services for the city. He followed Charles Elloie, who would later become a judge. These young African American men, well-grounded in civil rights history and active players on the local scene, were in Desire as tensions escalated. Each helped in important ways to avert what seemed like inevitable, massive bloodshed.

The move toward African American inclusion was a radical transition in a city where the voting majority was still 55 percent white. But the Voting Rights Act of 1965 had altered the political landscape. In 1964, 63 percent of the city's eligible white population was registered to vote, but only 28 percent of eligible black people were registered. Two years later, the number of eligible black people who had signed up to vote jumped to 42 percent.[1]

In 1965, in the wake of the Voting Rights Act, Robert Collins, Nils Douglas, and Lolis Elie had organized the Southern Organization for Unified Leadership (SOUL) to run black candidates for city and state office. SOUL's base was black homeowners and middle- and lower middle-class black citizens in the Lower Ninth Ward. In 1969, Collins, along with some Seventh Ward professionals, started Community Organization for Urban Politics (COUP).[2] By 1970, black people could exert political influence but only through discipline, organization, and a high degree of racial solidarity. COUP and SOUL functioned effectively to broker the black vote [3]

With strong support from both organizations, Moon Landrieu was elected as New Orleans' last white mayor in 1970. As he took office, Landrieu had two requirements for his new police chief. One was that the top cop be absolutely, impeccably honest. The other was that he have a "good, solid, rational attitude on race. Frankly," said Landrieu in a 2003 interview, "that was extremely difficult to find."[4]

On August 25 Landrieu appointed Clarence Giarrusso to replace his brother Joseph Giarrusso. He came highly recommended by Landrieu's friend Lolis Elie—who would later defend the Panthers in court. Said Landrieu: "Giarrusso was not only honest, he was incorruptible. He served this community very well."

Giarrusso had joined the police department in 1949. He was assigned to the motorcycle division, and five years later, he transferred to narcotics. Said one officer who worked with Giarrusso at the time, "There's a positive advantage to working narcotics because you come in contact with everything and every element of people. Narcotics is a vice that draws other vices."[5] Giarrusso stayed in narcotics, moving up from patrolman to sergeant to lieutenant, and then to captain in charge of the division. If anyone had dedication on the force, the officer said, Giarrusso had it. In night school he earned three degrees— in business administration, criminology, and law.

When Giarrusso was appointed chief he was forty-nine years old, a short, jowly man with a sharp grasp of diplomacy and warfare. An officer who had known him at the time of his appointment said, "He always considers all aspects of the situations he has to deal with. He tries to be fair, impartial." The officer went on to say that he expected the same of his 1,470 men. "He's not rank-conscious. He treats a man as a man and at the same time he demands their respect."

Another colleague said, "The chief seems to be the type to bend a little bit to prevent a loss of life. If there's a peaceable solution, he wants it. As an individual, he's one of a kind."[6]

When I interviewed Giarrusso in 2003, his health was declining, and his memory was clearer on some things than others. He was confined to a chair near the kitchen of his suburban West Bank house, but he talked spiritedly to me while his wife Catherine hovered nearby, anticipating his every need.

The aging chief still prided himself on his undercover work, boasting that in 1970 he had many dependable informants in the community. He considered Israel Fields and Melvin Howard, the undercover cops who had infiltrated the Black Panther Party soon after its inception, real heroes, some of his greatest assets at that time. "I knew what was coming, anticipated some things, and we could smooth things out. Information is very important for police work," he said, "and there were many pieces of string that I could pull at that time."[7]

From his vantage point thirty-three years later, he downplayed the drama of the confrontation. Fear is not part of his personality, he told me. "It didn't bother me that they called us pigs. I knew where they were coming from . . . I talked with the Panthers. They were dissatisfied people. The things they didn't like made sense. They were treated as second-class citizens . . . American society was in a revolutionary mood, a drastic changing mood."

In 2003, Giarrusso, despite his physical limitations, was still full of life.[8] He peered at me intensely, apparently reflecting a little more deeply on any apprehension he might have felt at the time. He remembered going into Desire before the confrontation with Mayor Landrieu and Ben Levy, the chief administrative officer for the city. He had second thoughts about trying to talk to the Panthers but said, "There's always some people with whom you can talk . . . America was engaged in social maturing at the time. In these last thirty years we've come a long way."

When Clarence Giarrusso assumed the top police position, he appointed Louis J. Sirgo, a white man and seventeen-year veteran of the NOPD, as his deputy chief.[9] Sirgo was a visionary. In a speech to civic leaders shortly before he died, Sirgo warned that "a thin blue line of police officers, working against the odds is able to partially contain the violence and prevent criminal anarchy." But that containment, he said, could not last for long. "Police forces were not designed for, nor are they capable of coping with the kind of [social ills] which exist in most of our urban areas, conditions which are becoming worse by the day."

He deplored what he called the "vindictive system" of crime and punishment. And he deplored "the greatest sin of American society— the status of the American Negro."

"If there were no 'Desires,'" he said, "there would be no Panthers. What I am saying is that we have to get our heads out of the sand, for, after all, it is an unsafe position. An ostrich buries his brains, and that part of his anatomy [that] remains visible makes a very good target for a sniper."

Unfortunately, it was Sirgo, the very opposite of an ostrich, who became the Howard Johnson sniper Mark Essex's target one week after his speech. Essex, a self-styled black extremist who had visited Panther headquarters but never joined the party, held hundreds of policemen at bay for ten hours, which climaxed in a week-long siege that paralyzed the Central Business District of the city. The twenty-three-year-old was killed during a rooftop gun battle with police sharpshooters who fired from a marine assault helicopter on January 7, 1973, but not before he had killed nine people, including Sirgo, and seriously wounded ten others.[10]

Moon Landrieu was born in New Orleans in 1930 and grew up in a racially mixed, working-class neighborhood. His father worked in a power plant, and his mother ran a corner grocery out of the front room of the family's shotgun house on Adams Street in the Carrollton area of what New Orleanians call "uptown." Landrieu family values stressed fairness and courtesy in the complex relationships with blacks who were their neighbors, maids, and customers. "But there was always that barrier. It's enough to confuse a child."[11]

At law school at Loyola University, Landrieu became active in student politics. He met two of Loyola's first black law students, Ben Johnson and Norman Francis. They became close friends. His experiences as student body president and his friendship with these two effectively changed his attitude toward racial segregation. His mentors at Loyola were Dr. Joseph Fichter, a sociologist who organized interracial projects, and Father Louis Twomey, a Jesuit who was active in race relations and labor education. In 1954, when the *Brown* decision ending school segregation was announced, Landrieu remembers "being terribly relieved that the decision was rendered."[12]

In 1957, after two years of army service, Landrieu opened a law practice on Broad and Washington streets. Roughly half of his clients were black. He served as mayor of New Orleans from 1970 to 1978, and as secretary of the Department of Housing and Urban Development from 1979 to 1980 under the Carter administration.

Landrieu is proud of having brought blacks into city government in meaningful ways. "We *moved* the system. We *moved* the system from an all-white system in which there was nobody [black] above the broom and mop level. We *moved* it. We moved it aggressively, beyond most people's wildest imaginations, beyond mine, to be honest with you." In 1970, black people occupied only 19.4 percent of the positions in the city's classified civil service; eight years later, they claimed 43 percent.

Landrieu broke with tradition on race. "I got to be known as 'Moon the Coon,'" he said around the time of his inauguration. "That was a common reference term. That's a badge of honor I wear with pride. People call you a nigger lover and I'd say, 'You're right, I am, without any shame or apologies.' But you don't get there overnight. Those kind of epithets in a Southern society will rock you the first time you hear them."[13]

Running a city presented some alarming challenges for the new mayor soon after he took office. The Panthers had recently come to town. Clarence Broussard, the owner of the Piety Street house where the Panthers lived after their eviction from St. Thomas, filed an eviction notice against them in August of 1970.[14]

In his 2003 interview with me, Landrieu described what happened: "The owner came to City Hall, as I recall, to see me and wanted to get them to vacate. I think he said they were Black Panthers. This was kind of new to us at the time. There had been no disturbance that I know of prior to that . . . I don't think there was any great concern on our part. The man came to see us and wanted these people out of his house."

I took note of his distinct understatement of the situation—"new to us," "no disturbance," "no great concern." As he continued, he began to describe the dilemma he faced about what to do considering the Panther reputation, the social anxiety, and the talk of revolution.

"And what could you do? After we looked into it, a group called the Black Panthers had taken over the place, boarded the place up, and put up their insignia or flag or whatever. It looked to us like it was more than a normal eviction. They, as far as I know, had not caused any trouble up to that point. I think the police were already monitoring them. I think the Panthers had already developed a reputation for being a 'militant,' hostile group, and I met with the police . . . At that particular time, there was a lot of anxiety about anti-American groups—the Vietnam War, the police brutality issue, running around the country. There was the youth movement. There was a whiff of revolution in the air . . . I wanted to make quite sure that we followed the law. So I advised them to go ahead and file this eviction notice with the court and have that eviction served on them, which they did. I don't know how they served the order, but I know it was served. I think it was just dropped on the front porch, because nobody would accept the order to vacate the house. Now bear in mind, they were occupying private property. This was not a public piece of property. I think this was an African American man as I recall. It was his personal property. They had taken it over, refused to pay him rent, refused to move out, and claimed it for themselves as a national piece of property, property of the people.

"We were then faced with the problem of what do we do with this legal situation. We can't let the law be ignored . . . It came to a head when they wouldn't get out and we were required by the law, our own moral commitment to the law, to evict them."

Landrieu, the experienced and scholarly lawyer, resolved the dilemma of what to do in his own mind by citing the rule of law and property rights.

Larry Preston Williams, a black officer in the Intelligence Unit, saw things differently. He thought the city's response to the Panthers was a result of politics. "You had Caucasians trying to evaluate a situation that they did not and could not begin to understand. In some ways they were probably more tolerant than most mayors and police chiefs would have been at the time, because Landrieu had run on a platform of including black people. In order to be an effective mayor, Landrieu had to be fairly liberal, and he was."[15]

Williams thought the police had it figured all wrong, too. He expected the Panthers to gain the confidence and respect of the Desire community. "But the funny thing, many of the white guys I worked for in Intelligence thought or wanted to believe that the people wouldn't [side with the Panthers]. Even if the residents didn't appreciate them being there, if it came down to choosing between the Panthers and the police, the people in large measure were going to take the side of the Panthers. And probably, had the police done it another way, it might not have come out like that. But even when the police were not trying to be heavy handed, they were making it seem as though the Panthers were the victims. And it only drew the Panthers and the community together. I thought white folks would understand that that's not a very good method . . . Clarence Giarrusso refused to believe that the citizens of New Orleans could form a relationship with a group that could come in to help them—which is not hard to understand because you didn't have a whole lot of other people helping. So the Panthers came in and fed their kids and tried to stand between them and police brutality and tried to make the place nicer to live in. It's only logical that they would form a bond with the Desire residents.

"The white people down at City Hall couldn't comprehend that. Seems strange that they could be so intelligent and politically astute and still be *so stupid!* Out of it completely! Not a clue! Just dumb! And things happen. You have a whole lot of confrontation that you don't have to have."

It was an amazing convergence of political events and personalities. At the same time a band of armed black revolutionaries formed in town, New Orleans had a new mayor who held progressive views about race, a new police chief who was humane, an assistant police chief who was a visionary, talented young black men in the city administration for the first time, and a black undercover cop who considered himself as far to the left as you could get. No wonder the defining racial event in New Orleans of the post–civil rights era didn't play out the way everyone thought it would.

6

The "Kidnapping"
of Ronald Ailsworth

When I first interviewed Malik Rahim, Marion Brown, and Robert King Wilkerson about the Panthers, they spoke fondly of Ronald Ailsworth, a Panther brother involved in the Piety Street shootout who now resides at Angola State Penitentiary. Marion praised him as an effective Panther organizer both inside prison and on the outside. As he serves his life sentence for a bank robbery, Ailsworth, Malik pointed out, has become a respected Imam, or Muslim cleric.[1]

Before he was arrested, Ailsworth was a strong supporter of the survival programs, especially the free breakfast for school children. I had the feeling in talking to Althea Francois, a female Panther active with free breakfasts and in charge of Panther children the night of the shootout, that she and Ailsworth were sweethearts at the time. But she never confirmed this. In any case, they have stayed in touch and visited over the decades.

When Ailsworth was arrested the day after the shootout for robbing the bank on the corner of Freret Street and Jefferson Avenue, it barely got a mention in the local papers. Malik said the money he took was probably intended for the breakfast program. But before he was arrested, the *Black Panther Newspaper* had already devoted substantial coverage to his hard work for the NCCF and the police harassment and brutality that it seemed to attract.

On September 12, 1970, here is what the *Black Panther Newspaper* had to say:

> On August 21, 1970, at 1:30 pm, Brother Ronald Ailsworth
> was kidnapped off the streets by two of the New Orleans pig

department fascist dogs. Brother Ron who is a hard worker for the NCCF here has been trying very hard to collect donations from the businessmen so that we can successfully implement the Free Breakfast for School Children Program. The pigs view the Breakfast Program as being a big threat to their capital and see it as being an effective tool in explaining the true nature of this decadent society. So in their all out efforts to sabotage the Breakfast Program, they moved in a fascist fashion to rip off the person whom they know is directly involved.[2]

The Panther writers did not mince words in conveying their take on what was going on. The article goes on to give the specifics:

On this particular day Brother Ron had just returned from collecting donations. He took the garbage across the street for the Project Sanitation to pick up. As soon as the brother put the box down he was vamped on by two pigs. Reed, who is known throughout the projects for his brutal tactics against Black people, and the other just being a commonly known White racist pig named Spong, stopped the brother and told him to go pick up the box. The brother being hip to pigs and not wanting to intimidate them, went and picked up the box of garbage. This is when the nigger pig asked his partner what could he arrest him on. The racist dog replied, "We can get him on putting garbage on a city street without placing it in a container." Pig Reed then made the statement to the brother, "You're the one who's been going around picking up donations. You're under arrest." Brother Ron didn't resist, he got into the car, and they drove off.

They took the brother to a back street and told him to get out. Ray Reed handcuffed the brother and started beating him in the back with his black jack. He began making statements such as "Why don't you resist nigger, so I can pop you in the head, you ain't nothing but a punk." After this he started punching the brother in the mouth. He then threw the brother in the car and took him to the precinct. There the pigs contin- ued their harassment, by trying to get information from the brother and threatening his life. They charged him with put- ting garbage in the city streets and refusal to put it in a con- tainer. He was then let out on parole.[3]

According to this account, he was threatened, insulted, and beaten up for putting out the trash, all the while exhibiting admirable restraint. But the cops didn't stop there.

"After getting out of jail, he was stopped again by the pigs and re-searched. During the re-search the pigs suddenly came up with a stick of reefer. These pigs have stooped to the low level of actually planting weed on the brother. He was then re-arrested and charged with pos-session of narcotics . . . The pigs thought they had for a while stopped the functioning of the Breakfast Program, but because of their pig men-talities, they don't understand that because they jail a servant of the people, a revolutionary, that they didn't jail the revolution."[4]

Although this story circulated nationwide in the *Black Panther Newspaper*, it was not the kind of news that would be mentioned in the mainstream media. The "kidnapping" would precede even more drastic legal events. On September 15, Ailsworth was arrested and booked with attempted murder in connection with the Panther-police shootout on Piety Street. On September 17, 1970, he was booked for armed robbery in connection with a $2,600 holdup at the International City Bank branch at Jefferson Ave. and Freret St.[5] I never drive by the building that used to be that bank, just blocks from where I live, with-out sending Ron a little jolt of sympathy.

To Ailsworth, the police in Desire were an abusive, oppressive invad-ing force. They harassed him and finally put him away for life. But some of the young people living in Desire experienced the cops in an entirely different way. One was Linda Francis.

7
A Pig or Officer Friendly?

In 1970 Linda Francis was a curious teenager living in Desire. She moved to Desire with her family when she was nine, the day after Hurricane Betsy in 1965. Desire was the only one of New Orleans' ten housing developments that was built for large families, and it was still fairly new. Linda remembers that people were clamoring to get in despite its many structural and other problems.

I met Linda Francis through Cecil Carter, who in 1970 was deputy director of the Human Relations Committee for the city of New Orleans and part of the team that Landrieu had charged with solving the Panther showdown peacefully. In 2003, Francis, a nurse, was helping him take care of his aging mother. Although Carter and Francis had not spoken much of Desire as they became friends, he thought that she would have some insights into the Panther story. While Cecil made tuna salad sandwiches, Linda and I sat around his kitchen table as she recalled Desire in the 1960s.

Desire was Linda's whole world. She was friendly with the black policemen assigned to the development. They would stop and talk with folks, she remembers, as they walked their beat. Sometimes she would speak with "long, tall Officer Friendly" (his real title), who later would use an unconscionable ruse to arrest the Panthers. He just thought he was doing a service to the community, according to Henry Faggen.[1]

Cecil paused from his culinary tasks to explain that by 1970, there were about fifty black officers on the police force. The force had been integrated in the 1960s, and this was the second wave. "The first wave were conscientious super-cops, good guys," Cecil said. "The second wave of [black] cops—who were still in the very gross minority—felt it necessary to out-cop the cops, tried to be bad-ass." But in general, he concludes, the police in Desire were well-known and fairly well-respected. "So when Panthers came in talking about the cops were pigs, that didn't altogether compute."[2]

The fear of infiltrators, instilled in Panther leaders from other places, didn't altogether compute either. In other cities the seeds of mistrust planted by local and FBI informants wrought havoc on chapters and played a large role in the demise of the party in the 1970s. But in New Orleans, the two young cops with the big Afros just *thought* they had infiltrated. The Panthers, tipped off by the little boys selling the *Louisiana Weekly,* knew who they were all along. Cecil cites another New Orleans example of an agent provocateur who planned civil rights protests and worked for the Marine intelligence—"Everybody knew he was talking trash. He lived down in the French Quarter with a Playboy bunny. People pretty much ignored him until he left town." In a town where most people know other people's business, the infiltration tactic wasn't as threatening as it was elsewhere.

Linda lived in the front part of Desire. "We couldn't go to the back [where the Panthers stayed]," she recalled. "But we snuck back there to see what was going on." Sometimes she'd go to the Panther classes, but she didn't pay much attention to what was being taught. "Marchin' and speakin' out" is how she remembers the Panthers. "They marched two by two around the project—just marchin' and talkin' about Black Power. We had to wear green and black and red bands around our hands or on our clothing. You made sure you had your green, red, and black attire on. They [Panthers] gave it out free and if you misplaced yours or didn't have it on, people said they were gonna get you. So you'd have to make one up. If you didn't have your wrist band, the school teachers had a ribbon and a stick pin and would pin it on you to make sure you had one on. The teachers said something about Black Revolution but I didn't pay much attention.

"My mom didn't talk about it. She was pretty much scared because she didn't know what was going on. She went to work and came home and that was it. It didn't faze most of us because they [Panthers] were not violent. It wasn't like a violent thing. They were just talking about the Revolution and Black Power and fight the pigs and the pigs are this and the pigs are that. It wasn't scary."

The day the police invaded Desire—November 19, 1970—Linda got to stay home from school. So while Carter and others were scouting to see who had hand grenades, relaying urgent messages to Mayor Landrieu, and praying that one false move wouldn't set off a massacre, fourteen-year-old Linda Francis was largely unconcerned.

8 Just before the Shootout

What was it like in and around Desire just before the cataclysmic shootout occurred? There seem to be as many stories as there were people down there that night. It was a Monday, the night youth from the project and elsewhere gathered in and around Panther headquarters for Public Education (PE). There was an unusually large crowd for PE this night, more than fifty. Police had been stepping up surveillance (some say harassment), residents believed, in an attempt to provoke a confrontation with the Panthers. For their part, the Panthers had had enough of pretending they did not know that Israel Fields and Melvin Howard were under cover. People sensed the tensions and gathered at headquarters to find out what was going on.

The Panther headquarters wasn't just an office; it was also their home. Panther families lived on Piety Street communally, sharing resources, labor, fundraising and organizing tasks, and responsibilities for parenting. They had a close relationship with many Desire residents. Additionally, many outsiders came to Desire that night, either curious or wanting to help.

I've captured descriptions of what that mean Monday was like from the perspectives of a white history teacher and his wife; a white Panther lawyer named Robert Glass; reporters from the alternative *NOLA Express;* Warren Brown, a black reporter for the *States-Item;* Israel Fields, one of the undercover officers; Panther Malik Rahim; and Panther Althea Francois, who had the horrific job of minding the children that night.

Another alleged kidnapping in Desire caught the attention of the media—this time the mainstream media—just before the shootout. A white couple had ventured into the project on the evening of September 14, they said, because they had been told that white people should come into the project area "to keep police from getting carried away." The *Times-Picayune* reported that the couple had been attacked by the people they tried to help. According to the report, neither Peter Wolslawski, a history teacher at L. W. Landry Junior High School, nor his wife, Evelyn, expressed hatred for those who beat them. "'How much must have been done to those people for them to hate so much?'" asked Peter, who received two black eyes and a fractured cheekbone. "'I'm not a saint, but I don't hate them.'"[1]

According to Evelyn Wolslawski, after she and her husband were pulled out of opposite sides of the car, her captors took her to a dark room in an old building where sandbags were stacked up to the windows and furniture was piled on furniture. She said a man hit her with a gun, causing her to pass out. "She said she did not remember if she provoked the assault."[2]

When she regained consciousness, she found herself lying alone outside. She then flagged down a car, she said, and a black man took her home to Gretna.[3] One report stated that she had been kidnapped and woke up naked from the waist down.[4] But many people who were in Desire, including Malik Rahim and Panther attorney Ernest Jones, say the newspapers were wrong. Mrs. Wolslawski was so drunk she didn't know where she was or what she was doing, according to them. Desire residents took pity on her and made sure she got home safely, they say. [5] The *Times-Picayune* reported Jones as saying that the allegation about the white couple being dragged from their car was an "absolute lie," because they had walked into the area. He didn't doubt that they were beaten, but he said it was unfortunate that the couple was there at a time when emotions were running so high.[6] Whatever happened, Mrs. Wolslawski's statement to the paper about not remembering whether she had provoked the alleged attack could be explained by an excess of alcohol, an excess of liberal white guilt, or both.

Mrs. Wolslawski's description of the room she had been taken to by her "captors" sounded a lot like the Piety Street Panther headquarters to the police. But eventually, the story of the assault, which possibly didn't hold together well under closer scrutiny, just seemed to go away.

On the evening of September 14 it was getting dark outside of Robert Glass's central city New Orleans Legal Assistance Corporation (NOLAC) office. NOLAC is a nonprofit free legal aid program for low-income people. Glass was working late to make sure that his files and his records were all in order, because he had a feeling that he wouldn't be working for NOLAC much longer. His current clients were too controversial.

The previous June when Judge Bagert had started eviction proceedings against the revolutionaries on St. Thomas Street, the Panthers had asked Bob Glass and fellow attorney Ernest Jones to represent them. Even though it cost Glass and Jones their first jobs out of law school and they had no idea how they would get paid, neither one thought twice about defending the Black Panthers.

Thirty-three years later, Glass was working late again, this time in an elegant but comfortable downtown office with brick walls, wide plank floors, and plenty of New Orleans charm. Although he was a busy man, in demand as a defense lawyer, with the reputation of having an acerbic personality, he was willing to give a lengthy interview that evening. He ended it with this story, almost as an afterthought:

"I got a call that some trouble had occurred down in the Desire Housing Projects. I called Ernest [Jones] at home, and we agreed to meet down there. I got down there. And on the edge of the project was a liquor store called Champs. I walked into the store—I was a little young and prideful. After law school I had bought a Mont Blanc fountain pen, and that's what I used in my office late at night to write. They cost thirty-five dollars at the time. And so I had the pen with me when I drove down to the Desire project.

"I walked into Champs liquor store and there was a young black man with a bandolier—That's what those things are with bullets across the chest? It's called a bandolier? I think that's what they are—and a gun. He said, 'My kid sister could use that pen at her school.' And he took it. It took me five years—the prices kept going up. It took me five years before I could buy another one."

Jones met Glass at the Panther headquarters. "We went to the house in which somebody had been injured by a bullet," Glass recalled. "One of us took the person to the People's Health Clinic on Decatur Street."[7]

Glass said he never saw Evelyn Wolslawski at Panther headquarters or anywhere else that evening. However, he was unwillingly drawn into her story when his plaid sports jacket with his bar card (identifying him as a lawyer) in the pocket was found in the Piety Street house after the shootout. Glass says he must have taken it off when he was there that night right before the shootout and forgotten it. That was reason enough for a grand jury, which has broad powers of questioning, to subpoena him as a witness about the white couple.

The *States-Item* reported that "the district attorney's office wants Glass as a material witness to the beating . . . The grand jury is considering the possibility that the woman was the victim of certain crimes, among them simple kidnapping, attempted rape, rape and aggravated battery."[8]

Glass declined to answer the subpoena on the grounds that he had acted—and was still acting—in an attorney-client relationship with people on Piety Street. He refused to testify and was held in contempt. He appealed it all the way to the U. S. Fifth Circuit and lost. By the time he was forced to serve his five-day jail time in 1972, the Panther case was history and the Wolslawski story had just seemed to disappear.[9]

When asked if he was scared that night in Desire, Glass says, "No. Not that I was particularly brave. I was young. I don't remember physical fear. [The guy with the gun] created some apprehension. But he left. And when he left he brought me from the liquor store to the Piety house. He walked me over there. I think he said, 'If that's where you want to go, I'll take you there.'"

What went through my mind as I interviewed him was, "How could you have not been afraid? You're a white lawyer in a black housing project on the tensest night in its history. Someone with a gun took your pen and then offered to escort you to Panther headquarters. There were rumors of white people getting beaten up and raped. Somehow it made sense to you to meet your black law partner in Desire when you must have had a pretty good idea that it was getting ready to explode. Moreover, you were ready and willing to go to jail rather than have to answer questions that might damage your clients, though you knew you'd be seen as a race traitor, and probably never get paid."

As a psychotherapist I've learned to let such argumentative inner dialogues just play out in my head, concentrating instead on trying to get a glimpse of the situation from the other person's point of view. The view I was getting was "through a Glass darkly," as the verse from Corinthians goes. No doubt from the vantage point of eternity, it would all become clear.

The two lawyers who were called to Piety that night first met at NOLAC, where they were both Community Lawyer Fellows. Ernest Jones had moved to New Orleans in 1969 right out of Howard Law School. He had missed the Vietnam War "by the skin of my teeth."[10] His interest and training were in poverty law. "Everything was changing and everything was possible. That was the way everybody looked at it. The Panthers just burst onto the scene when I was in college. In 1969 Fred Hampton [a national Panther leader] was murdered by police in Chicago. Riots and assassinations popped up all over the place. People started to look around and notice that something was very much wrong. Nobody knew what was going to happen, but everybody believed that something had to change." Jones would later play an eloquent role in the Panther defense.

Glass had finished law school in 1968 and come to New Orleans from Philadelphia also on a Community Lawyer Fellowship program for NOLAC. He never intended to stay. "The Panthers and their families couldn't pay," Jones recalled, "but we knew it would work out some kind of a way because we thought we were doing the right thing. There was not a lot of soul searching. This is why I had become a lawyer."

Soon after Glass and Jones took the Panther case, they had to quit their NOLAC jobs, because "you [couldn't] be on the federal payroll and defend these people," Jones explained. "People raised some money so we could survive."

The public response to the two lawyers was markedly different. It was tougher on Glass because he was white. Jones was seen as just doing what black lawyers do, whereas Bob Glass, according to Jones, "got vilified because he was white . . . Bob was seen as a traitor, a race traitor. Everybody who qualifies for the benefits that were given with white skin was presumptively going to take them. And part of that meant that you didn't give any aid and comfort to those folks who *didn't* have them. But Bob never wavered. Never, never."

Rumors swirled all around New Orleans just before the shootout, and many were skeptical about the accuracy of the reports that appeared in both daily papers, the *States-Item* and the *Times-Picayune.* The *NOLA Express,* which came out every other week, offered a truly alternative point of view. Considered one of the most outrageous papers put out anywhere during the 1960s, it was published by two young white poets, Darlene Fife and Robert Head, and produced by a dedicated band of activists, poets, and illustrators based in the French Quarter. *NOLA Express* was profoundly opposed to American imperialism, racism, and materialism.[11]

In September of 1970, the *Express* complained that everything fed to the media about the situation in Desire was scripted by the police department. They said only certain reporters were allowed in at certain times to witness certain events:

> One thing they don't tell you when you go to journalism school is how cozy you'll get with the police department. Why some of your best friends will be police. They'll provide you with leads, give you copy for stories and most important give you just the right slant for your objective reporting . . .
>
> It's a script. We don't know who wrote it, but whoever directs has all the players trained enormously well. Some of us people here at *NOLA Express* were silly enough to think we might be able to make a few alterations in the script, and believe it or not we actually thought the New Orleans media might want to help out. We thought the local reporters might not like the parts they are supposed to play, but it turns out they'll even ad lib their parts whenever they get a chance.
>
> Just two weeks ago we called a press conference to let the media know that two NOLA staff members were stopped and searched by the police as they left the Panther office and that the Panthers were under 24 hour surveillance and harassment, a potentially explosive situation.[12]

To the mainstream media, that was a nonevent. The daily papers ignored the press conference and Darlene Fife's editorial challenge to them. But that only increased Fife's determination to capture every detail of the unfolding historic events.

The day before the shootout, September 14, *NOLA Express* reported, "One of the members of our tribe managed to finally get out to Desire this morning. He was allowed to get no closer than 8 blocks from the NCCF Headquarters, so was unable to see what was actually happening. Hundreds of local residents stood along Florida Ave. and he was able to speak with them. 'As many observers as I spoke with denounced the police as deliberately trying to provoke violence by making harassment of local residents' routine. Generally, residents expressed a strong desire to fight the pigs and their rulers.' When asked what whites could do, they responded, 'Tell the truth and bring some artillery with you next time.'"[13]

One *NOLA Express* article is merely a record of a phone conversation that occurred during the night of September 14; one of the participants, apparently, was the *New York Times* reporter Roy Reed, who was based in New Orleans. The cryptic report is included here just as it appeared in the *Express,* because each line or fragment, although sometimes confusing, seems to hint at the terror of what was going on:

> Reed—*New York Times.* Hello, I'm sorry to call you so late but . . . will you go? It is. You are. You will? That's great. I hope it's not too late. Wonder what kind of person he is. Keep trying doctors. Nothing.
>
> Talk to friend again. Two police reported wounded. Don't know how many Blacks. Taking people to charity hosp. By the way, I just learned Landrieu has been in conference with Giarrusso. They have governor on the phone mobilizing the national guard. I also just found out that there was a briefing with the press. What press? The mayor and Giarrusso had a briefing with the top people from the papers and stuff. Did they give a release or something? No, they aren't making any statements yet. I see, just a cozy little power structure pow-wow.
>
> Reports from the hospital confusing. No one seems to know what has taken place. People and police everywhere. Police separating family and friends of wounded and talking to them alone. No one can find out anything from anybody. Still getting

calls for doctors. You just don't know how much I want to get one for you. I promise you I shall never be this impotent again. If you'll just stay alive, I promise you, next time . . .

Peculiar news. The police have decided to call it a night and come back at dawn. What does that mean, what's supposed to happen at dawn? Don't know, that's all I heard. Going home now, will call you if I hear anything else. But don't go out there, just stay where you are. Sure . . . You don't have to worry about that . . . I'm too tired now to even feel guilty about it [not going to the scene of the action].

Dawn. Phone wakes me from my 30 second doze. The police are now processing reporters who want to go into the area to wait. You have to go down there to get police identification and then you can go out. . . . Planning a raid. What do they call what they've been doing.[14]

That same night, the black *States-Item* reporter Warren Brown managed to get into Desire, but his white colleague was turned away by police. Brown filed this report:

Accompanied by fellow *States-Item* reporter Chris Shearouse, I was preparing to go into the project about 2:30 a.m. to check out reports of disturbances. As we turned off Florida Avenue onto Desire Street, we were stopped immediately by four or five policemen, two with shotguns.

They asked to see our identification. Then we asked the policemen if we could go as a group into the project. They said we could not; they weren't allowing whites to go back in but they told me I could go in at my own risk.[15]

Brown went in, apparently with another black person. He said that a shot was fired, "either at us or very, very near us . . . We fell to the ground and I lost my glasses," Brown continued. "I asked who the blacks were shooting at, since they must have seen that we are black. 'Cops and Uncle Toms,'" a young man answered.

According to all reports, the immediate precipitating cause of the September 15 shootout on Piety Street between the police and the Panthers was the outing of two undercover policemen. Local and national newspapers featured headlines about the mock trial and beatings of infiltrators Melvin Howard and Israel Fields at the hands of the Panthers. But thirty-five years later, Israel Fields said that there was no trial. Inside the Piety Street house, there was "not much at all, just a little scuffle" with people shouting accusations. Fields remembered three other NOPD undercover officers being there that night, as well as at least one person from the FBI. "We never admitted to being undercover."[16]

"Tyrone Edwards hit both of us in the head with a pot. When he hit me a second time, that started a fight." Fields and Edwards fell to the floor—neither would let go—and both of them took some kicks. But others intervened to stop the fight, and the Panthers ended up putting Fields and Howard out on the street. Once out of the Piety Street house, Fields says he was stabbed in the back and hit by a two-by-four with nails in it. He didn't know who his assailants were. When he looked at the blood coming out of his head, he almost passed out. "If I had, I probably would have been dead." But instead, he picked up a metal garbage can to shield himself against blows from a metal pipe and started running. "I was out on my feet. As soon as I realized I was running, I fell flat on my face." Somehow, he got to Foreman's grocery store, which was next to Broussard's. From there he called headquarters, and they sent someone to take him to Charity hospital, where twenty-seven stitches were required to close up the gash on his ear.

Fields had joined the force in 1969, when he was twenty years old. He became part of the narcotics squad when Clarence Giarrusso was in charge of it and Joseph Giarrusso was police chief. "I had a narcotics buy on one of the guys." Fields had bought marijuana from Ron Ailsworth on St. Thomas Street, after which he was encouraged by both Giarrussos to hang around Panther headquarters. He officially went undercover in August of 1969. Young and still very green to police work in 1970, he mused in 2005, "Maybe I was trying to stay out of the war and I wound up in another war." He and Melvin Howard worked independently, and it took him some time to figure out that Howard was undercover also.

Fields says that his escape from Piety Street was quite frightening. He hadn't completely realized what he was getting into. Comparing his stint with the narcotics squad to his undercover work, he reflected, "I would rather buy drugs."

Malik Rahim recounted the events leading up to the shootout this way: He said two little boys selling the *Louisiana Weekly* on the corner of Tulane and Broad—right outside of police headquarters—had tipped off the Panthers weeks before the shootout when the observant children spotted Howard and Fields. In late July, they said to a party member, "Hey, them two is police, pigs," setting in motion a hair-raising chain of events. "Those kids knew just about every police that came in and out," said Malik.

The Panthers knew how to handle the obvious undercover police. "We'd call them Uncle Toms and we'd run 'em off. But the two young ones with big, gigantic bushes [Afros], Melvin Howard and Israel Fields—there was a lot of debate about what to do with *them*.

"First we said we were going to expose them. But then Charles [Scott, the nineteen-year-old New Yorker who had inspired Malik with Panther principles,] said, 'No, we won't expose them 'cause then they gonna send some more and it might take us too long to find out who they are. Let's just keep them here. We're gonna feed them with a long-handled spoon and we're gonna use them up.'"

At that same meeting, a Panther imposter who had not yet been discovered, a federal agent who had infiltrated the unit said, "Kill them."[17]

"But Charles said, 'No. We'll either educate them or use them until they realize they are Uncle Toms. Maybe they'll see the light.'" So that's what they did.

As the weeks passed, it became more and more obvious that the police would find some excuse for a raid on the Piety Street Headquarters. But the Panthers still pretended not to know that two of their "brothers" were NOPD cops.

Malik remembers that the night before the shootout, the police cordoned off the project, restricted access, and were flying over it in a helicopter. There was sniping all night long, probably from Broussard's store, Malik believes. The Panthers evacuated all the children from the headquarters. Anyone who wanted to leave could.

Althea Francois was surprised at the number of people who had come for the public education class conducted by Charles Scott that night. She noticed that he was rushing through the class. Then he said, "There are two pigs in the office." Althea felt a chill go through her body. He told her to take Olga, her two-year-old, to the back. He then instructed her to take all of the children to the safe house and wait for more instructions. So she gathered up the five or six children, all under the age of five, and headed with them for a house less than a block away from the headquarters.

"It was a very strange night," Althea recalled. "I didn't sleep at all; but the children slept through because they were too young to know what was going on."

"If things get really hairy, throw a mattress over the children and lie on top," Charles told her.[18]

According to the *States-Item,* on the day of the shootout, "During early morning hours, many Panther sympathizers in Desire pleaded with the leaders to 'lose themselves' in the project's labyrinthine complex of buildings to avoid police arrest." But the Panthers had their own way of doing things. "They stayed to face the riot squads," the paper reported.[19]

Malik Rahim had a plan for getting out. There were bunkers all through Desire. "Get as close to the Gulf as you can," he thought, "take a boat, and go to Cuba."

But again, Charles saw it differently. He said, "No, man. This is political. And we gonna make a political stand." He wasn't moving the group into the projects, either, because "they gonna destroy a lot of people's houses. These people are poor. They can't afford to lose nothin.' We gonna stay right here in our office."

Malik remembered that even with the sniping, people from Desire were coming over to see if they needed anything and to help get the children out. One lady came over and put a prayer cloth, a plain black cloth, on the wall and said, "Ain't nothing' gonna happen to y'all."

As tensions rose, it became harder to deal with the so-called Panthers who were cops. A month and a half of pretending not to know had created a strain. According to Malik, the night before the shootout, he lost patience with Fields and punched him straight in the mouth when Fields claimed not to be a cop. But Charles, the principled strategist, said, "No man, don't hit him. Don't beat him. Don't do anything to him."

Meanwhile, a crowd had gathered around the Piety Street Panther headquarters. Monday was the regular night for the public education class, and word on the street was that something was about to happen on Piety. "Charles reasoned that Fields and Howard, if they were all right, if what they were standing for was right, if they were there to protect their people, they wouldn't have any problem going out of the Panther office and walking in front of the people. So [the Panthers] tossed them out there," recalled Malik. "Howard and Fields tried to run through the crowd, and some Panther members even opened up a way for them so they could try to get away. Charles figured, if they get jumped, that's just the excuse the police want to come in here and raid. When the Panthers opened up the way, one ran straight for Broussard's store."

According to the *New York Times,* "Mr. Fields said he took refuge in a grocery store and waited to be rescued by other policemen. Mr. Howard said he jumped a seven-foot fence and outran his pursuers."[20]

Malik continued, "As soon as they got to the store, the police opened fire. That's where they killed a young brother [the next day] who just happened to be there. He didn't even have a rock." The first shots of the thirty-minute volley, according to Malik, came from Broussard's store.

The *States-Item* reported that patrolmen Reed and Orticke, the black policemen who patrolled Desire not under cover, had driven by the Piety headquarters shortly before midnight Monday and had seen two men who looked like they had been beaten running toward Broussard's grocery store. Reed and Orticke had come to investigate a car burning.[21] The car belonged to Fields and Howard, according to the *NOLA Express.*[22]

The *States-Item* report went on to say, "Gunfire then sent bullets ripping through the patrol car, injuring Reed and Orticke."[23]

During the Monday night of sporadic shooting Althea was awake all night at the safe house. Around 7:00 a.m. on Tuesday, the children, including Donald (Malik Rahim) and Barbara's two, were just waking up. They wanted their breakfast, their bottles, their mamas and daddies. Althea could see the Piety Street house from where she stood in the doorway, but she didn't know whose parents were still there; and she had no way, at that moment, of finding out. She didn't know if Ron Ailsworth, whom she admired greatly, was in the house. She turned around and scooped up the littlest, fed them all a breakfast of oatmeal, and pretended it was a normal morning.[24]

But there was nothing normal about what was about to happen.

9
The Shootout

After the undercover cops escaped and after several people in Desire were wounded by snipers during the night, after the white couple and attorneys Ernest Jones and Robert Glass had gone home, there was a lull in the shooting for several hours. But in the morning, the police plan started to roll.

The police plan was partly a response to Broussard's legal right to evict the Panthers from his private property, as Landrieu explained. But according to Larry Preston Williams, it had more to do with surveillance information that two undercover cops were soon to be outed. Giarrusso apparently wanted to protect them in the conflict that he knew would ensue.

Malik Rahim and Williams described the shootout from two completely different points of view, and yet their stories do not conflict factually. Both were amazed at the absence of bloodshed. Was what kept both police and Panthers alive the prayer cloth, blank bullets, Giarrusso's control, or dumb luck? Who knows.

Another mystery was Steve Green's role in the New Orleans Panther chapter. Geronimo ji Jaga Pratt, a Louisiana native and national Panther leader, told me that he sent Steve to New Orleans. Williams, however, thinks that Green was sent by the FBI. In any case, Green left New Orleans before the shootout, according to Malik and Green himself, yet the *New York Times* reported him injured in the shootout and gave details of his injury. Where did that story come from and why?

Here is how the drama unfolded:

"The scene of the Central Lockup as police geared up for the raid was grim," reported the *Times-Picayune* on September 15, 1970. Also in that article: "'It's a job,' a black policeman said simply. 'It has to be done by somebody.'"

A convoy of police buses, police cruisers, and newsmen in private cars made its way through the downtown morning rush-hour traffic and onto Interstate 10. The first bus pulled out of police headquarters at 8:04 a.m., reaching Desire shortly after 8:30, just as the winds from the nearby tropical storm Felice churned up a black cover of clouds that dumped a downpour of rain on the city. Several hundred New Orleans policemen and twenty or thirty state policemen descended on Panther headquarters, a large old frame building decorated with posters of Panther heroes.[1] By 8:45 a.m., the battle was on. "My god, it sounds like a war," one policeman exclaimed as automatic rifle and machine gun fire punctuated the early morning stillness.[2]

Malik Rahim told the story of the shootout on Piety Street in this way: "There were twelve of us in the party office at the time, and almost a hundred police with everything from a .50-caliber machine gun and armored cars down to their revolvers. We had about nine shotguns and a couple of handguns, .357 revolvers. But everything we had was legally purchased, and it was registered to our office. Our position was that African Americans should no longer be lynched or beaten or attacked and have their rights taken away without any form of resistance. We believed that you had a right to defend yourself. You had a right to defend your community. You had a right to defend your family. And you had the right to defend your honor as a human being."[3]

Malik continued to tell the story as if he were watching a movie in his head: "The police came in busloads. They got in their positions and just started shooting. They shot up in the office maybe twenty minutes straight. It seemed like it was all day. I said, 'Boy, they gonna kill us.' The firing was coming in so fast we literally had to pour water on the walls because you could see the sheet rock expanding from the heat till you could touch it and it would just pop. The tear gas came in constantly as fast as we could throw it out. We put bread in wet towels. The yeast in the bread helped with the tear gas. The front door weighed about three hundred pounds." It was constructed from drain covers scavenged from the nonfunctional Desire sewer system.

Among the revolutionaries and defenders of the people was a fourteen-year-old in the Piety house when the shootout occurred whom the Panthers hadn't been able to get out in time. In the middle of all the shooting, he rose up and uttered a plea that probably voiced the fears of the slightly older people as well. "I want my Mama!" Everyone was taken aback. Someone yelled, "Get down, fool!" and tackled him. Seconds later, the place where he had been standing was riddled with bullets.[4]

Time Magazine described it this way: "Shots of unknown origin were heard, and police opened fire with automatic rifles and shot-guns. Some of the ammunition was powerful enough to rip through three rooms and emerge from the building's opposite wall . . . The besieged were presumably saved from death or injury by sandbags they had piled against their walls."[5]

"All of a sudden the shooting stopped." Malik continued his story, peering out the window in King and Marion's living room as if looking for an explanation on their porch. "After about three or four minutes, Charles asked me to crawl to the different rooms and find out how many was injured and how many was dead. I went to the first room. I asked, 'How many people in there are shot? How many is dead?' Ron [Ailsworth] told me, 'Ain't nobody in here shot or dead.'

"I crawled to the next room—Leah and T. I asked them. Nobody shot or dead. Elaine and Ed. 'Who's shot and who's dead?' Nobody. The back room—Cathy and Brokie. 'Who's shot, who's dead?' Nobody.

"I went back to Charles and he asked, 'Who they done killed?' I said, 'Nobody.' He said, 'What!? All that shootin' and they ain't shot nobody!?' I said 'no' and we all bust out laughin.'

"He said, 'Well, we done did all we can do in here. Now we gonna take it to court. Tell everybody to come down.'

"I said, ' No. I ain't gonna let them take me out anywhere and hang me, beat me to death. Whatever they gonna do to me, they gonna do to me right here.'

"Charles said, 'That's not what we here for. We gonna come out of here *as men and women* and we gonna take it to the court. Whatever happens from there happens. If they take us out of here and kill us, everybody in this community, they gonna know what happened because we gonna walk out of here *as men and women.'*

"We all gathered up in the second room and that's when Charles gave to me one of the greatest inspirational speeches I ever heard. He said, 'We're the Black Panther Party and we ain't gonna bow down and we ain't gonna allow anybody to degrade us or what we stand for. We gonna let everybody know that we stand for our rights as human beings and we gonna take it to court. If they convict us, we gonna let everybody know that in this country there's two kinds of justice. There's justice for the rich and powerful and there's injustice for the poor and the disenfranchised. When you walk out of that door, everybody raise their hand and holler POWER TO THE PEOPLE.'"

The prayer cloth—or something (the sandbags, the three-hundred-pound door?)—had worked. So had Charles's inspirational speech. Malik prepared for the surrender: "Charles told me to tie a white flag on my shotgun and put it out the window. As we started walking out, I said, 'Hey, Charles, they might not honor that white flag.'

"Charles said, 'Well, hey, if that's what they gonna do, let me be the first one to die.'

"Charles was the first one to walk out. He raised up his hand at the door and called out POWER TO THE PEOPLE. I was the last one to leave the office. The first policeman that had me put a gun in my ear and tried to trip me to make it look like I was gonna run so he could shoot me. A sister named Charlene Duckworth was in her window and she yelled, 'Don't you shoot that brother!'

"When Charlene started hollering, another police, a lieutenant [Rahim thinks it was Sirgo], jumped that police who was trying to shoot me and made him leave. He put another police with me and brought us through the house. They took Ron and me back in and kept asking us, 'How many up in there is dead? How many is left in there?'

"Ed (one of the brothers) hollered 'FIVE. Get two of them big ones!'"

The Panthers were taunting the police even at this very tense time. Malik laughed as he remembered it because at the time of the shootout, he was the biggest, at a whopping 147 pounds.

Malik continued: "That's when I was able to get a look, a real look, at how everywhere you looked there were bullet holes. I looked and I said, 'Boy, how in the world did we survive this? Lord have mercy.'

"They had Ron [Ailsworth] and I to sit on the porch and it started raining. The police that was there with us, the white guy, he said, 'Hey, I respect that that's what y'all stand for, that's what y'all believe in. But this is what I believe in.'

"I said, 'Well, I respect that, too.'

"Then we talked about the Saints [the New Orleans football team], about the season the Saints was havin.' Then they took us to jail."

The arrested Panthers marched out of the headquarters with arms raised. They were ordered to walk across a narrow bridge over the Higgins Canal and told to lie on the ground, spread-eagled, while they were searched. They were then taken in a police van to Central Lockup for booking.[6]

Larry Preston Williams's view of the shootout is quite different from Malik's.[7] Williams, like Malik, was twenty-two, African American, and had grown up in New Orleans. But instead of going to Vietnam, as Malik had, he joined the NOPD and was assigned to the Intelligence Division. This is Williams's account:

"I arrived there in the afternoon, if I remember correctly. There were large numbers of police officers standing outside. We were there because we understood that the Black Panther Party was prepared to confront two men that they thought were undercover agents, that they thought were New Orleans police officers. The assumption was that that would cause some kind of conflict. The FBI told us. The chapter was well infiltrated with police officers and undercover agents. I think at any time there were probably at least five—at the high point maybe eight or nine—police officers and/or paid or leveraged informants. And we didn't know if the people they were going to accuse were really *our* police officers. But in the event that they did accuse our officers and in the event they were in danger, there was a contingent of officers prepared to go in and rescue them. So our presence there was really not to move the Panthers out of the premises but to be there to rescue our officers in the event they needed to be gotten out, extracted."

When Williams came into the Intelligence Unit, Fields and Howard were already undercover. He never debriefed them. "I would hear people say that they were two cops and I figured it out because they just kind of stood out. They didn't have the rhetoric. They didn't have the background. They were not from the same kind of home life. They just stood out. I just kind of suspected; but I wasn't certain."

The Piety Street office was bugged, but whether the transmitter was planted or whether undercover officers had body transmitters, Williams didn't know. In any case, from police headquarters he was able to hear the discussion in the Panther office:

"Somebody said, 'There's a pig in here!'

"And Mr. Fields said, 'Off the pigs!' Mr. Fields was at the time one of the NOPD undercover officers. And my memory is that shortly after that, Mr. Fields and the other undercover officer, Melvin Howard, left Panther headquarters and took refuge at a grocery store across the street.

"Later on, there was some firing back and forth. I'm not clear as to who fired the first shot. I didn't get any specific instructions. When I arrived, officers were standing around pretty angry, but at the same time under control. You didn't have officers—angry as they were—totally out of control, running around, storming the place, trying to kill people. I attribute that to Clarence Giarrusso's leadership.

"His brother [Joseph Giarrusso] was entirely different. He was old school—reactionary, rule by force. I think if it had been up to Joseph Giarrusso, the cops would have stormed the place. There would have been a bloodbath. That's the way you did it in those days. You didn't let people like the Panthers dictate what you did. You didn't give them a break. Not that you order people to kill suspects, but you understand that in that kind of frenzy—with setting that kind of example and tone—that someone was going to get killed."

"Well, Clarence's tone was just the opposite," Williams continued. "He had always had the reputation for being an easygoing, sensible, compassionate person. He would avoid violence if he could.

"Miraculously, no one was injured. I probably came as the shooting was winding down. I had a carbine at the time and I do remember firing some shots—but not many shots. I don't think I fired more than two or three shots. Our information was that somebody had switched out live ammunition for blanks. The reason I believe that was the case is that as we stood and fired at the Panthers, it would have been impossible for them to shoot into this large gathering of police officers and not hit anyone. Of course our ammunition was live.

"I was there when they surrendered. They came out with their hands up. We cuffed them and took them to Orleans Parish Prison . . . The Panthers *did* give up—to their credit—because that was not a confrontation that they could have won. It would have been impossible. With all the grenades they had, it still would have been a bloodbath, and the people who would have shed the most blood would have been the Panthers . . . When it came down to it, they put their hands up and walked out of their headquarters like any bank robber. They just gave up. They weren't ready to pay the ultimate price. Not ready at all . . . I mean, what kind of serious Panther just gives up? . . . Now to me that was a miracle. I am *glad* that they surrendered. But serious Panthers would have fought to the end. These guys were different. It's *good*."

Williams, of course, had not been privy to Charles Scott's inspirational speech.

Neither had Althea Francois from her post at the safe house with the children, so maddeningly close yet so far away. She recalls twenty-five minutes of nonstop shooting. "I didn't know which of the parents were in the building. Hearing the gunfire and the way it happened, I knew nobody was alive. It suddenly stopped. I had to just wait."[8]

After the Panthers filed out of the Piety Street house with their white flag on the rifle past the plain black cloth, the prayer cloth, that was pinned to the wall, and after they were searched and taken to Orleans Parish Prison, Chief Giarrusso called a press conference at 1:30 p.m. at City Hall. A reporter asked the chief, "What does an incident like this do to the man-power situation, working around the clock?"

Giarrusso answered, "I think that this community should recognize that we are terribly, terribly short of men. What it does to us . . . some of us have been up thirty consecutive hours."

"How long can you keep up at such a pace?" the reporter wanted to know.

"I don't know but we will if we have to. These people will not get a foothold in this community," the chief vowed.[9]

When the shooting stopped, neighbors drifted out to the front yards of their small houses across the street to watch. About four hundred people gathered behind the committee headquarters and shouted antipolice slogans.[10]

By 2:30 p.m. calm had returned to the Desire area. Public Service buses crossed the creaky bridge and headed into the project.[11] A young man with two companions sauntered by the firehouse, and he was blowing on a clarinet. Another man, his chest bare, frolicked past while holding his umbrella high to ward off the September sun.

And yet people were edgy. As a reporter left the general area in a cab, the driver said, "You are lucky; the first cab driver who had this call got cold feet and wouldn't come down here."[12]

The next day, life in the project appeared normal, with women doing their wash and hanging it in the backyards and children going to school or playing among the buildings. However, many people gathered in clusters and talked of the violence and, in hushed tones, about their extreme hostility toward the police.[13]

The *New York Times* was reporting almost daily on the details of life in Desire. The national media seemed fascinated with the danger, violence, and racial tensions playing out in New Orleans. Local papers carried several stories each day.

Thirteen people (including three women) were arrested when police stormed the Black Panther headquarters. On September 21, they were charged with five counts each of attempted murder. Bond was set at $100,000 per person.[14] The youngest, who had cried out for his mother, was released.

In her editorial in the *NOLA Express,* Darleen Fife asked, "Are the Panthers charged with attempted murder because 14 men and women between the ages of 14 and 27 tried to defend themselves from 200 armed men who were besieging their office?"[15]

A very good question.

Steve Green is one of the lingering mysteries of the shootout. Although he was originally from New Orleans, until the shootout, he was referred to by the media only as "Steve from the West Coast." He had contacted the Human Relations Committee in May to announce that he was setting up a Black Panther headquarters and to ask for assistance with a free breakfast program for children.

On September 19, 1970, the *New York Times* reported:

> Sources in the black community have disclosed that a Black
> Panther party organizer, the man the police particularly wanted
> to apprehend in their raid Tuesday on the party's headquarters,
> was severely wounded in the raid and has since been receiving
> shelter, protection and medical care somewhere in the city.
>
> The Panther organizer is Steve Green of Compton, California.
> He was known here only as "Steve from the West Coast" until the
> police made his full name public yesterday.
>
> Sources reported that Mr. Green was receiving "professional
> medical care" and that a tracheotomy—a surgical incision of the
> trachea, or wind-pipe, to prevent suffocation—had been per-
> formed. He was reported to be "doing O.K.," but some concern
> was expressed about his condition.
>
> The sources said one bullet went through Mr. Green's neck
> and another hit him in the shoulder. He has been unable to talk
> since the injuries.[16]

Malik, however, tells a very different story. Steve, that "brother who
had no fear," had actually left New Orleans before the shootout,
prompting some who survived the police assault to wonder whether
Steve was a part of the FBI. But Malik admired Steve Green and has
defended him to the other Panthers over the years. He didn't see or
hear from Steve again for thirty-three years, but he continued to
believe that Steve had not deceived or betrayed them.

Larry Preston Williams, however, thought that Steve worked for
the FBI. "It was always reputed," Williams told me, "that Green Stevens
[a.k.a. Steve Green] was a person who came to town at the request of
the FBI to start a Panther chapter so that the FBI could identify those
people who had those revolutionary tendencies, thinking that if they
created a Panther Party, those people would surface and they would
be identifiable. And there may have been some other reasons NOPD
thought that he was the person . . . Then things would happen, and
he'd always be in the midst of them."

Two years before I met Williams, as I wrote about the shootout, I
mulled over the Steve Green mystery. And then, out of the blue, as our
committee prepared in 2003 for the Panther forum, Malik arrived late
with two friends. When he introduced them as Lil Man (a former

Panther) and Steve Green, I almost fell out of my chair. I felt like the very act of writing this story had materialized one of the characters who had seemed to disappear under disputed circumstances thirty-three years ago. The real explanation was that Geronimo ji Jaga Pratt had called Steve to tell him about the forum and suggest that he might want to participate.

I couldn't wait to ask him about the *New York Times* story and what really happened. Steve claimed that none of what the *New York Times* said about him is true. He confirmed that he left New Orleans before the shootout; afterward, it was too dangerous for him to contact the group or return. He said his real name is Green Stevens Jr.[17]

But Steve didn't participate in the forum. He and Malik worked together, and their mothers prayed together. It was just the kind of fairy-tale conclusion that I wanted to put in the story, until Steve and Malik had a falling out and Steve left town again to farm a plot of land in Mississippi. When he left, I still had a lot of questions. Why did he have an alias? Why did he leave New Orleans just before the shootout? Why did he wait so long to contact his old comrades? Why did he agree to be a speaker at the Panther reunion and forum and then change his mind? Why did the joyful reunion between Malik and Steve after thirty-three years end in a falling out?

After the shootout, the citizens of New Orleans were wary, gun-shy, and quick to react. Chief Giarrusso and Mayor Landrieu held a press conference and attempted to soothe fears and quell rumors. They tried to normalize what was not normal at all. "The city is fortunate that out of this tragedy there were as few injuries as there were. This city has all the resources to meet any situation that arises. I feel the worst is behind us," said Landrieu.[18]

But only hours later, the lifeless body of a shooting victim was lying on Piety Street in front of the grocery store belonging to Clarence Broussard. That victim was Kenneth Borden.[19]

10

After the Shootout

New Orleanians Speak Out

On September 17, two days after the shootout, community leaders held a news conference to castigate the police, the city administration, and the news media for their handling of the "racial violence" earlier in the week.

The group included Johnny Jackson, director of the Desire Project Community Center; Sidney Duplessis of the Sons of Desire, a "black capitalist organization"; Barbara Allen, on leave from the Desire Area Community Council; Henry Faggen of Concerned Residents of Desire; and Mrs. Clara Prater, the mother of sixteen-year-old Kenneth Borden, who was shot by police in what the media would dismissively call "the firebombing incident."

The group unanimously adopted a statement that read, "If police are going to serve warrants on the Panthers . . . they should also serve warrants on everyone who is exploiting the black community." They named Clarence Broussard—owner of the store—specifically as an offender.

Jackson asserted that the news media had interviewed individuals at random during the violence, and that the people who were interviewed were not community leaders. He said that the Panthers were not the real issue, but rather the bad conditions in the project.[1]

THE KILLING OF KENNETH BORDEN

The *States-Item* reported that the group sharply disagreed with the police account of the killing of Kenneth Borden by police near

Broussard's grocery store the night of the Piety Street shootout. Police claimed that Borden was among a group attempting to firebomb the store, which four black police officers had been sent to protect. Chief Giarrusso said his policemen, when they fired, had aimed at the legs of those who advanced.

Mrs. Prater, however, said that her son had not been armed the night of the alleged firebombing, as police charged, and that he was only out to get some beer.[2]

According to *Time Magazine,* "When the shooting was over, three blacks were wounded and a fourth lay motionless under a street lamp for more than two hours; both police and residents feared to present themselves as targets in the light. The man, Kenneth Borden . . . was dead when residents finally reached him."[3]

Ruby Richards and Doris Smith, two eyewitnesses, claimed the young men had not been carrying bottles or weapons when the police, who had been stationed in the store, opened fire. "Those kids were shot down in cold blood," Miss Richards declared. She said she had been sitting about sixty-five feet from where they fell. Kenneth Borden was killed by gunshot wounds to the head, neck, and shoulder. There were no traces of glass in front of the store.

Roosevelt Lee was the first man who got there. Two and a half hours had passed between the time he first saw Borden's body in the street and when he and several neighbors were allowed to remove the body. By then it was 1:00 a.m. "The impression they [police] gave me," said Lee, "was that the cat was just going to lay out there forever."[4]

"'We were curious,'" said Jefferson McCormick, one shooting victim, explaining why he and his friends were in front of the store. "Everyone else in the city was curious, I guess."

Then he added in a low voice, "Curiosity kills the cat."

Kenneth's father, a security guard for the federal government for fifteen years who had just been appointed special officer for the New Orleans Police Department, declared on the Monday after the shooting that he would return his special appointment "because I cannot see myself being a part of a killer organization."[5]

The death of Kenneth Borden at Broussard's store is the one part of the Panther story that Moon Landrieu still seems unsettled about.

Looking back thirty-three years later, Landrieu said, "We were just very fortunate that there were no other deaths and no serious injuries other than one. Still, to this day, I don't know what happened that night. According to the officers inside that store who were protecting the property, they felt that the kids were trying to firebomb. That's where this person was shot. We were sick at the stomach over it. I remember that."[6]

A WHITE PASTOR

After the shootout, the Panthers seemed increasingly threatening to many. However, they, and particularly their breakfast program, garnered support among a wide spectrum of New Orleans citizens. Reverend Joseph Putnam was the white pastor of St. Francis De Sales Church. Speaking just five days after the Piety Street shootout, he had this to say from the pulpit on Sunday, September 20:

> Black Panthers, your platform and your program embraces what every self-respecting man wants for himself and his people: Freedom, power to the people, full employment, decent housing, education. To achieve these basic goals you demand an end to capitalist exploitation and robbery of black people, an end to compulsory military service for black people, an end to police brutality and murder, an end to unfair and unjust trials of black people, and freedom and amnesty for all blacks who have been convicted unjustly. You want land, bread, housing, education, clothing, justice, peace and self-determination for the black community. In all of these things I too believe. For all of these things I too work daily. It is for these things that I live and struggle and suffer. And yes, like you, it is for these things that I will gladly die.
>
> This is why I welcomed a free breakfast program at the Church I serve with full knowledge that some members of the sponsoring group were Panther sympathizers.[7]

After describing the church politics that brought the program into being, Putnam continued:

> During the months that have followed, these young people demonstrated their ability to feed about one hundred to one hundred twenty hungry children every weekday and to deal

with the problems and details that accompany such a program. Perhaps their greatest trial came from the internal turmoil caused when one of their helpers tried to cause conflict between the black children and the five to ten little white children who were hungry and were also being fed. The group had sufficient character to make the decision to feed the hungry no matter what the color of their skin, and sufficient self discipline to deal with the dissident brother. I must confess, my experience has not always been the same in some white church groups when black children have come to participate.

Putnam then ended on a cautionary note:

But, Black Panthers, in spite of your magnificent platform, your great goals and objectives, if what I read, hear and see in news reports and in reports from the community is true, I cannot agree that your attempt to arm yourselves with guns and bombs will bring better conditions. I cannot agree that strong-arm, fascist-like tactics will effectively combat fascism. I cannot agree that police-like methods will eliminate police brutality. I cannot agree that exploitation of black brothers will eliminate exploitation of black brothers. I cannot agree that freeing your will on the minds and hearts and bodies of black people is the way to freedom for blacks. Many blacks who are working in breakfast programs and in other fine programs and who love your goals but do not agree with your strategy and tactics are now suffering considerably because of your actions. Somehow your actions are not liberating but enslaving to those who associate with you.

Nevertheless, in spite of our differences of opinion, I hope we can continue to work together on things where we agree. Thank you.

THE NATIONAL COUNCIL OF JEWISH WOMEN

In this climate of deadly confrontation, yet another group remained hopeful. On the same day as Putnam's sermon, the Greater New Orleans section of the National Council of Jewish Women wrote to Mayor Landrieu to urge him to read and act on Robert Tucker's study. The letter stated, "We must assure every citizen in the Desire area that the administration, police, and other citizens in New Orleans not only understand their situation but are willing to work together to alleviate the deplorable conditions in which they live. In this way frustrations can be diminished and perhaps the young can turn to constructive methods of self-improvement which will not only benefit them personally but will benefit the entire community as well."[8]

In 1970 a wide variety of people could venture outside of their own experience to feel empathy and hope for action. They could envision, just around the corner, the alleviation of suffering for the city's poorest. Moreover, that vision could be held and articulated in the very midst of a deadly confrontation between the symbols of white authority and black men and women with guns, a confrontation that would take two more months to play itself out.

THE HUMAN RELATIONS COMMITTEE (HRC)

After the shootout, the HRC was quick to say that it deplored "the use of violence as a means of social change," but it also deplored the "violence done to human lives by years of racial discrimination and poverty." It appealed to the blacks and whites of the city "to unite in building a New Orleans where the quality of life will so enrich all that none will be tempted to use violence."[9]

In 1967 the New Orleans City Council created the Human Relations Committee on the day Martin Luther King died in Memphis. Subsequent members were elected by popular vote, with blacks and whites each choosing half of the members. It had a full-time staff, which in 1970 was headed by John Pecoul, who was white.

Pecoul was quoted in the *States-Item* two days after the shootout as saying, "If you deal with the underlying grievances—the drug problem, the sanitation and health problems, the economic problems—you can limit the growth of racial violence. If not, it becomes a police problem, one of confrontation.

"The Panthers would like us to shoot at them. We would rather eliminate them by removing the frustration and hate on which they feed." Pecoul further stated, "The Panthers' goals, which center on ultimate control by blacks of the systems that govern blacks, are not as extreme as their methods."

Bill Rouselle, a twenty-four-year-old African American who had recently served on the HRC, offered this analysis to the *States-Item:*

> I think the over-all feeling about the Panthers in the Desire community was not resentment. There is a wellstream of psychological reasons for that. The Panthers represent a radical view of society—one in which people are oppressed by conditions they can't control. And the police are the symbols of authority, the status quo. The attraction for disadvantaged young people is their deep commitment to bring about racial changes in America.
>
> They [Panthers] don't attempt to go underground. They denounce the system publicly and are willing to suffer the consequences. That is obviously a suicidal tendency.

Rouselle did not see that the Panthers had made significant inroads on local college campuses, but he did believe that "their influence could spread in other underdeveloped black neighborhoods in New Orleans."[10]

MAINSTREAM MEDIA

The television station WWL editorialized on the day after the shootout: "New Orleans is fortunate that there is strong leadership within the project. The people, themselves, want something better. And so far the people, themselves, have sought improvement sensibly, logically—and peacefully. Now the Mayor has just had a study made about conditions in Desire and what should be done to change them or improve them. This should become a key project. And planning should begin now—short range and long—to make Desire a good place to live—and not the feared thing it is today."[11]

The station's editorial the following day, after the community news conference in Desire, was a step more strident:

> Negro leaders in the Desire Project spoke out today. And we believe New Orleans would be most wise to listen to what they have to say . . . and then take it to heart and do something about it. The crux of what they had to say was simple: the violence between the Police and the Black Panthers was intense and disruptive. But it came and now it is gone. And it doesn't compare to the daily violence which goes on constantly throughout the

Desire Project . . . as they put it "the violence of crime, of dope addiction and also of poverty, and of unemployment." It's a simple message. New Orleans is outraged because of the shootout and because of Panther rhetoric and the Panther threat. But the people of Desire are hurt and angry because New Orleans so far has not become outraged at all about the daily misery of Desire . . . the muggings, the almost nightly violence upon the people who live there. I suppose you'd have to live there to realize just how bad it is. Most in New Orleans can't identify with such problems. But the problems are there. And New Orleans had better begin doing something about it. And soon.[12]

The *Times-Picayune,* however, still seemed to have its head in the sand. Its editorial on September 16, 1970, acknowledged that "material and spiritual desperation can bring restiveness" in an "evolving biracial community." But it insisted on seeing incidents such as the shootout as "exceptional, exotic growths that can be pruned away" and "not representative of New Orleans' citizens or reflective of New Orleans' real condition." The horticultural imagery struck some as a bizarre spin.

Michael H. Kulka wrote a letter to the editor of the *States-Item* chastising the mainstream media for dereliction of duty: "The police of the nation have presented a false picture of the Panthers and its support organizations as violent terrorists within the black community so that the repressive attacks on the Panthers and the rest of the community will be accepted as justified by the white community. The press has helped the police in this endeavor, constituting a complete dereliction of journalistic responsibility."[13]

On September 20 the *New York Times* was still watching closely: "The raid and the violence that followed is regarded by some young blacks as the first heroic chapter in the life of the New Orleans party. Teenagers and younger children have been drawn to the headquarters to help 'get it together for reopening.' And the general feeling is that the nearby community is heavily armed to protect the Panthers."[14]

HORSEFEATHERS AND LITTLE ANGELS

In 2003 Malik Rahim looked back to the shootout with awe and gratitude for divine intervention. He thought of the four little girls who had died in the bombing of a Birmingham church in 1963 on that same date, September 15. His spiritual journey over the years brought him for a time into the Muslim faith. After Hurricane Katrina, he became a Christian again. He had come to feel sure that the Panthers had four little angels watching over them that day on Piety Street.

Clarence Giarrusso, on the other hand, at the age of eighty-two, eschewed the theory of miracles. At the suggestion of such a phenomenon, he said, "Horsefeathers! It wasn't a miracle. It was good police work, an intelligent mayor, and the Americanism of the people of New Orleans." Catherine Giarrusso, his wife of fifty-four years, listened as she tidied up the kitchen. New Orleans is sometimes called "The Big Easy," a tolerant, creative, fun-loving place. She added: "We're not a rioting kind of city."[15]

MOON LANDRIEU: "IF I HAD BEEN BLACK . . ."

How did the Mayor assess the upheaval? In 2003, Moon Landrieu remembered it this way: "The Panthers apparently had won a good bit of support down there by giving out meals and breakfasts and becoming part of the community in the time that they were there [in Desire]. And they developed a good bit of sympathy, both from the standpoint of 'charity' work they were doing as well as this whole question of race, which was and still is today (not as much today) a boiling question. Minority rights, the repression of blacks, police brutality, poverty—these played a huge part in it.

"I got a minority of the white vote, a vast majority of the black vote. There was no reason for me to be frightened of black people. I just wasn't. I felt comfortable with black people. Still do, always will. But, I was going to enforce the law. You can't have anarchy. Whatever the social injustices of the time were, that wasn't the way to solve them."

Landrieu paused a moment as he deftly shifted his point of view. "I actually had a grudging respect for the Panthers—not for what they did, not for how they did it. But they were willing to put it on the line. I often thought if I had been black, I might have been a Black Panther myself. You had to respect the fact that however wrong they were, however misguided I thought they were, they were never just mouth. They were willing to put something on the line. They were willing to put their lives on the line for what they believed and what injustices they felt existed."

Several things struck me about the public reaction to the shootout. One is the quick, strong, and organized response of Desire residents. Another is the concern and insistence on solving the problems of the people of Desire by white protestant and Jewish leaders echoed by one of the daily papers. But more than anything, what struck me was a widely shared refusal to tolerate poverty, discrimination, deplorable living conditions, and the violence that they breed. This was coupled with a hopeful belief that dialogue could happen across neighborhoods, generations, and socioeconomic strata to alleviate these conditions.

Before Hurricane Katrina, I sensed a deep resignation on the part of both black and white citizens about the intractability of poverty and crime. Katrina changed all of us in important ways. And though it is too soon to know for sure, I think I now detect a communal understanding that we can better care for each other, that our neighborhoods and their inhabitants are all connected, and that our survival as a unique city depends on finding a way—or many ways—to put that caring into practice.

The lessons of 1970 could be instructive. Would the level-headed responses of a large cross-section of New Orleanians be enough to de-escalate the conflict? It turned out that even with stellar behind-the-scenes efforts at mediation by black and white clergy and people in the Landrieu administration, the answer was no.

PART II
Desire Heats Up

11

The Rematch

After the Piety Street shootout, the confrontation between the Panthers and the police seemed to end for a time. Malik Rahim and the other Panthers in the Piety Street house were locked up in Orleans Parish Prison. But Althea Francois and several other Panthers had gone straight back to the Piety House after the shootout as soon as her mother and Malik's mother had picked up the kids. They found "awful stuff." Althea recalls, "When we went in, sun was shining through the holes in the building. The tear gas was thick. The police had urinated in the refrigerator. We had no weapons. But we decided to sleep there anyway, in the other side of the house. We called Central and told them we were still open."[1]

The next day, they tried to wash the smell of tear gas out of the salvageable clothes, and they fed children with their breakfast program. In the weeks that followed, they continued their other activities, meanwhile polling residents as to whether they wanted them to stay. Claiming a mandate from the people, the Panthers set up their headquarters in apartment #3315 in Desire on October 25, 1970.

The interlude of quiet would soon end. Noted Landrieu, "Now we've got the Housing Authority [involved—HANO]. It was like a rematch. We'd already been through the first one [the Piety Street shootout]. So we were well aware of how dangerous these things can be. And the first one exceeded anything we could imagine.

"We started negotiation all over again. I remember going down to Desire at nighttime to meet with Johnny Jackson, a young activist in the Desire project. There was a great deal of concern among my security people and the police department about my meeting with them. But I insisted on meeting with them. So I met with them and we had a discussion to try to resolve the matter. And we went through the same process again. We had to evict them by force.

"I think before we tried that, some people, young members of the administration, tried to negotiate them out. Bob Tucker, as I recall, was in that group. They were treated like the enemy, too, because they were part of the administration and part of the establishment. They were not attacked or anything. It came down again to a question of eviction."[2]

Larry Preston Williams again takes issue with the mayor:

"I would have paid less attention to the Panthers as long as they remained in the Desire area. Sometimes they came to Canal Street to distribute their literature. But he gave them, I thought, too much status by trying to move them out of the apartment complexes, especially the one in Desire. I don't think that was necessary. I think that had he just let them remain there, the Panthers probably would have just dissipated on their own. It wasn't a real strong organization.

"I mean, if they were smart, they would have let the Panthers have that little apartment. I mean, who needed to collect rent? I think people were paying like nine or thirteen dollars a month. Who cared? I can only assume that Landrieu was getting pressure maybe from people in the white community. But he should have known better."[3]

The *Black Panther Newspaper* had this view of the third eviction:

> Still trying to get rid of the Party, once again the pigs had another eviction notice sent, charging the occupants of Desire Project House #3315, the Black Panther Party office, were violating a criminal trespassing law and had to leave. The members of the Party passed out a petition in the community and the people willingly signed it. The petition asked for the consent of the people who live in the community for the Party to stay in the Desire Projects. And, the permission was granted by the people. A contradiction arose, because the Housing Authority in New Orleans said that the Party would have to leave because, they claimed, no rent had been paid; but, in fact, these pigs had refused the money. So again a confrontation between the Party and the reactionary New Orleans forces was anticipated on any day.[4]

On the local scene, the *NOLA Express* seemed to be the only news outlet telling the Panther side of the story:

> If they try to force you out of the neighborhood—move in next door. Or so goes the theory the local NCCF is now trying out. They were forced out of their bullet-pocked house on Piety St. last Thursday night and immediately took up residence inside the Desire Project in an abandoned apartment which they promised to repair and redecorate. The NCCF circulated petitions throughout the project explaining the move and asking the project residents to sign if they were in favor of the action and would support their attempts to remain there. The housing authority, meanwhile, had already decided to get them out, and the following morning reports came that HANO was negotiating their removal, forceful and/or otherwise.[5]

The next edition of *NOLA Express,* in a piece entitled "More Than a Foothold," explained that Harold Holmes, acting for the NCCF, had offered to pay rent to HANO. But HANO had refused the money on the grounds that the NCCF was not a cohesive family unit. HANO claimed that it rented only to cohesive family units. Groups providing a community service could sometimes acquire an apartment rent-free. But that status only came with special federal permission. Holmes then abandoned his efforts to pay rent, and the NCCF took the position that the community wanted them to remain and that as a community-service organization, they should be allowed to stay rent-free.[6]

On November 14, based on information supplied by Israel Fields and Melvin Howard, the two policemen who had infiltrated the NCCF, narcotics charges were filed against nineteen Panthers who were not incarcerated. Some saw this as harassment, but Chief Giarrusso denied that the charges had anything to do with "attempts to remove Panthers still at large from the Desire area."[7]

A flier circulated throughout Desire by the Panthers announced political education classes. It stated:

> The Housing Authority of New Orleans (HANO) has charged the NCCF with criminal trespass, and has stated publicly that they will be evicted. HANO claims they can house only 'cohesive family units.' This is a lie! A Tulane Social Service unit, Catholic Charities, and other outside groups have been housed

at Desire for the past five years. These groups are obviously not cohesive family units. Nevertheless they are there with the approval of HANO. The NCCF is there with the approval of the community.

HANO encourages the Tulane School of Social Work *to use the community* for its own educational purposes. HANO refuses to house the NCCF, a group which seeks to enable people *to control their own community*. Who does HANO serve? The rich or the poor? White moneyed interests have never been kept out of the Desire Project . . . The facts show that these powerful people are the real trespassers on the basic right of the NCCF to exist.[8]

The Tulane University Student Senate News Service was quick to state its position. It put out a bulletin urging immediate action to "prevent disaster to the entire community" and "to protect the rights of the NCCF." They implored people to send telegrams to the mayor and to HANO requesting a "cooling off" period. "In short," they said, "there will be a gun battle that is likely to spread throughout the city *if* preventive action is not taken *immediately.*"[9]

It had been two months since the shootout, and a showdown was looming again. The whole nation was watching Desire as tensions escalated. The *New York Times* continued to follow the story closely: "Because of the armed resistance they had met in September, the police approached the eviction task with increased armor and with somewhat greater caution."[10]

This was no ordinary eviction. This third eviction for the Panthers was shaping up to be a confrontation larger than the one on Piety Street. A small army, including a newly purchased "tank," was ready for use in Desire to enforce a trespass law that carried a maximum fifty-dollar fine.

In an attempt to avoid this larger confrontation, frantic negotiation efforts ensued.

12

This Time We Ain't Movin'

The evictions from St. Thomas and from Piety Street had only increased the Panthers' determination not to be evicted from Desire. Their programs had continued without interruption after the shootout, and the police stance had strengthened support for the Panthers in Desire. Despite more than a dozen Panther arrests, a core group of armed Panthers living in a Desire apartment said they would fight to the last person to defend their "home" if the police interfered. In early November, five clergymen, two black (Jerome LeDoux and William London) and three white (William Barnwell, Harold Cohen, and Joe Putnam, who had preached on the shootout), decided to see if they could help.

Fearing a racial Armageddon, Chief Giarrusso and Mayor Landrieu asked the members of the clergy to join the negotiating effort on November 16, a month and a day after the shootout, to try to get the Panthers to leave peacefully. In 2003, two of the clergymen—the Rev. William Barnwell and Father Jerome LeDoux—recounted the story.

Until Easter of 2007, Jerome LeDoux, S.V.D., pastored St. Augustine's Catholic Church in Tremé, the oldest mixed-race Catholic church in the city. The Reverend William Barnwell, a retired Episcopal priest, teaches and consults nationally on church outreach work.

In 1970 Father LeDoux, who is black, had been to Desire many times. He had scheduled the Panthers to speak at his theology class at Xavier University. For his part, Barnwell, who is white, saw Desire as alien territory. "Will they take us hostage?" he asked himself on the drive into the development in mid November. "Of course not," he repeated, as if it were a mantra.[1]

Both priests remembered the Panther headquarters as a fortress. According to LeDoux, it had "window-high sandbagged walls, scores of grenades, dozens of assault rifles, and numerous bandoliers of ammunition occupying most of the space of the floors of both stories."[2] Panthers were making a statement with their fortifications and also with their rhetoric.

Barnwell, in his memoirs of that time, quotes one of the Panthers as saying, "You've moved black people with your urban renewal programs so you can build shiny new buildings we never see the insides of. You've taken us from our homes to beautify our city as though people don't matter. You moved us to build Interstates that we can't afford cars for. This time we ain't moving."

According to Barnwell, the mediation went like this: "Look," said a black priest, "if you will just leave this apartment for a few weeks and make formal application to the Housing Authority, I think we can arrange for you to have it legally. Already some people have agreed to pay the rent."

Father LeDoux confirmed this for me. "Yes, I said that. I said it to Poison [Harold Holmes]. He was leaning out of the door without his shirt on. He wouldn't look at me."

Barnwell's amazingly detailed memoir contains this dialogue: "Man," said George [a Panther spokesman that Barnwell recognized from coverage on TV], "you haven't been getting the message. We don't have to make *no* formal application to *no* housing authority. This is our housing project, our community. We are here because the Desire residents want us here. Ask them, if you don't believe us. That's all the authority we need."

"The police are going to come in here and shoot up the whole place and kill every one of you. They mean business. I can promise you that," LeDoux responded, according to Barnwell.

"It ain't no different from any other time," responded a Panther, as recorded in Barnwell's memoir. "They're always coming in here and shooting up everything. The only difference is this time they are going to have to kill a whole lot of us. And for every one of us they kill there'll be ten more right from this project to take his place. It ain't no different."

"Will you listen to reason?" another member of the clergy asked.

"Your reason is white man's reason," said someone Barnwell doesn't identify. "Look at what your reason has got us: bad housing, rats, wall-to-wall roaches, schools that don't teach you nothing but how to smoke dope, and no decent jobs. If the pigs are so concerned with law and order, why don't they get the dope pusher who's ruining our children?"

LeDoux recalled that Poison finally said, "We're not talking."

That was the end of the mediation.

Barnwell remembered an elegant young woman in a long dress in the Panther apartment saying, "You know what a panther is? A panther is an animal that attacks only when attacked." He wanted to wipe away the tear that crept down her cheek. He realized she was the tender age of the students he taught. He thought as he listened to her, "Tomorrow she'll probably be dead," and he was struck by the contrast between the Panthers' tough political rhetoric and the gentleness with which they treated each other and the visiting clergymen.

In 2002 LeDoux would make a similar observation about the Panther stance: "Ever careful to avoid being aggressors, the Panthers always kept themselves in a protective mode only. Not very many whites believed them or trusted them, especially given their strident tone, their constant taunting and challenging of the white world, and their ominous flaunting of arms." He added, "They were not racist baiters of whites and others, but staunch, fearless protectors of the poor, the abused, the disenfranchised and the helpless."[3]

Barnwell's memoir continues, "The Panthers repeated their refusal to move, repeated their Ten Demands, then shut the door. 'One: we demand that all political prisoners be freed. Two: we demand that all black people be given jury trials by their peers . . . '" Noted Barnwell: "It looked as though the Panthers would be totally destroyed."

Negotiation proceeded on multiple fronts. Before he sent in the army of police, Mayor Landrieu had been dead set on using negotiation to get the Panthers out of Desire. He wanted to avoid bloodshed at all costs. The group that Landrieu sent to negotiate included Cecil Carter, deputy director of the Human Relations Committee, and Don Hubbard, who directed the neighborhood center in Desire, as well as Bob Tucker, the mayor's special assistant. All were men of color. Henry Faggen, the

"Mayor of Desire," coordinated the effort on the Desire end. In a group interview in 2003, they remembered it this way[4]:

According to Carter, "Moon had asked us to go and see what we could do. So we had some conversations with residents and Panthers. The conversation went like this: [He quotes the Panthers.] 'We have occupied. We claim nesters' rights. We ain't movin.'"

"Moon really got on our case," Tucker recalled. "He thought we should have been able to talk them out of the project."

Hubbard: "We just looked at the Panthers like they were another community organization. We weren't in awe of them or what they were doing—the uniforms and the Tammies and the combat boots. The Panthers came to the Center one day and announced that they were going to liberate my office. And I didn't know what the hell they were talking about. So I listened. I said, 'Well, look. If you want to use the facility here, it's no problem. You can register just like the Better Young Men's Boys Club or whoever, get a night, come in, and have your meeting or your rally. I don't know what you mean by 'liberate.' If 'liberate' means run me out of here, you got a problem because this is my job. You can't liberate my job."

Hubbard continued: "We had been part of CORE. We weren't in awe. What they were doing—all that military stuff—was no problem because it was just another phase of a foundation that had already been laid. It was just another group in the neighborhood. But certainly they escalated it to another level.

"We had some differences with the Panthers. Some of the smaller neighborhood grocery stores, Mom and Pop stores, complained about them coming into the stores demanding food for their feeding program. We had a meeting with the Panthers and suggested they not do that. We said, 'Look. We got a whole bunch of white folks round here y'all could shake down. We got Schwegmann's; there was Canal Villere, Mackenzie's doughnuts.' Without giving you all the details, it was just suggested that they do things differently."

Ultimately, the negotiations didn't work. Henry Faggen recalled the conversation he and Hubbard had with the Panthers: "They just talked crazy about revolutionary suicide. I gotta wipe my hand off. You know I wasn't for that."

Mayor Landrieu was under increasing public pressure from the white community to exert control over Desire and evict the Panthers. But it was clear to Hubbard, Tucker, Faggen, Carter, and others that this would not be an easy thing to do. The Panthers were holed up in a fortified apartment with lots of Desire residents supporting them.

As Hubbard and Carter were standing around talking to residents in Desire that tense fall, a young man came over to them and said, "If they put that tank on these kids [Panthers], we got something for 'em."

"You got something—like what?" inquired Hubbard.

The man opened a Schwegmann's grocery bag and showed off a half a dozen hand grenades.

"At the point where the deal went down," said Tucker during the Hubbard Mansion interview, "I [thought] the pins on those grenades were going to get pulled. A grenade has no conscience and particularly a frag." He pointed out that Desire had over 10,000 inhabitants, and many more were streaming in every day to be part of the action. With most of the people being children in this veritable war zone, leaders in a position of responsibility were concerned about collateral damage.

Tucker explained to Landrieu on the phone from Faggen's house that when the people in Desire wanted the cops, they never could get them. They had to wait four or five hours for an ambulance. "There are a lot of adults today," Tucker told me, "who were babies born in ambulances trying to get out of Desire, locked in by bridges, a train track, and a canal. Now that the Panthers were there organizing for black self-determination, though, the cops came swarming."

Faggen added, "They were there to hurt, not to help. The police would come into Desire and do like they want. You'd be sittin' on your porch and they'd tell you to go inside. All that resentment just built up. And when these guys [Panthers] confronted them [police], that brought people to them [Panthers]. The people were *willing* to protect the Panthers with their *lives*. But I didn't want to see that."

Hubbard saw a kid sprinkling cayenne pepper around the Panther apartment, creating a perimeter to deter the police dogs. And he saw Johnny Jackson (who later became a state legislator) come out of the Desire Community Center, sit down on the steps, put his head in his hands, and moan, "Man, I never thought it was going to come to this."

Tucker recalled a meeting at City Hall, a last-ditch attempt to avert the looming catastrophe in Desire. "It was a meeting of essentially white males. Somebody volunteered me to go with Landrieu to police headquarters to direct the operation. I said, 'Mr. Mayor, with all due respect, I don't think that's gonna work out.' Moon kind of went off," Tucker remembered. Landrieu reminded Tucker that he and other white people had stood up for blacks when Leander Perez, the arch segregationist from Plaquamines Parish, was oppressing them. "Now y'all gotta stand up for us," Moon said.

"So I said, 'Mr. Mayor, could you and I go over in that office over there for a minute?' So we went into the office. I'm not gonna get into detail about what I said to Moon. But it was in clear and clean terms of what I wasn't going to do, and what he could do with the job. I said, 'I'm not going to be involved in an operation designed to kill black folks. Where I'm going, I'm going down to the streets and see if we can avoid anybody getting killed.' I said, 'I just want you to understand that the corollary to an anti-Panther position is a pro-police position, and the history books won't let black folks be pro-police in this town.' So they gave me an unmarked police car with a radio in it. I parked that sucker about five miles from Desire and walked in because I didn't want anybody thinking I was under cover. I walked into Faggen's place and we began to try to sort it out." Faggen lived a few blocks away from the apartment that the Panthers had taken over.

Don Hubbard was also at Faggen's house. According to Hubbard, when Chief Giarrusso decided to back off and give them a chance to talk to the Panthers, "that's when it got real. I didn't know who was in the building," said Hubbard. "I didn't know how volatile the situation was. I didn't know if somebody wanted to be a hero and blow the top off of one of our heads. The talk about going in there trying to reason with the brothers? To me that was a long walk from that side of the street to the other side of the courtyard to get with these guys with guns asking, 'what do y'all want?'"

When they got there, Tucker remembered, the Panthers were respectful, but determined to do what they had to do.

And what they had to do was defend their Desire apartment home.

13
The Massacre That Almost Occurred

It was a Tuesday, November 17, when the men of the cloth realized that the Panthers could not be "negotiated out" of Desire. "These people [Panthers]," the Rev. William C. London, an African American Methodist minister, told the press, "believe they are the vanguard of the revolution and that the vanguard must die, and they are prepared to die."[1]

Although rhetoric swirled around the concept of revolutionary suicide, at face value the conflict came down to a relatively simple point of law: criminal trespass, the act of being in a building illegally, a misdemeanor. Remaining in the apartment had become an integral part of the Panther cause. The Panthers said they were willing to pay rent for the apartment but that all other residents should refuse to pay rent until conditions in Desire were improved.[2]

The reporter Clarence Doucet noted in a local paper, "Some people say it is misguided, but no one seems to challenge [the Panthers'] dedication."[3]

The news reports from the time were quite detailed, fueling a pervasive sense of alarm—especially among white citizens. Personal remembrances of Faggen, Tucker, Hubbard, LeDoux and Williams—all of whom played strategic roles—fill in the picture of the showdown in Desire. Landrieu's analysis as he remembers calling the shots from police headquarters provides a somewhat more detached overview. Marion Brown's perspective illustrates what it looked like through the eyes of a hopeful teenager.

Chief Giarrusso warned that his police would evict and arrest the Panthers from the Desire apartment if it became necessary. However, he made it clear that he did not want another confrontation. "We're doing things to let these people get out of there," he said. "Reasonableness will be the controlling factor."[4]

Early Thursday morning, November 19, during a press briefing at police headquarters, Giarrusso stated that police would make "a last-ditch effort" to remove the Panthers from their new headquarters. "We are going to do our damnedest to get them out without any violence," Giarrusso told reporters.[5] He said police intelligence had learned that between five and fifteen NCCF members were holding out in the project, possibly in more than one building. Tucker, Giarrusso, and Landrieu discussed the Panthers' possible use of hand grenades, and how Panthers might occupy sniper positions in various apartments. As a result of the long Vietnam War, some Panthers, like Malik Rahim, had joined the armed forces or been drafted and had become skilled, if reluctant, warriors.

After the press briefing, approximately 250 police boarded buses for Desire armed with riot guns and wearing bulletproof vests. They marched into the project at about 11:30 a.m. behind an armored vehicle, dubbed the "war wagon," that had been acquired after the September shootout. Three helicopters circled a few hundred feet above while state police stood ready nearby. "For your own safety, please move out of the area," a voice from a loudspeaker urged.

"More power to the people!" came the reply in unison.

The army of police were determined to serve the eviction notice. They accused the NCCF of violating the state trespass law—with its maximum fine of fifty dollars. The letter of that law, so important to Landrieu, was soon to become moot. Panthers' attorneys were at that moment in court arguing that it was unconstitutional.

As the police occupied buildings surrounding the Panther fortress and attempted to evacuate residents from them, people began throwing bottles and rocks. The officers warned newsmen that they were "on their own." Most of the reporters made a hasty retreat when bottles began falling and shattering around them.[6]

At one point, a sign on the Panthers' headquarters reading

"National Committee to Combat Fascism" fell to the ground. Neighborhood residents put it back up as police looked on.[7]

At 11:45 a.m. hundreds of young African Americans blocked the police and the tank as it neared building 178, the NCCF stronghold. During the yelling and the mayhem, one enterprising young man made the best of the situation, selling ice cream from his truck parked some fifty yards from the community center, close to building 178.

At 12:20 p.m., the armored police tank again rolled up to the NCCF building. Police announced from the war wagon that the building's occupants were in violation of the law and would be given eight minutes to clear the building. The tank immediately withdrew. Confrontation seemed imminent.

Eight minutes came and went, but police did not advance on the building. The NCCF members remained inside. Yet another warning was issued at 1:45—with the same results. The crowd of Panther protectors had moved out of the way, but within minutes of the last warning, they filled the street in front of the Panther headquarters. Any earlier advantage held by the police seemed to evaporate.

At one point an angry sea of Panther supporters was less than thirty feet from the police. They were being restrained by Desire leaders, who locked their arms together to prevent the crowd from advancing. Meanwhile, other project leaders met with Chief Giarrusso. The chief warned community leaders that the situation "is damn near getting out of hand."[8]

Charles Foti, the city attorney assigned to the NOPD, would go on to become Orleans Parish Criminal Sheriff and later Louisiana State Attorney General. He appeared in Desire the day of the showdown riding atop what Detective Williams called "some sort of a mobile device" like an urban cowboy. Tucker and Hubbard described it as a machine that could move earth. He was riding high, waving his hands, and sending out signals. Williams said, "He had the bright idea to ram the Panther apartment complex, which would have been a total disaster." Someone talked him out of it.

Williams also said, "What the [street] cops didn't know but we [the Intelligence Unit] knew was not only did the Panthers have weapons, but they also had grenades. And if they would have lobbed some of those grenades, it would have been a bloodbath. During that time we didn't have SWAT teams. In fact, we didn't really have SWAT training until after the Mark Essex incident. So the cops down in Desire didn't have military training. As a police unit, they were not prepared to storm and secure residences. And it would have been horrible. It would have been a massacre."[9]

Throughout the afternoon, Father Jerome LeDoux and Rev. William C. London held private conversations with the police chief about every fifteen or twenty minutes on the Alvar Street neutral ground. Meanwhile, police manned several project buildings adjacent to the NCCF headquarters. They stood in second-story apartments aiming their shotguns out open windows.

At midafternoon, Rev. London emerged from the project to report to Landrieu, Giarrusso, and the press that Desire residents had taken a vote and "unanimously" decided to back the NCCF holdouts as long as police remained on the scene. "It is surprising to note the number of people who are supporting this movement," said Rev. London.

Asked if he thought NCCF members were giving any serious consideration to giving up without violence, the minister thought for a moment and replied, "My frank answer is no . . . They would rather die for the cause."[10]

While Faggen and Tucker, as well as the clergymen, were circulating around Desire, Father Harold Cohen, a Jesuit from Loyola University, placed himself between the Panthers and the police and was reciting psalms. Panther George said to him, "Man you don't want to do that! You might get killed."

Father LeDoux advised "that white boy amid all those black people to move out and pray in private."[11]

Responding to dire warnings coming from several sources, Giarrusso called for his men to withdraw. The cops were tense and angry amid shouts of "Death to the Pigs!" They resented the insults, the hours of tension with no action. It did not sit well with them to leave without doing what they had come there to do. They walked past one building on which "Power comes from the barrel of a gun" was crudely written in black paint. That may have been one sentiment upon which they and the Panthers agreed.

When Giarrusso made his decision to withdraw, a key to the

agreement he made with community leaders, including Faggen, was securing the safe passage of his men from the apartments they had been occupying for more than four hours. As Giarrusso left his command post to enter the project in the company of about a dozen Desire leaders, there were awkward moments of uncertainty on both sides. Bob Tucker was part of the group. He told the chief point-blank: "I'm putting my life on the line."[12] "Is it worth it?" Tucker was wondering, "Is the chief willing to put his life out there too?"[13]

The mayor asked Bob Tucker to go building to building with Giarrusso to tell the cops it was time to leave. Tucker said to Landrieu, "You tell Clarence to take his coat off, and take his heater off, his weapon off, 'cause I don't want none of the brothers shootin' at him to hit me. So he did that and we went together."

As Giarrusso marched into the project, the crowd of people in front of the Panthers' headquarters began shouting louder and raising clenched fists, the symbol of black power and defiance. Giarrusso cast a few glances over his shoulder in the direction of his men about two blocks away. As he emerged from each building escorting his men out, the crowd shouted and gestured for the police to leave. Tempers were running high. A rain shower doused the scene as the police boarded their buses and left at 3:50 p.m. followed by their war wagon and helicopters.

The reporter Clarence Doucet had a "nagging feeling that a confrontation was not necessarily avoided, but possibly just postponed. There was a feeling that the underlying causes responsible for the rise of the Panthers and the support they appear to be receiving did not vanish as did the police."[14]

HENRY FAGGEN'S ACCOUNT

Desire resident and community leader Henry Faggen ran a methadone clinic. He had seventy or eighty people to take care of. Bob Tucker, who had just finished a late-night staff meeting with Landrieu to plan the arrest of the Panthers, called Faggen at about 3:00 a.m. and told him to get his people to the clinic and get them medicated.

As he was hurriedly putting on his clothes and going down the steps, Faggen heard groaning. "I saw a guy lying there," Faggen told me in an interview three decades later. "He was shot. I didn't know what to do with him. I definitely didn't want him hanging around, but I didn't want him to die. We got the boy to the hospital, and when we got to the hospital, to my surprise they had four or five other people who had been shot *in Desire!* But nobody had heard no shots. And that just surprised me."[15]

As Faggen finished caring for his methadone patients and the wounded man, the sun came up, and he went back home to meet Tucker. They, along with Don Hubbard and Charlie Elloie of the Division of Youth Services, huddled to decide what to do next. Tucker stayed at Faggen's house to be in phone contact with the mayor and the police chief. Hubbard, Faggen, and Elloie walked the streets.

Faggen told me the police had not come into Desire like trained troops. "They just came in runnin'—runnin' right past that building [where the Panthers were headquartered]. That's when the shit hit the fan," he recalled. "The police came in with tanks. The people had hand grenades. The [white] officer driving the tank, we called him Big Red. Big Red knew me and he was a straight shooter. He said, 'Man, you better get these people off of the street 'cause it's gonna be bad.'"

Faggen remembered an old lady, about seventy years old, who had one leg. "They [police] throwin' her down the steps right cross from the center. They had forty, fifty, sixty people lookin.' People seen that and they started hootin' and hollerin' and cursin.' Wasn't no leadership there until Bob and Don and them came out.

"When we got over to Pleasure Street, we heard a loud scream. It was a friend of mine named Geraldine, and they [police] had jammed her in her house. She just screamed and screamed, and when she seen me she said, 'Faggen, help me, please help me.' Well then my adrenaline started runnin' and the police they got their guns crossed but that didn't move me. I just pushed the guns away and went up to the step to cool her down. The shouting stopped. We got out the back door some kind of way. That's when I seen the tank in front of the center and the people moving about, everybody real excited. Except for that incident of throwing the lady down the steps, the police was kind of calm.

"As the day progressed, [the police] got real, real, real agitated. And I'll never forget the longest day I live. We were walking on Pleasure and Alvar and they had police lining up everywhere. I was talking to the chief of police and this cop was looking at me. And I seen he just wanted to shoot me. He had all the venom in his eyes and in his mouth. I said, 'Go ahead, shoot me. That's what you want to do. Shoot, you coward! You just taking over our community. Just shoot!' Clarence [Giarrusso] told me to cool it. I had a lot of respect for him.

"Whatever was happening, I'd go back to my house and I'd tell Bob. Bob would confer with the mayor, and whatever him and the mayor was talking about really didn't interest me. Then Bob put me on the phone with the mayor. It had to be getting just about dark. The only thing I could tell him was it was a bad situation and if the police didn't get out of there by night, there was going to be some action. I knew there was going to be some action. Those boys [Panthers] was playing. But the people were not playing. I don't want to downgrade them kids [Panthers]. They were just young kids doing a good job in the community, feedin' the children, teaching them discipline. What got me was they were talking about revolutionary suicide. Now here my community's at stake. A lot of people fixin' to get hurt, hurt *bad, bad, bad!* Young kids with their own philosophy and ideology that to me were not concerned about the *masses* of the people."

When Landrieu and Giarrusso issued the order for the cops to leave, the cops were furious—at the Panthers, at the Desire residents, at Landrieu, even at their chief. Faggen remembers not one or two but many calling Giarrusso a "nigger lover" on the way out. "He just took it," recalled Faggen. "He had plenty of heart to take that from them.

"After the police left and the sun went down, the people in Desire brought out the food and the beer. They carried the Panthers on their shoulders all the way to Florida Avenue, just like a second line. Folks partied all night long.

"The Panthers were the heroes, not us," said Faggen. "But we prevented the killing. I don't like to pin no roses on myself, but it would have been a very tragic day had it not been for us."

FATHER LEDOUX'S ACCOUNT

Father LeDoux is a slim, white-haired, attractive man in his seventies with chocolate-colored skin. In 2003 I sat with him in his rectory in the oldest church in Tremé, filled with books, prints, and writings. Between phone calls and knocks on the door from parishioners who needed something, this is what Father LeDoux told me about the standoff:

"Policemen were very nervous. And if you are nervous, there's no way you can conceal it, especially if you are light-complected. I was looking at 250 policemen with no blood in their faces. They were all blanched. All those boys were having problems. We had some clenched fingers, no doubt—a bit trigger-happy. One got a little cramped or whatever and accidentally he pulled the trigger. The guns were pointed up. The policemen were standing at attention when this gun went off. These were shotguns. They had buckshot. The shot went up naturally because the guns were pointed up. A single BB went through a second floor (apartment) window and struck a very young black man. And luckily it just grazed his neck, just drew a little bit of blood, did no serious damage. But when the gun went off, I didn't expect to hear a gun go off. But within a second or so, I realized a shotgun had gone off. I expected either the police to react or the crowd to rush the police or a mixture of both. Nobody moved. I couldn't believe it. I thought the whole place was going to explode. Frankly, I thought it was all over. I thought there was going to be a massacre. There would not be one policeman left alive and a lot of people would die also."

As LeDoux remembered it, it was standing room only in all of Desire, with the crowd numbering "far into the thousands." He was circulating through the crowd as best he could. The residents were all outside moving around, and black supporters from around the city had come into Desire as well.

"Reverend London and I were walking back and forth between the buses and the officers and the people, walking back and forth talking to Chief Giarrusso. I said, 'Captain, you're in trouble. You're in deep trouble. If you don't get your men out of here you're going to see blood and it's gonna be from both sides, the police and the people. These folk will get wiped out.'

"Somewhere around 4 o'clock in the afternoon he began to see. He called his men off. And they marched in file back to the buses. It looked like a military retreat. In fact, it was a military retreat. It was quite dramatic. It was so dramatic that at first people didn't much notice at all. They were startled, stunned."

MAYOR LANDRIEU'S ACCOUNT

Mayor Landrieu wasn't in Desire that day, but he was closely connected to the events going on there by phone and police radio. In an interview with me, he told the story of the standoff this way[16]:

"I discussed it with the chief of police. He told me what his plan was. I authorized him to go on in. Gave him one bit of advice, which you could call instruction, because it was more than just advice. And that was: I did not want any of those police officers in there after dark; negotiate [the Panthers] out before dark, or they were to vacate that project, because I did not want a police officer shot. The fact of the matter is I didn't want anybody shot. And I knew that if a police officer got shot, the imagination can run away with you. When a police officer gets shot, there's an enormous reaction from all the other officers who themselves had guns and were prepared for battle. It's not just a question of pride. It's a question of protection, of asserting your authority, and, in some cases, unfortunately, as we've seen so often, of retaliation.

"So I was dead set on those officers getting out of there before it got dark. I forget what time they went in, but it lasted a good bit of time. As I recall, I talked to Superintendent Giarrusso over the telephone, over the radio. It was getting dark. I essentially said: *Get those people out of there!!*

"Well, it was a source of enormous disappointment and embarrassment to the police, because they were being heckled and yelled at and humiliated by some of the residents down there, particularly kids, I'm told. I wasn't down there personally. But I was at police headquarters when the buses came back. The cops were furious—furious at me, furious at the superintendent. I suspect more furious at me for having insisted they get out of that project because they were at a stalemate. They had hundreds of people in between them and the Panther complex, I'm told. So they really couldn't take it by force without hurting some innocent people . . . So the officers withdrew.

"The Panthers apparently had won a good bit of support down there by giving out meals and breakfasts and becoming part of the community in the time that they were there. And they developed a good bit of sympathy, both from the standpoint of 'charity' work they were doing as well as this whole question of race, which was and still is today (not as much today) a boiling question. Minority rights, the repression of blacks, police brutality, poverty—these played a huge part in it."

Landrieu went on to say, "We were not precipitous about this. There was no chest-beating. There was no sense of posturizing. I knew this was a dangerous situation. I knew there was a real possibility of injury and death in each one of these instances. There was no political capital to be made. First of all, I had been elected with essentially 95 percent of the black vote. These were my constituents. And I'd lived through the civil rights era. And I didn't have any racial fear. Not that I was brave. I didn't have racial fear. That didn't mean I didn't fear the Panthers. The Panthers were a different make-up, a different group. I didn't know much about them. I knew that they were militant. I knew what they said, and I knew their public stance."

Roy Reed, one of Rev. William Barnwell's parishioners at the Chapel of the Holy Spirit, was in Desire on Thursday, November 19. He sent this special report to the *New York Times:*

> The New Orleans Police Superintendent called off an armed four-hour confrontation with a Black Panther group today to prevent what he saw as an impending "blood bath." Neither side fired a shot.
>
> The move, believed to be unprecedented in police-Panther relations, forestalled what could have been a serious clash between hundreds of tense policemen and an angry portion of the black community here.
>
> Three to four hundred emotionally charged young Negroes had stationed themselves between the police and the Panther group, which was garrisoned in an empty apartment building. It was concern for the young crowd, not for the Panthers, that caused him to withdraw his officers, Superintendent Clarence Giarrusso said afterward.[17]

The *Black Panther Newspaper* reported it this way:

> On the morning of November 19th, approximately 600 pigs, in armored vehicles (new ones having been recently bought by

the New Orleans Pig Department), moved in to assault the office in the projects.

Three to five thousand Black people, men and women old and young, stood between the pigs and the office demanding that the fascists leave their community immediately. The fascists frustrated themselves trying to get the people to leave, but the people continued demanding they withdraw from the community. Finally, after four hours, they retreated. It was the only thing they could do in the face of the power of the People. And the People sang and danced in the streets.[18]

The black-owned *Louisiana Weekly* reported on the "solidarity and strength" of the black residents of Desire as they joined together in front of the Desire project apartment that served as Panther headquarters. "One of the members of the residents proclaimed their stand a victory when the police left at nightfall; they had successfully 'protected our brothers and sisters of the NCCF' (National Committee to Combat Fascism, an arm of the Black Panthers)."[19]

The city's Human Relations Committee issued a statement offering "special praise to the thousands of citizens of Desire who kept the peace in their own neighborhood. Their contribution to limiting injuries and loss of life to a level far below that of similar incidents elsewhere must be applauded gratefully by all. Similarly, the restrained and judicious use of force by the Police Department . . . kept destruction to a minimum."[20]

Marion Brown was a nineteen-year-old freshman at Newcomb College of Tulane University on that November 19 of 1970 when she caught a bus to see what was going on in Desire. After the police left, she told me in 2003, the residents went wild. They couldn't believe the New Orleans Police Department had been faced down by the Panthers supported by Desire residents and people from all over the city. "I had never seen such partying and celebrating," she told me.[21]

"One thing is sure," a young man living in Desire told the *Louisiana Weekly* right after the standoff: "the problems of black people will not be dealt with in the usual manner, the last say being had by white folks."[22]

At least for that day, he was right.

14

The Day after the Standoff, Revelations in a Pig's Eye, Kinship, and Luck

A second miracle had occurred. In yet another, even bigger, police-Panther confrontation, no one had been killed. The "hero" status of the Panthers was increasing, and Desire residents were in a good mood.

But still, there was the morning after. Don Hubbard, over in the Desire neighborhood center, had to field the complaints from residents about what the police had done. Hubbard remembered these calls: "This is so-and-so in apartment such-and-such. Somebody came in and ate up our liver cheese—made a sandwich and drank up all the Barq's Red." Another call: "They ate all my bologna." Somebody else called and said, "I had a pot of beans on. The police ate it." After the people talked about the missing food, they'd mention the kicked-in doors, the stolen clothes and jewelry.[1]

New Orleanians take food very seriously. But Henry Faggen remembered complaints that anyone anywhere would take seriously. He recalled people talking about who got beat up and whose furniture was thrown out of windows. He said, "Geraldine, the girl who screamed—they shot her son. He's paralyzed now from that."[2]

Misses Edith Harrison, Lucille Thomas, and Marie Burton, residents of Desire, filed a suit against the city for $25,000 each for damages they said resulted from police taking over their apartments while surrounding the Panther headquarters. According to the *Louisiana Weekly*, "The ladies accused the police of humiliation, intimidation and embarrassment, damage to furniture and violation to the right to be secure from unreasonable search and seizure. They asked that

113

a restraining order be issued in order that police may not use their apartments again in case of future confrontations."[3]

Public response to the standoff was just as varied as the aftermath stories. The mayor got a handwritten letter from Carl Jones from New York City dated November 19, 1970. He wrote: "I saw your example of 'statesmanship'—the police did not shoot down the residents of the Desire Street housing project to get to the militants entrenched in an apartment in one of the buildings . . . Your restraint is remarkable in view of the fact that shooting down 'niggers' would be generally (speaking of the 'American' attitude) acceptable. This Northern-born Afro-American is impressed—the pressure on you, both attitudinal and social, must be heavy. I salute your 'individuality.' Very truly yours, Carl Jones"[4]

The mayor also received a telegram from a former supporter, C. M. Rhodes, who said he was too old to write: "Your handling of the Black Panther Incident smells to high heaven. I think you should have enforced the laws . . . I think you have sealed your political ambition. Respectfully."[5]

In a 2003 interview with me, Bob Tucker recalled sitting at a bar in the French Quarter called In a Pig's Eye sipping cognac with Mayor Landrieu the night after the standoff. After the massacre that everyone thought was inevitable had been averted, the mayor said to Tucker, "Now I understand what you were saying—that if you didn't maintain your credibility as a black person in this administration, then you would be of no benefit to what we were trying to accomplish."[6]

Tucker also remembered Landrieu saying, "You know what? I admire the hell out of those kids."

"What kids?" asked Tucker.

"The Panthers," Landrieu told Tucker. "To find a seventeen-, eighteen-, nineteen-year-old who had a cause he was willing to die for. That's something. For a young person to be so committed to something. I disagreed with what they were trying to do. But I admired that kind of commitment."[7] Thirty-three years after that night at the Pig's Eye, Landrieu used almost exactly the same words.[8]

Charles Elloie was also part of the group taking stock at the Pig's Eye. In 1970 he was thirty-two, a new assistant to the mayor and the director of Youth Opportunity. In 2003, in his chambers between prayers (an activity to which he gives time every morning) and the convening of court, Judge Elloie remembered sitting off in the corner of the bar, "just quiet, uncharacteristically quiet." Landrieu noticed and wanted to know why.

"It was the first time I had reflected on what could have happened," recalled Elloie, who had been part of the late-night meeting to decide how to enforce the law in Desire. But he saw more than law breakers. When he saw the Panthers and all those Desire residents, many of them children, surrounding and protecting Panther headquarters, Elloie saw himself. "I'm a product of the projects. I grew up in the Lafitte project. I spent twenty years in the projects. So I never had any fear of me. Everything in there was me."[9]

The fear didn't come until that night while Elloie was sitting a little apart from the group in a corner of the Pig's Eye. Before that, he couldn't remember being truly afraid. "I'd been careful," he told me, "but not fearful. But on that particular night I reflected on what could have happened and I was *scared*. I sure 'nuf dodged the bullet. That's the very first bullet I dodged.

"When Moon asked me why I was quiet, I said, 'You know someone could have banged on a garbage can cover or a garbage can could have turned over and BOOM, right out front.' 'Cause Don and I were really right out front . . . I imagine if I'd stopped to think about what I was doing, I probably wouldn't have done it. I don't know."

Since many considered the outcome of the November 19 confrontation a miracle, I asked Judge Elloie what he thought it was that saved the day.

"Police restraint," he said. "There were a lot of policemen, a lot of firepower, and a big tank . . . Two people I gained a *lot* of respect for on that particular day were Deputy Chief Louis Sirgo and Clarence Giarrusso."

Sirgo, said Elloie, was the man really in charge. "He was a take-charge kind of a man. That's how he wound up getting killed in the Mark Essex matter. He was an on-the-line kind of man.

"I have a lot of friends and associates who are police officers but *none* that I have more respect for than Louis Sirgo. Sirgo and Clarence Giarrusso were both reasonable people on that day, and fortunately, the Panthers in the development at that time—they were cool, too. Several of us had conversations with them. For some reason it all worked and peace prevailed. That night I just reflected."

How did New Orleans avoid a race riot while so many other cities had recently exploded? According to Cecil Carter, although New Orleans had a high concentration of African Americans and a lot of poverty, poverty doesn't necessarily create an uprising. "Poverty was so severe in New Orleans. The uprisings occur in communities where there is some measure of hope and the rate of change is not fast enough, or there has been some change and there's an effort to repress it."[10]

Bob Tucker added, "The expectation bar never really got raised in New Orleans because people just kind of accepted the Big Easy mentality . . . Mardi Gras was always a way to let the build-up of frustration out so that by having this big, crazy celebration once a year, people could go act out."

William Barnwell recalled the 1971 Mardi Gras as being normal —that is, normal for Mardi Gras. "The whole city was extremely tense from the near-massacre, but blacks and whites intermingled as usual, going to parades, vying for beads."

Carter added that New Orleans had always been the "R & R" place for the civil rights movement.

They have another theory, too, one that has to do with proximity. "Geographically," said Tucker, "there was never 'across the tracks.' To cross a race barrier, you only had to cross the street."

Other barriers were often crossed as well. Carter noted, "We are all kin. If we had a riot," he said, "we'd be killing our cousins. That's my blood. You ain't gonna hurt your *blood!*" I thought of the Klansman that Larry Preston Williams had told me about with the biracial grandson.

Don Hubbard remembered a guy at Charity Hospital called Noonie whose job it was to declare on a baby's birth certificate whether he or she was black or white. It was a nuanced gate-keeping job, because race wasn't always easy to tell.

To test Carter's kinship theory, I asked about the undercover cops, Melvin Howard and Israel Fields. "Howard used to be my brother-in-law," said Carter.

"His sister used to be my secretary in City Hall," Tucker added.

When I interviewed him in 2003, Moon Landrieu didn't take personal credit for averting a race riot. And he took a broader view of the law than he had in 1970. "There were grievances that weren't being addressed. If government doesn't rectify grave grievances, somehow people feel forced to take action on their own . . . African Americans had a legitimate complaint and still do about the aftermath of slavery and reconstruction. It's horrible. We are paying the price to this day, and we'll continue to pay the price for a long time. I don't think any of us have been able to estimate the impact, the full impact, that's had on our society today."

Landrieu went on to say, "I'm not making a comparison, but when you look back at the founding of the country, we wouldn't have an America if the founding fathers hadn't decided to say 'We're going to take the law into our own hands because we've kept appealing to the law and the law won't give us any relief.' Then came the American Revolution, and of course our side won. And so they all became heroes. Otherwise, they would have all been hung as traitors. So [people in] social movements, when they win, they become the heroes of the day, rather than the criminals of the day. The Panthers, having [eventually] lost in these confrontations, not just with us, but across the country, became the enemy."

Landrieu, evaluating the whole Desire Panther episode, said "I suspect that it turned out about as well here as it did in any community in America. It could have turned out just horrible. I thank my stars that we were very, very lucky."

15

Double Dirty Tricks

On the fifth and sixth days after the standoff, the police pulled what many considered to be two dirty tricks. A lot of New Orleanians remember the first one, probably because it involved a celebrity. But amazingly, very few remember the second, the final arrest of the Panthers. Even the man who ordered it has forgotten.

A few weeks before Thanksgiving, a notice had circulated throughout Desire entitled "The Revolutionary People's Constitutional Convention." It stated: "The structure of legality in America rests upon the Constitution of the United States. The U. S. Constitution was written by propertied men, many of whom were slave-holders who wanted to keep power and property for themselves and for future generations of their class. To do that they elevated property rights above human rights."

The notice concluded with the announcement, "The Black Panther Party has called for a Revolutionary People's Constitutional Convention to be held in Washington on November 27 through 29. The major purpose of the Convention will be to write a new Constitution which will meet the needs of all oppressed people in the United States—Black, Red, Yellow, and White." On the flier was a number to call for transportation.[1]

On November 24, five days after the showdown, Jane Fonda arrived in New Orleans to protest HANO's efforts to evict the Panthers from their apartment in Desire. Her career as an actress had taken an activist turn in response to the Vietnam War. As reported by the *States-Item,* Fonda, wearing a green turtleneck sweater, brown buckskin pants, and a navy pea coat, appeared at the HANO office shortly before noon to "help arouse the public consciousness as to what is happening to the black people." A hundred or so sign-carrying demonstrators chanted, "Kill poverty, not Panthers." She urged her audience to "find out for yourselves" what was happening there instead of believing what was in the newspaper.[2]

Expressions on the signs carried by picketers read: CRIMINAL TRESPASSERS—HANO, GIARRUSSO, LANDRIEU; WHITE PANTHERS SUPPORT BLACK PEOPLE; GUNS KILL PEOPLE; HANO, GIARRUSSO, LANDRIEU WANTED FOR MURDER; POWER COMES FROM THE BARREL OF A GUN.[3]

According to the *States-Item,* "The marchers, mostly college-age but including some older persons and mothers with children, were about evenly mixed racially. The demonstration was peaceful and there were no incidents except for some heckling from bystanders."[4]

Praising the NCCF efforts in resisting the police attempt at eviction, Fonda told the paper, "How can we smug white people say what black people should do? We have done nothing for centuries to stop the violence perpetuated against them."

She said she had been working with the Black Panthers nationally, raising money for their cause for about a year and a half. She called them a "disciplined organization."

The *States-Item* reported that from the demonstration, Fonda went to Loyola University's Field House, where she told a large group that "Desire is a concentration camp where a reign of terror exists." She said that the terror was being perpetuated by the New Orleans police, not by members of the NCCF.

The next day, November 25, Fonda rented four cars from Hertz to transport the Panthers and their supporters to the Revolutionary People's Constitutional Convention in Washington D.C. Before they got out of town, they were stopped by the NOPD, and all were arrested.

In a special edition on December 1, the *NOLA Express* reported: "The pretense at legality was very thin. The police thought, or at least would have the public think, that they captured a gang of 'militants,' including the bulk of the NCCF chapter. In all, two members of the NCCF were in the caravan. The other 23 arrested, including a mother of two, seven juveniles, and six whites, were proclaimed guilty of walking into the NCCF headquarters earlier in the day to sign some papers. For this they were charged with two counts of criminal trespass and one count of criminal mischief each."[5]

Former intelligence officer Larry Williams remembered it this way during an interview with me in 2005[6]: "When Jane Fonda came to town, I was assigned to follow her around. She got nasty. She called me an Uncle Tom. She called me a sellout. She'd stop what she was doing. She'd point me out—'cause there was more than one of us following her. We're following her to see who she makes contact with.

"She comes to town and she rents the automobiles. There are people who get into the automobiles. They are leaving New Orleans and going to Washington D.C. We arrest them. They are leaving town. To this day, I have no idea why they are arrested. I don't even remember what we charge them with. But I do know when I arrested a group, my English teacher from Xavier got out of the car. He and I chatted. I could not imagine what law they had violated.

"But, see, we would do stupid things like that. Everything is going good. You had these groups we had infiltrated. They're not doing anything to anybody. We were in a position where if they did something serious, we'd know it in advance. And we do something damn stupid like arrest them for nothing. Bring them downtown. No charges. The District Attorney would never take the charges. There *are no charges* [laughter] for getting in a car and driving out of town. It's not illegal. But that's the kind of stuff we would do on a slow day. We had nothing to do."

Williams's final analysis of the event: "You had a white mentality that just didn't comprehend that you'd do more harm than good. They had to react. They just couldn't let it go. They had to do something, and it accomplished nothing."

The *Louisiana Weekly* reported, "The Superintendent of Police has thanked the Fonda woman for her assistance needed to evict the NCCF members."[7] Is this sarcasm or a joke? If so, is it the *Weekly*'s or Giarrusso's, and at whose expense? There was speculation that Fonda was in collaboration with Giarrusso despite her denunciation of the establishment. There was also speculation that the plan went bad because a person with fame and white-skin privilege, though well-meaning, couldn't fathom the requirements of revolution, couldn't foresee the booby traps to which she was usually immune. Williams stated unequivocally that Fonda was in no way assisting the NOPD.

The *NOLA Express* responded to the next bizarre turn of events with more sarcasm and more information:

> After the arrest, Giarrusso went to see the Mayor "and we discussed it, and quite honestly, the mayor said the operation wasn't complete." What would Thanksgiving dinner be without a good raid under the belt?
>
> Phase two came at 1:30 that morning. A force of 25 undercover police, allegedly "led" by Giarrusso, entered the Desire project. Six black policemen approached the NCCF apartment. As Giarrusso puts it, "there was some subterfuge that was used in terms of the clothing that was worn." Sgt. Robert Frey of the Red Squad, dressed as a priest, knocked on the door saying he had money for the NCCF. When someone inside opened the door a crack, police burst in firing their weapons. A woman, Betty Powell, was wounded and the six occupants were arrested. While taking their prisoners to the police vehicles on Desire Parkway, the police grabbed three community people and attempted to use them as hostages to secure a safe getaway from the project.[8]

One of the hostages was Johnny Jackson Jr., executive director of the Desire Community Center. In an open letter to "All Black People and Concerned People" printed in the *NOLA Express,* he called the arrest of the people trying to go to the Panther convention a conspiracy and a "plot by the Housing Authority of New Orleans, City Hall, the Police Department, the News Media, the Courts, and Undercover colored people." He said, "This is happening every day to black people who attempt to get out of their place. Things haven't changed since Black people came to this country."

Describing the early-morning raid, he said,

> The police department disguised themselves in many ways, from Public Service repairmen, mailmen to a priest. It was this

policeman disguised as a priest offering a donation for the Breakfast Program with the other policemen hidden in the hallway with all sorts of guns that lured one of the occupants to open the door a little. At that point, they [the policemen] burst into the office and began shooting, wounding a young Black woman. Many of this strike force were "COLORED" policemen who later were called "AMERICANS" by the Superintendent.

Some of these "instant americans" (sic) have grown up with people of this Black community. Some have been to our schools, teaching our children about "Officer Friendly" and community relations in the day and raiding our community by night. [One had befriended Linda Francis.]

Two other Black people of this community besides myself were kidnapped from the community center and used as shields/ hostages to get them out of this hostile community and booked firstly with a city charge and then a state charge of resisting arrest and interfering with Police officers. More trumped up charges like these and others are just part of the systematic games run on Black people.[9]

After reporting the Jackson story, the *Louisiana Weekly* opined, "Even fancy titles and membership in prominent organizations does not change anything in the eyes of the police, the enforcer of the white man's rules."[10]

Jackson indeed had titles and memberships. In addition to directing the Desire Community Center, he was on the Model Cities Advisory Commission and a number of other panels and boards. He had lived and worked among the people of the Desire project all his life. He had been active in establishing community support programs in drug rehabilitation, education, and health care, and a talent showcase.

On the night of the final arrest of the Panthers, he was working late into the morning at the Desire Community Center when he heard a noise and went to investigate. He thought the noise had come from a group of kids preparing for a Thanksgiving party in the back of the building. When he got to them, they told him they had just seen priests, police in disguise, leading members of the NCCF from their headquarters, which was next door to the community center.

Jackson stepped out onto the porch to see if he could figure out what was going on. Someone called to him from the shadows. As he stepped around the corner, he was thrown up against the wall, and someone stuck a shotgun in his chest.

"Get us out of here safely," he, Joseph Lewis, and John Cook were told, "or you won't be a shield, you'll be a target."

When they refused to cooperate, they were handcuffed and taken to the police cars with the NCCF members. Residents began shouting, "Pigs in the community!" and "Power to the People!"

As Jackson put it, "I belong to all these organizations and have these titles, but when you get down to it with the police—I'm just another nigger."[11]

Jackson would go on to serve as a state legislator and New Orleans city councilman.

Larry Preston Williams had this to say about the final arrest of the Panthers: "The Intelligence Division decided to use the disguise of a priest to get into the place because about a week before, the Panthers had some negotiations with a priest. This was Woodfork's idea. [Warren Woodfork was head of the Intelligence Division and would go on to become police chief.] So a police officer by the name of Robert Fry made contact with the Panthers. I think he told them he had some money or something. He identified himself as a priest and made some arrangements to meet them.

"They opened the door, and then a group of officers rushed in. I was down the street. There was some shooting. Obviously, the Panthers were caught off guard, and a woman by the name of Betty Powell was shot. They were taken outside. I don't know if they were put in the mail truck or if we only used the mail truck to transport our officers. There was a black officer driving the mail truck by the name of Herbert Warren. And we obtained the mail truck from a postal inspector whose name I don't know.

"For the longest time NOPD denied that it happened. I think it was mainly the involvement of that mail truck [that was controversial]. But there were some priests who thought that by using a priest in that way, it would damage the credibility of priests in that community. And it probably took us two or three years before we even admitted that it happened."

Williams got to the scene after the shooting, "after the place was under control. Betty was lying on the floor; and there were other police officers around her. I think she was the only one that was shot. It's miraculous that more people didn't get killed. I'm not saying that the NOPD was the best police department in the world, but when it came to those incidents, they showed a lot of restraint, for whatever reasons. Good leadership. Clarence Giarrusso, at the time working with a liberal mayor, understood the value of keeping officers under control."

NOLA Express in its special edition about the standoff ran a picture of the mayor's home on Thanksgiving Day: "A modest home in a quiet, clean neighborhood just off Napoleon Avenue." It was the same house where I interviewed him in 2003. The picture shows Landrieu talking to Poison (Harold Holmes), with Landrieu's children, nine in all, and other family members sitting on the porch watching. In 2008 several of those children had gone on to public-service careers of their own: Mary was a U.S. senator, Mitch was Louisiana's lieutenant governor, Madeleine was a judge in Orleans Parish Civil District Court, and Maurice was an assistant U.S. attorney for the eastern district of Louisiana.

As the children watched what must have been a memorable Thanksgiving interchange, thirty-one angry black men and women stood in the front yard across the street. Suddenly, the mayor was among them, shaking hands and fielding hostile questions. He stood on his liberal record. He "rapped" (a 1960s term for conversation) for nearly half an hour. "In fact the only indication from Moon that these little people hadn't come to wish him a pleasant Thanksgiving was the trembling in his hands," said the *NOLA Express*.

"Many things can be justified in the name of the law," the paper chided. "Like moving a small army into the Desire project to enforce a misdemeanor statute carrying a maximum fine of $50."[12]

The *Black Panther Newspaper* had also been watching the story closely. It reported:

> George Russell and Harold Holmes, members of the Party, along with 25 other people from the community, left to go to the People's Revolutionary Constitutional Convention in Washington, D.C. Before having hardly left, they were arrested by heavily armed members of the New Orleans Pig Department. Harold Holmes was charged with criminal anarchy and criminal trespass-

ing; George Russell was charged with criminal trespassing, criminal anarchy and criminal property damage. And on the morning of November 26th, at 1:30 a.m., members of the New Orleans Pig Department, numbering approximately 50, donned the uniforms of priests and U. S. Postal workers, thereby gaining entrance to the doors of the Desire Project address which was the office of the Louisiana State Chapter of the Black Panther Party. They shot one member of the Party, Betty Powell, in the chest, and arrested a total of six people. The six arrested were: Godthea Cooper, Leon Lewis, Marshall Kellen, Odell Brown, Larry Jackson, and Betty Powell. All were charged with attempted murder and violation of the federal fire arms act. These brothers and sisters are presently incarcerated in the Orleans Parish Prison, awaiting trial.[13]

A year later at the awards program in Superintendent Giarrusso's conference room on November 23, 1971, "class A" medals of valor were handed to Patrolman Israel Fields, age twenty-two, and Patrolman Melvin Howard, age twenty-one, who were nicknamed, respectively, "Legs" and "Bush." According to an NOPD internal newsletter, "for over a year these officers served in the capacity of undercover agents for the Department, infiltrating the hippie underground, the so-called peace movement, the college intellectual group and the Black Panthers." What, one must wonder, did the "college intellectual group" consist of, and why did it need infiltrating? The NOPD further explained," Their initial objective was to make narcotics cases, however, they became the primary source of intelligence information to the Department on the Black Panthers, knowing the Panthers were police haters and that discovery could mean death. They eventually were discovered, placed on mock trial and then brutally beaten by the Black Panthers. Fields and Howard performed an act considered extremely hazardous and beyond the call of duty. These officers acted as truly professional police officers."[14]

"Class A" medals were also given to six policemen who, as volunteers during an "armed confrontation between a militant organization and the police department . . . placed their lives in grave jeopardy in order to serve our community. These officers entered an apartment residence of these militants who were heavily armed and whose precept of philosophy was death to the police. These officers were engaged in a brief volley of fire between themselves and these militant leaders. In performing this extremely hazardous assignment, these officers displayed exceptional courage."

Nine officers received "class B" medals because they assisted in the operation. The NOPD stated, "These officers have cover and immediately went to the assistance and aid of the officers inside the apartment when a brief exchange of gunfire occurred."[15]

In 2003, Landrieu remembered the final Panther arrest this way: "Sometime after [the Desire standoff between the Panthers and police], the chief devised a plan to evict them with a kind of a ruse, decoys. He had a cop dressed as a postman to go up to try to deliver mail. And then he had somebody dressed as a cleric. I don't think I knew that part—of the cleric—before it happened. I don't know enough about police work. I was not a cop. I had no training. I knew enough about the law to feel somewhat comfortable. None of these things were done without discussion and ball-parking ideas. What options do we have? What kind of injuries, if any, will we have? What will the repercussions be to the people there? To the people in the projects? The police officers, etc.?

"This seemed like the only way you could do it without serious bloodshed. As I recall the incident, the occupants who answered the door suspected some kind of trick. They fired on the officers. The officers fired on them . . . It was surprising and miraculous that no one was killed.

"Sometime later, we received word that Jane Fonda had provided a bus to take some of the Panthers to a meeting in Washington D.C. It was our only opportunity to arrest these people with the least amount of bloodshed, hopefully without any. Chief Giarrusso told me about it. I said, 'Fine. Do what you gotta do.' And he had some cars get in front of the bus. They stopped the bus and kicked them off. As far as I know, that was the end of the whole thing."[16]

In the 2003 interview Landrieu had the order of the Fonda incident and the Desire arrest switched in his memory, recalling the Fonda incident in the 2003 interview as "sometime later." And he remembered a bus instead of rental cars.

At the Hubbard Mansion interview, everyone remembered the Jane Fonda incident. Tucker, alluding to perks of privilege, said, "Jane Fonda was probably sittin' on a Delta airline in first class sippin' on a martini, and they were taking the Panthers off to the slammer."[17]

Hubbard, Carter, and Tucker, however, didn't know about (or had forgotten) the trick that led to the final arrest of the remaining Panthers in the Desire apartment.

But the real priests and the Panthers remembered it very well. In Malik Rahim's words, "It took them to do a deed that is about the greatest betrayal of morality that I have ever witnessed to get us. They came and raided the office dressed as priests."[18]

Father LeDoux, who hardly ever says a bad word about anyone, in a 2002 interview still considered Sergeant Robert Frey, the policeman who wore the priest garb, "the scum of the earth."[19] In 1970, LeDoux told the *Louisiana Weekly*, "For the past two years and especially during the recent crisis in the Desire Housing Project, the clergy played an important role as mediators. This subterfuge seriously undermines future effectiveness of the clergy."[20]

The real men of the cloth felt that their credibility had been stolen. They felt vulnerable, mistrusted by the community. Protesting the use of the clergy collar as a disguise, the priests and pastors said in an open letter to the *Louisiana Weekly*, "We could compare this police action with the use of the white flag of truce or the Red Cross symbol in the same way." The group said two detectives had borrowed the clerical garb from a Notre Dame Seminary student and used it to help police sneak into the housing project and raid the Panther headquarters. Several other theories floated around about where the clerical garb had come from.

The mayor and the police chief gave their assurance to the clergy that "this impersonation will not be used again under similar circumstances."[21]

F. Winter Trapolin, president of the Catholic Human Relations Commission, wrote a letter to Superintendent Giarrusso. It said,

> We protest the use of clerical disguise in the raid made by police on Thanksgiving Day in the Desire Project . . . This misuse of priests' garb has added risk to the lives of ministers and clergy in all future cases where police or other authority may wish to

use them as intermediaries. The trust people have for clergymen is built upon their service to man and God, and this has in the past been recognized in any man who wore the cloth. We are sure that there were other disguises which could have been used for the protection of police in the raid . . . From now on the clergy will have good reason to suspect police motives and this will cloud future relations. It seems in this instance that the police granted clergy access to NCCF headquarters in order to establish a pattern of trust which could then be utilized as a cover by police forces.[22]

Trapolin went on to say that his organization was expressing the concern privately rather than publicly (the letter was marked "confidential") because "You and the entire city administration have your hands full in dealing with the problems of this city, and we wish to support your efforts in every way possible."

Sister M. Harriet Waldo, R.S.M., also wrote to the mayor to express outrage about the misuse of clerical garb: "Such practices can only confirm the young people who listen to their [Panthers] revolutionary doctrine in the belief that the system is evil and rotten and must be destroyed."

She said she and others like her had been placed in "genuine physical danger" and that it would take "very little of this type of thing to make clerical and religious garb the object of suspicion and hatred to the people among whom we live and work."[23]

When I interviewed Clarence Giarrusso at his home in 2003, he was eighty-two. On the day of the interview, he remembered nothing about the final arrest of the Panthers. Reasoning that objectivity in regard to one's personal history accrues with forgetfulness, I described the events to him as matter-of-factly as I could, leaving out his role in it. When I got to the part about the cop disguising himself as a priest, Giarrusso seemed genuinely shocked. He said, "That is not something I believe in."[24]

Nevertheless, it was something that he ordered, and it finally accomplished what a shootout and an invasion of Desire could not. It eliminated the Panthers as an effective organizing force in the city.

16

The Year After

Did the Panthers Make a Difference or Were the People "Tricked as Usual"?

The problems didn't go away after the last group of Panthers was ousted from Desire in the post-midnight arrest on Thanksgiving of 1970. Bob Tucker reflected on this in 2003 with Cecil Carter, Don Hubbard, and Henry Faggen at the Hubbard Mansion Bed and Breakfast owned by Don Hubbard and his wife Rose.[1] "But there was an effort on the part of the administration to get more resources into the project. Ms. Ursula Spencer was appointed to the Housing Authority Board, the first resident from public housing to hold such a position.

"It was the first time in my life that we had a mayor we could talk to, a can-do attitude. Not only would he listen to what you brought him as a problem, but he was prepared to work with you on a solution. All that was good news and fresh news for us. That's why we had so many organizations that were functioning in the community."

Hubbard explained that every block in Desire had its history, every building its personality. "If you were going to survive down there, you had to understand and respect the personalities."

That kind of understanding paid off with Desire residents. In 2003 Faggen still felt a strong connection with Carter, Hubbard, and Tucker. He described himself as "just basically a street guy running a drug program and a boys' club [in 1970]." But he said Tucker and

Hubbard were "my own, my boys. Don would give me different directions for different programs. I would tell Bob. Bob would do what he had to do and get things done . . . Don was the man the whole time he was there—and this is not flattery . . . It's a fact. He had all the connections. He had plenty of nerves. He wasn't gonna let nobody bully the community. He kept a strict staff. He had them all in shape. We had the Desire Area Community Council. He would sit on the board with us and he would dictate things that needed to be done in the community to the council. We had never had a director to do that before. The others would just take their little bread and go home. But Don was a mover and a shaker. Bob was the executive assistant to the mayor. He was the only black in City Hall with that kind of power, and he was not afraid to use it."

Hubbard, Carter, and Tucker were trusted by the Desire community. They were also trusted by Landrieu. And that trust went both ways. Carter said, "It never really occurred to me to distrust Moon. We didn't always agree with him. And Moon had a temper. Sometimes he would fly off. But he would eventually come around and you could talk to him. He'd still disagree. But it never occurred to me to not trust Moon."

The three agreed that there was no other white man in power that they trusted at that time. "It was the first time we as black people could turn to anybody other than ourselves," said Tucker.

"Moon the Coon," white detractors had goaded. "And we were Moon's Coons," chuckled Hubbard.

In the wake of the Panther incidents, Cecil Carter said that community organizing efforts were enhanced, the Welfare Rights Organization was founded, and the range of municipal services improved greatly. Residents had garden clubs. They were planting fruits and vegetables in common courtyards. The city did a better job of policing and picking up garbage.

"People saw Desire as just as much a part of the city as any other," said Tucker. Referring to his report on the conditions of Desire, finalized immediately before the shootout, he contended, "The Panther encounter highlighted the problems in Desire better than any report."

Faggen, the only person in the Hubbard salon who wasn't a former city administrator, acknowledged that quite a lot of resources came into the project, but he also pointed out that some of those resources were misused by contractors. He summed things up: "We got tricked as usual."

Unlike Carter and Tucker, Hubbard still had to work in Desire after the Panther confrontation. He said the "mature people" thanked him and his colleagues for what they did. "The young ones, the hot heads, never said anything, but they gave me their respect when I walked the streets. And they made sure our cars weren't vandalized. They were grateful that nobody actually lost their lives."

But on January 11, 1971, in what police and fire officials described as "a night of violence" characterized by "a rock and bottle throwing melee," both the Piety and the Desire NCCF headquarter buildings were burned to the ground.

The city's chief administrative officer Bernard B. Levy said of the firemen: "Their service is especially noteworthy in that it was carried out in the face of continued harassment from several hundred irresponsible rock and bottle throwing youngsters who hampered their fire fighting activities. We intend to protect life and property in all neighborhoods regardless of the obstacles encountered."[2]

The next day, the *Times-Picayune* editorialized in favor of a proposed thirty-million-dollar project to convert some Desire buildings into townhouses with patio backyards and a shopping center to "give the residents a basic sense of pride and dignity, a feeling that they have their own homes."[3] A special consultant had been hired after the shootout. But the thirty-million-dollar price tag was deemed too expensive, and renovations were postponed.

A year after the Piety Street shootout, Warren Brown, the reporter who had lost his glasses that night in Desire as he wondered who was shooting at him, said the following in a story for the *States-Item:*

> Raindrops fall on the Desire Housing Project in slow cadence, producing a dreary rhythm which seems to be in keeping with the general appearance and mood of the community.
>
> Your empirical observation tells you the place has not changed much since last Sept. 15 when police and members of the then-called National Committee to Combat Fascism confronted each other with guns and bullets.
>
> The burned-out hulk of the building at 3542 Piety St.,

where the first NCCF Desire headquarters were located, remains as a grim reminder of the shooting, the angry shouts and, most of all, the general feeling of desolation which seems to pervade the current project mood.[4]

According to Brown's report, the old Delta Theater was crumbling and boarded up. So was the bowling alley. But the Desire Neighborhood Development Center in the same block housed various Model Cities programs, the community food stamps programs, and facilities for other community services. Several of the programs had begun soon after the police-Panther confrontation. But directors and staff members were quick to emphasize that they were not a result of that confrontation.

One official who asked not to be quoted told Brown, "Nothing has changed. All of the programs you see around here are gimmicks to placate people. The programs only benefit people who have jobs administering them."[5]

A police car marked "Urban Squad" cruised along Desire Street Parkway. There were four such cars in Desire each day. Brown noted that the Urban Squad, created specifically to handle the problems of the housing project, came into being after the confrontation, but not *because* of the confrontation, as police chief Giarrusso hastened to make clear.

Of the Urban Squad, Brown wrote: "Desire residents have mixed feelings about the squad. Some feel it has cut down on drug traffic, purse snatching and rapes in the area. Others, mostly the youths, regard the squad as a 'police army of occupation' . . . Revolutionary graffiti—'Kill the pigs,' 'Death to the Fascist Pigs,' 'Power to the People,'—still cover many outside apartment walls."[6]

An article that ran in the *States-Item* on January 12 explained that the twenty-six-man biracial Urban Squad had been proposed to Giarrusso by Sergeant Rinal Martin in December of 1970 and went into operation on February 7. "The men in the Urban Squad are volunteers. They were chosen for their sensitivity to community concerns and needs and they were given training by professors at Tulane University . . . 'I think that the program is people oriented,' said Giarrusso."[7]

Indeed, the police seemed to have gone to great lengths to put an optimistic face on their endeavor: "Though some Urban Squad members were reportedly the targets of sniping after they first began patrolling Desire, police officials appear pleased with their efforts and say they are being increasingly accepted in the community." One would never have known it from the snipers. In a typical miscalculation made by white planners, Tulane professors were deemed the best advisors on how to deal with the Desire unrest. How could professors who probably had never set foot in Desire be better advisors than the residents themselves? Accounts didn't mention whether people were eager to volunteer for the squad.

Carter, who was acting director of the Human Relations Committee in 1971, told the *States-Item* that whites in New Orleans had become more aware of black concerns in the year since the Desire shootout. "There does seem to be more responsiveness from so-called Establishment-types," he said. He noted that there was no excessive backlash. "I thought that the city responded in a rather cosmopolitan way."[8]

City officials interviewed for the anniversary story credited Landrieu, his contacts, and his rapport with both black and white community leaders with keeping the city on a good course following the confrontations in Desire.[9]

Major renovations did not take place in Desire until 1975 through 1978, when workers put new steel doors at the entrance to every building, new kitchen sinks and cabinets in apartments, and decorative iron bars on second-story windows. But the doors and bars and sinks, a far cry from town homes with patios and a shopping center, did not give residents that illusive sense of pride in home.[10]

In February of 1995 the U.S. Department of Housing and Urban Development approved a HOPE VI grant to HANO to redevelop Desire. HANO subcontracted much of the work to Tulane University. Subsequent Congressional hearings and investigations as well as a recent lawsuit by current and former residents against HANO for their implementations of the HOPE VI grant all point to broken promises, poor management of funds, superficial planning, and continued hardships for the residents of Desire. Some things never change.[11]

17
Panthers and Principles on Trial
"Somebody Has to Not Have Fear"

Awaiting trial for eleven months in Orleans Parish Prison (OPP) was a trial in itself for the Panthers. The bail, set by Judge Bernard J. Bagert, owner of the St. Thomas Street house that was the first Panther head-quarters, was $100,000 apiece. In spite of continuous pleas from their attorneys that the bond was exorbitant, none of the Panthers charged with attempted murder went free. By late September Judge Bagert had recused himself from the case.[1] The Panthers were segregated from other prisoners. Even the Panthers' visitors were kept separate from the other visitors.

Bill Rouselle, who as deputy director of the city's Human Relations Committee had received that first phone call from "Steve from the West Coast," commented about Mayor Landrieu and Chief Giarrusso for a group calling itself "a cross section of concerned black citizens." He said, "It is our feeling that Mr. Landrieu has made certain statements concerning the Desire area and the Panthers which will certainly prej-udice the community against those persons arrested. Both Mr. Landrieu and . . . Giarrusso are lawyers and should be aware of how statements which create a climate of hostility and repression can make a fair trial impossible."[2] Rouselle also noted that "the average maximum bond set for attempted murder in this state is $5,000—$95,000 less than the bond set in this case."[3]

William M. Kunstler, the attorney who defended black militant H. Rap Brown, was in New Orleans a week after the shootout to address students at what was then the Louisiana State University in New Orleans. He described a "legal lynching under way" and characterized the Black Panthers as "those who dare raise their heads above white men's knees." He said that Judge Israel Augustine—the only black judge on the bench, who supposedly had been chosen for the Panther case by lottery—was "very much a part of the white system. They know he will react in a way to safeguard his own status."[4]

On September 26 Judge Augustine said there probably would be no more hearings on the bail issue even though Miss Hodges, one of the Panthers arrested on Piety Street, testified that she was one of twelve children, her father was disabled, and her family lived on welfare payments. She said that she could not raise more than $500 for bail.[5]

By Christmas, additional lawyers had joined Robert Glass and Ernest Jones for the Panther defense—Lolis Elie, Charles Cotton, Alvin Bronstein, and George Strickler. For Elie, this marked a stark departure from a career path that had heretofore aligned him solidly with Moon Landrieu.

The day after the Piety Street shootout, Charles Cotton had invited his fellow black attorney Lolis Elie to a meeting to discuss the Panthers. "There was a group of African Americans condemning the Panthers without knowing anything about them," Elie recalled when I interviewed him in 2003.[6] But he saw the Panthers as "people who had suffered from a level of oppression such that they were prepared to do something about it, including not let the police brutalize them. Desire was a slave-like community. So my heart was with the Panthers . . . The more I read and the more I learned, it became easier rather than harder to take the Panther case. I had pretty much gotten disgusted with electoral politics."

Elie had achieved a measure of material success by then. But he didn't like what he saw material and political success doing to many of his black colleagues. He was reading Abraham Maslow's books on self-actualization. Consciousness rather than material wealth was his priority.

When asked if he had gone to the meeting with Cotton expecting to represent the Panthers, Elie responded, "No. Lord, no. I was probably the closest African American to Moon Landrieu, and I was in the perfect position to get some serious economic benefits from that."

Elie and Landrieu had met at Dillard University and become friends in 1963. Both were born in 1930. Both grew up in the Carrollton area of uptown New Orleans, just blocks apart. But in those days, Black Pearl (where Elie's family lived) and Adams Street (where the Landrieus lived and had their store) were worlds apart. Landrieu grew up in a working-class family. Elie grew up downright poor.

In fact, when Elie was a boy, the Magnolia project (a housing development not far from where Elie lived) looked posh to him. It had "nice brick houses with indoor plumbing. They even had hot and cold water. They had a lot of things the Black Pearl didn't have."

From their meeting at Dillard onward, Elie and Landrieu developed a close relationship. "From the beginning Moon and I talked straight to each other and talked to each other in black and white terms." When asked if it was rare back then for black and white people to speak frankly to each other about race, Elie replied, "Still is."

Taking the Panther case put Elie squarely at odds with his friend Landrieu and with Clarence Giarrusso, the police chief that Elie had helped Landrieu select. But Elie said there was no conflict in his mind. "I was an advocate for the Panthers. I was 100 percent on the side of the Panthers. I was close to Landrieu before I became involved with the Panthers. But, after that, at no point did I compromise." Principles rather than people were paramount.

Protest about the incarceration of the Panthers began right away. The night of the shootout, Sheriff Louis Heyd and Warden A. J. Falkenstein reported getting three threatening phone calls. "One caller said that if any of the prisoners were harmed the jail would be blown up. Another said the prisoners would be freed."[7]

The women Panthers weren't taking things sitting down, either. The *States-Item* reported, "A criminal sheriff's deputy was bitten yesterday in a scuffle with three women arrested last week during the police raid on Black Panther headquarters. As the deputy was escorting Elaine Young, 22, to her 10th floor cell at the House of Detention after she had conferred with three lawyers on the second floor, two other women, Leah Hodges, 18, and Catherine Bournes, 19, left the cell. All three attacked the deputy. He was treated at Charity hospital for a bite and the three were charged with two counts of simple battery."[8]

Warden Falkenstein tried to allay the fears of the public. His assurances were probably aimed most directly at the white public: "We put them in a secure place . . . we located them in an area where it would be highly improbable that they could create any disturbance in the jail . . . They're all in an area where they can't possibly cause any havoc."[9]

But creating havoc in the prison was perhaps less the purview of the Panthers than of their keepers. Police detective Larry Preston Williams remembered when the attorney Etta Kay Hearn came to OPP to consult with the female Panthers. He described her as "light-complected with a big bush." "I was duty officer that night in Intelligence. The desk commander called me at home and told me to go to Parish Prison. They needed me to identify Angela Davis. When I got to Parish Prison, Etta Kay Hearn had fainted. She had gone there to consult with some of the female Panthers who had been arrested and [the guards] stopped her and detained her and accused her of being Angela Davis."[10]

In 1969 Angela Davis had been removed from her teaching position in the philosophy department of the University of California at Los Angeles as a result of her social activism. At the time of the New Orleans Panther incarceration Ms. Davis was on the FBI's Ten Most Wanted List on false charges. She was the subject of an intense police search that drove her underground before her acquittal in 1972.

Recalled Williams: "As I'm in OPP there's this big white matron who argued with me and kept saying that that was Angela Davis even though she had Angela's 'wanted' picture—the old-time wanted pictures you put in the post office. There's Hearn passed out. There's the white matron with the 'wanted' picture—and still insisting that Hearn is the 'wanted' picture. And then someone suggested that I didn't want to book [Hearn] because both of us are black. The white detective came over and tried to convince [the white matron]—no, that's not Angela Davis. This is *not* Angela Davis, but she wouldn't hear of it. But finally he convinced her to let [Hearn] go and the next day we straightened it out."

Referring to cases of misidentification, Williams went on to say: "When I was in the district, I saw that happen a lot. I would sit in a police car. There was a white officer who had a mug shot of a wanted guy. He'd get out of the car and go stop a guy that looked *nothing* like the guy in the mug shot and put him up against the wall."

Eleven months seemed like an eternity for the group arrested on Piety Street. In November they were joined by the Panthers arrested in the cars rented by Jane Fonda and in the Desire apartment by police in disguise. They were also joined by Robert King Wilkerson, a childhood friend of Malik Rahim's; Albert Woodfox; and Herman Wallace, who had been recently recaptured after a jailbreak.

The OPP was a hellhole, according to King and Malik. King told me, "The sewerage was real bad. Rats and roaches were running around like they owned the place. Guys were sleeping on foam rubber mattresses on the floor, on tables, in the hallways. If you were lucky you got an old Army blanket that had been used thousands of other times. And that was if you were lucky."[11]

Malik remembered the constant tear gas on their tier: so thick that the guards had to wear gas masks. "The guards had broken up the porcelain toilets and dumped trash in the cells. Then they tried to make the prisoners clean it up. The guards put mace on the end of fire hoses so the mace would go as far as the water would go."[12]

A flier circulating in Desire entitled "Do not be alarmed, but do be informed" stated, "Any day now the residents of Desire may be reading that members of the National Committee to Combat Fascism (NCCF) have died a natural death. But let us be well informed that that natural death might also be classified as murder. The kind of treatment and cruelty that is employed on our devoted Brothers who are being held at Parish Prison as Political Prisoners on a special made Tier (C-1) for NCCF members and their sympathizers are inhuman."

The flier went on to document the atrocities:

> The first attempt came on Monday, December 3, 1970, when the police gassed their cells. Because the gas smell was still present the Political Prisoners were not able to have visitors. The second attempt came on Monday, December 14, 1970, when the police could not break the spirit of the members of the NCCF and sprayed them with mace. Still not able to break the spirit,

they forced the members to the yard and sprayed water on them through a fire hose for two (2) hours. (The temperature that day was 42 degrees.) As a result of this attempt one Brother (political prisoner) was hospitalized, but Harold Holmes is in grave need of medical treatment and because the police have a personal thing with Brother Harold they have not permitted him to get any medical attention, and he has swollen twice his natural size and they constantly harass him telling him to let that "All power to the People Cure Him."[13]

During the Christmas holidays, a priest who had helped with the Panther breakfast program came to OPP to visit, Malik Rahim recalled. Panthers had suspected this priest of assisting with the ruse in which policemen had disguised themselves as priests to accomplish the final arrest. "When the priest took a long look at how the Panthers were living, one of them, Ed, said, 'This is what you gave your collar for—for them to come and do this to us.' After Ed said, 'And you call yourself a man of God?' that priest started crying."

The Panther case finally came to trial on July 8, 1971. According to Elie, the lottery that chose black judge Israel Augustine was rigged. "He was the only one we could intimidate," Elie recalled. "He used all his power against us, but he wanted to be perceived as being on our side . . . He wanted to satisfy white people at all costs while pretending he was a civil rights person."

As the case progressed, every time court was in session, it was packed with Panther supporters. Family and friends played an important role. In addition to visiting the Panthers in prison, Marion Brown and her roommates attended the trial. Her parents were not pleased with her involvement with the Black Panther Party. They saw her rebellion as a sabotage of their hope that a first-class education at Tulane University would propel their daughter effectively toward the achievement of the American Dream.

Althea Francois's parents also constantly tried to pull her away from the party. They told her she wasn't being fair to her child. Althea didn't fully understand what her parents had been through until she was sorting old pictures and papers after her mother's death. She found a picture of herself and her young daughter at a protest demonstration attached to a threatening note from the FBI.[14]

Malik's mother took care of his two children when he was in OPP awaiting trial. "From the time my mother took my children, the FBI kept questioning her," Malik said. His mom, Mrs. Lubertha Johnson, gave them some unexpected answers.

Mrs. Johnson was seventy-seven years old when I crossed the Mississippi River in 2002 on a ferry to speak with her at her home in Algiers. She had thirty great grandchildren, three of whom were in her care that day. It was just before Christmas, and entering the tranquil neighborhood with its modest, well-kept houses and gardens was like going back in time. Mrs. Johnson's home looked like a family museum, with pictures everywhere and treasures from Africa and the Far East brought back by her seaman husband.

We sat in a kitchen decorated for the holidays and filled with handmade Biblical reminders where she served us home-baked treats. The great grandchildren, four-year-old twins and a seven-year-old, cheerfully complied with each of her requests, including reciting the Pledge of Allegiance.

"I've always supported my children if they were doing the right thing," she told me.[15] "They [Malik and the Panthers] were trying to make it better for our people. I and some other mothers, Brokie's, Betty's mom, used to cook for them and make little clothes-pin bags to sell. We went every day to their trial when they were in jail. We would march around outside the jail singing." One mother with three sons who were Panthers had fought the arch-segregationist Leander Perez in Plaquamines Parish for years. She was solidly behind the young revolutionaries.

Lubertha Johnson was one of those rare mothers who could support the principles of her son, Malik Rahim, even knowing that they might cost him his life. In her peacock print dress and leaning on an African walking cane, Ms. Lubertha, as the many people that she mothered called her, was the perfect mixture of old-fashioned family values and revolutionary verve, a true Mother of the Revolution.

Mrs. Johnson grew up during the Depression with "half beans and half rice rations and a little lagniappe. I just thought that was the way it had to be, blacks and whites separate. But we're all human. During those days, you couldn't holler 'You wrong!' because you could get killed." Then she added, thoughtfully, "But I couldn't die but once. And that's OK if it's for the right thing."

Of the Piety Street shootout, she said, "When I saw it on TV, I thought they were all dead. It was nothin' but a miracle that they survived. They were for good things, trying to do good things as young black people. If I had my life to live over, I'd do the same thing they did.

"Somebody has to not have fear."

Maybe that's why it was okay with her for Malik to do what he did. When the FBI came to her house to get information about him and the other Panthers, agents asked why the Panthers wore their hair plaited. She thought it was such a stupid question that she came back at them with "Why do the KKK wear pointy hoods and sheets?"

On Easter Sunday of 1971, Mrs. Johnson dressed Malik's toddler Donald in his suit and little white shoes and took him to see his dad at Orleans Parish Prison. She stood in line with the others who had come to visit Panthers, cordoned off from visitors of other prisoners. Donald got away from her and went tearing down the hall. Mrs. Johnson remembers three guards bulging out of their uniforms in hot pursuit, yelling, "Catch him! Catch him! It's a Panther baby!"

Of the Panther activities in New Orleans at that time, Mrs. Johnson concluded, "I believe in myself that God was pleased."

The Panther defense team effectively argued that the Panthers had acted in self defense. Assistant district attorney Numa Bertel Jr. countered, "If it was the intention of the New Orleans Police Department to slaughter these people, they could have dropped a bomb on them."[16]

By all accounts, Ernest Jones's closing arguments were eloquent. "When in the history of New Orleans have 150 men gone down there with a tank to serve simple arrest warrants?" he asked, and reminded the mostly black jury that after the Panthers surrendered, the police took posters, typewriters, newspapers, and leaflets from the Panther headquarters. "Why?" Jones asked. "Because these things were doing what they [police] feared most. They were giving ideas to black people."

The highly publicized trial culminated on August 7, 1971, when a jury of ten blacks and two whites returned a unanimous verdict of not guilty after barely half an hour of deliberation.

The friends and sympathizers who jammed the courtroom greeted the verdict with a single shout of joy, pounding each other on the back and hugging. Defendant Leah Hodges buried her face in the shoulder of defense attorney Robert Glass. The seventy-five or so sympathizers who lined the corridor as the defense attorneys left pressed near to convey their gratitude. Ernest Jones nearly disappeared under the crowd that swarmed around him.

After Judge Augustine quieted the shouting in the courtroom, Assistant District Attorney Bertel asked that the jury be polled. As each of the jurors rose and pronounced the defendants "not guilty," Kenneth Weaver, a white juror, one of the first to be picked, rose and said, "In the spirit of Martin Luther King, not guilty!"

Judge Augustine said that the decision proved that "fair trials can be had by any black people in the South. If ever there was a fair trial in the community, this trial was it." As he emerged from the courtroom in a shirt and tie, the crowd in the corridor began chanting "Here come de Judge!" Several times he was stopped and kissed by spectators.

18

"Better Off in the Penitentiary"

When Malik Rahim came out of Orleans Parish Prison in 1971 there was no person he trusted quite like Lolis Elie, one of the lawyers who had won an acquittal for the Panthers after eleven long months in OPP. Just five days after Malik was released from that "hellhole," he was picked up on kidnapping charges. The last thing he wanted to do was go back to a cell where his toothbrush reeked of tear gas. But Elie convinced him to do just that, promising that he would get him out soon.

Malik had been accused of kidnapping two guards during the time when prison guards were making life almost unbearable for the detainees. Elie had the charges reduced to "false imprisonment," to which Malik pleaded guilty and was released after a week and a half for time served.[1] Malik may have been guilty of false imprisonment, but he was also falsely imprisoned himself.

After he was finally free, Malik implored Elie to spend a day in the projects with him so he could see for himself how the people there lived. Elie protested. He already knew about poverty. Poverty was where he had come from. "You don't need to tell me. I come from Niggertown." (That is what many of the people who lived in Elie's neighborhood called the Black Pearl area.) But Malik wouldn't let up. It took him a year to convince Elie to go with him to the Fischer Housing Development near where Malik had grown up.

When the two finally made the trip, they were an odd couple. Malik is tall and imposing. He looks tough, but he has another side that is caring and gentle. Elie, twenty years Malik's senior, is a small man who looks gentle. He is, in fact, quite tough. "Malik was the disciplinarian. When he spoke, people obeyed," Elie said, remembering the incident that was still so vivid to him thirty-three years later when I interviewed him that he related conversations word for word.[2]

The first thing that happened down in Fischer was that a man came up to them and wanted two dollars to buy heroin. The man had ten dollars, but the heroin cost twelve. Elie remembers Malik saying, "Let me talk to the seller and see if I can get him to take the ten." In addition to being a disciplinarian, Malik was also a mediator and a problem-solver.

But the prospective buyer was in no mood to negotiate. He'd just go hold the seller up and that would be that, he reasoned. Malik said, "No, man. If you do that, he's gonna come back at you." So Malik talked to the seller and got him to take ten dollars for the transaction. The police sat parked no more than fifteen yards away, observing everything and doing nothing, Elie remembered.

Then another person came up and asked Malik to loan him ten dollars, just until the next day when he could hold up a 7–11 convenience store. At this point Elie jumped in. "Look, man, don't you know if you do that you gonna get caught and go to the penitentiary?"

The man said, "Yeah, man. I've been to the penitentiary. I'm better off in the penitentiary than I am out here. When I was in penitentiary I got three meals a day. I had a place to sleep. I was in charge of something. My folks wrote me letters. They came to see me. I ain't got none of those things out here. No one pays any attention to me. I'm not in charge of anything."

Elie said it stuck in his mind that "there are people who are so bad off, their lives are so hopeless, that prison is no threat." Ever since then, he has continued to question the premises of a society where a "significant portion of its citizens believe they are better off in prison than in the so-called free world."

Elie says he learned another thing in Fischer that day. He learned that "people who live in the projects don't associate with other people. They are ashamed. They feel stigmatized, not so much by whites as by other African Americans. I wasn't aware of this."

Elie and Malik didn't see each other again after that Fischer trip until a chance meeting at a Juneteenth 2004 celebration. As they hugged, all that Elie had learned from his client that day flashed back into his mind. Malik, at the same time, expressed to the lawyer the depth of his gratitude for the sacrifices that Elie had made to defend him.

N C F F

P I G S

above: Young black men stand between heavily armed police and the Black Panther headquarters in the Desire Housing Project the day of the standoff, November 19, 1970. Courtesy of the *Times-Picayune.*

left: Cartoon from *NOLA Express* depicting the extreme hostility as well as the up-and-down nature of the confrontation between the police and the Panthers. Donated to the author's archives by the former *NOLA* editor Darlene Fife.

above: Malik Rahim
(Donald Guyton) is
escorted by two
policemen back into
the Piety Street
Panther headquar-
ters (raised build-
ing) on the day of
the shootout,
September 15, 1970.
Courtesy of the
Times-Picayune.

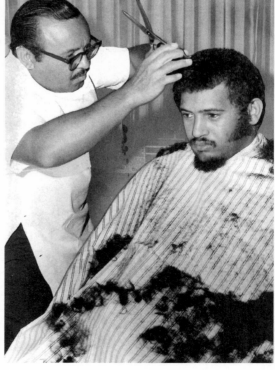

right: Undercover
agent Israel Fields,
twenty-one, gets his
first haircut in four-
teen months.
Courtesy of the
Times-Picayune.

Melvin Howard and Israel Fields infiltrated the Black Panther organization. Courtesy of the *Times-Picayune*.

Police chief Clarence Giarrusso examines a firebomb the day after the Piety Street shootout. Courtesy of the *Times-Picayune*.

Headline from September 17, 2003: "Recalling Strife in '70." From left: Sherman Copelin Jr., Robert Tucker, Charles Elloie, and Henry Faggen walk past "the War Wagon" in the Desire housing complex during a standoff between Black Panthers and police on November 19, 1970. *Times-Picayune* caption: "The potentially explosive event that was defused peacefully is the subject of a forum today in Central City." Courtesy of the *Times-Picayune*.

Police Chief Clarence Giarrusso instructs his officers to leave the Desire Housing Project the day of the police-Panther standoff on November 17, 1970. Courtesy of the *Times-Picayune*.

above: Robert King Wilkerson leaving Angola State Penitentiary on February 8, 2001, after thirty-one years of incarceration, twenty-nine of them in solitary confinement. Donated to the author's archives by the National Coalition to Free the Angola Three.

left: Robert King Wilkerson bagging Freelines in his midcity house in New Orleans in 2004. Photo by author.

above: Albert Woodfox (left) and Herman Wallace (right), two of the Angola Three in solitary confinement at Angola State Penitentiary in 2007. Donated to the author's archives by the National Coalition to Free the Angola Three.

right: Herman Wallace at Angola State Penitentiary, 2006. Donated to the author's archives by the National Coalition to Free the Angola Three.

Robert King Wilkerson, Brandon Darby, and Geronimo ji Jaga (from left to right) at Herman Wallace's hearing in 2006. Donated to the author's archives by the National Coalition to Free the Angola Three.

Robert King Wilkerson (left) and Geronimo ji Jaga at Herman Wallace's hearing in 2006. Donated to the author's archives by the National Coalition to Free the Angola Three.

right: Steve Green (Green Stevens Jr.) at a Panther forum planning meeting in New Orleans in 2003. Donated to the author's archives by the photographer Nijme Rinaldi Nun.

below: Althea Francois at a Panther forum planning meeting in New Orleans in 2003. Donated to the author's archives by the photographer Nijme Rinaldi Nun.

above: Henry Faggen at a Panther forum planning meeting in New Orleans in 2003. Donated to the author's archives by the photographer Nijme Rinaldi Nun.

left: Malik Rahim at a Panther forum planning meeting in New Orleans in 2003. Donated to the author's archives by the photographer Nijme Rinaldi Nun.

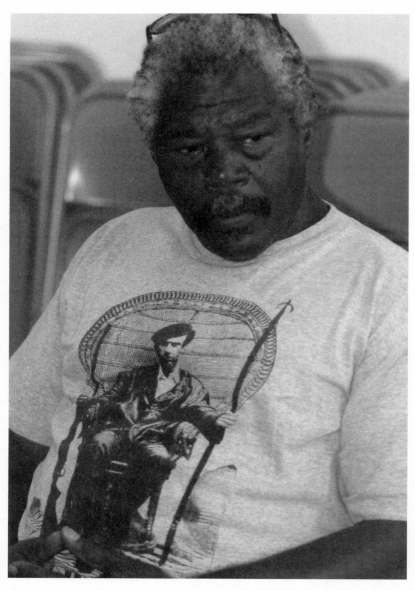

Malik Rahim at a Panther forum planning meeting in New Orleans in 2003.
Donated to the author's archives by the photographer Nijme Rinaldi Nun.

Bob Tucker at a Panther forum planning meeting in New Orleans in 2003.
Donated to the author's archives by the photographer Nijme Rinaldi Nun.

Royce Osborn, film documentarian for the New Orleans Black Panthers and New Orleans' black culture, at a Panther forum planning meeting in New Orleans, 2003. Donated to the author's archives by the photographer Nijme Rinaldi Nun.

Former Panthers Lil Man, Malik Rahim, and Steve Green (left to right) at a Panther forum planning meeting in New Orleans, 2003. Donated to the author's archives by the photographer Fred Plunkett.

Lil Man, Bob Tucker, Malik Rahim, and Steve Green (left to right) at a Panther forum planning meeting in New Orleans, 2003. Donated to the author's archives by the photographer Fred Plunkett.

Moon Landrieu, Panther forum, New Orleans, 2003. Donated to the author's archives by the photographer Nijme Rinaldi Nun.

Althea Francois and Malik Rahim, Panther forum, New Orleans, 2003. Donated to the author's archives by the photographer Nijme Rinaldi Nun.

Malik Rahim, the Reverend William Barnwell, Ted Quant, and Moon
Landrieu (left to right) at the Panther forum in New Orleans, 2003. Donated
to the author's archives by the photographer Nijme Rinaldi Nun.

Panther forum participants, New Orleans, 2003. Back row, left to right: Malik
Rahim, Cecil Carter, Don Hubbard, Robert King Wilkerson, Father Jerome
LeDoux, Bob Glass, William Barnwell, Charles Jones, Bob Tucker. Front row:
Ted Quant, Charles Elloie, Henry Faggen, Marion Brown, Althea Francois.
Donated to the author's archives by the photographer Nijme Rinaldi Nun.

Al "Carnival Time" Johnson and Malik Rahim at the Ernie K-Doe Mother-in-Law Lounge, Mardi Gras Day, 2004. Photograph by author.

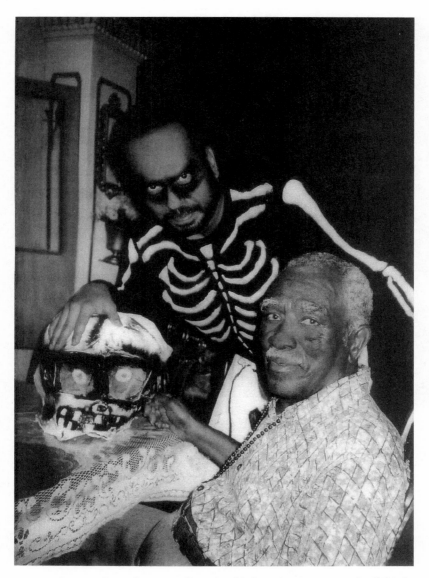

Royce Osborn and Mardi Gras Indian Big Chief Tootie Montana at the "Chief of Chiefs'" last Mardi Gras, 2005. Montana and his devoted wife Joyce attended St. Augustine Church. He died June 27, 2005, of a heart attack as he was lambasting the police at a city council meeting for a recent disruption of Indian ceremonies. The chiefs, spy boys, flag boys, and queens of the assembled tribes launched into a somber rendition of "Indian Red," a ceremonial Mardi Gras Indian song. He was eighty-two. (*Gambit Weekly,* July 5, 2005). Donated to the author's archives by Royce Osborn. Photograph by Pat Jolly.

Father Jerome LeDoux celebrating mass at St. Augustine Catholic Church in New Orleans in 2006. Donated to the author's archives by the photographer Alan Pogue.

PART III

Prisoners and
Those Who Love Them

19

The Escapees—
Now Known as the Angola
Three—and the Panthers
A Long-Term Relationship

Four of the people I interviewed for this story, Malik Rahim, Robert King Wilkerson, Henry Faggen, and Geronimo ji Jaga, had been incarcerated for various lengths of time—sixty-one years combined—because of their Panther activity. All were innocent. Their prison experiences form instructive side stories to the Desire narrative, illuminating the vindictive strategies of FBI and police intelligence in targeting the Panthers as well as the inhumane prison conditions they endured. One question that I still ponder is how these men triumphed against seemingly impossible odds. Instead of dying, giving up, or going crazy, as many did, each has remained tenaciously engaged in the struggle for liberation in its broadest sense. They have made enormous contributions to freedom and self-sufficiency for their comrades on both the local and global level.

In the middle of September in 1970 Robert King Wilkerson was watching a guard's television in the hall through the bars of his cell in Orleans Parish Prison. What had landed him in that cell—this time—was a jailbreak from OPP with twenty-five other prisoners. When he found out he had gotten a thirty-five-year sentence for an armed robbery of an uptown supermarket that he says he didn't commit, he decided "the slaves have a right to rebel. Many of us felt we were unjustly confined," he told a group of students at Tulane University in 2003. "I began to see that I had no moral obligation to a system that oppressed me. To run from injustice did not mean that I was guilty of a crime."[1] He was at large for two weeks before he was recaptured.

On the small television, the announcer cut from the regular programming to inform viewers that a group of black militants, men and women, had barricaded themselves in an apartment in the Ninth Ward and were "shooting it out with the police." King says in his autobiography: "This caught my attention. It was something that was unprecedented in the city of New Orleans, and as each scene unfolded, and with every word passed by the commentator, the kinship I felt with the group—whoever it was, grew. And if it was possible that I could have undergone a transfiguration, I would have transfigured myself to that scene, into that house with whomever it was that was shooting it out with the police."[2] He felt an emotion beyond anger. It was a huge empathic "companionship," as King describes it, with the cause of those militants.

King soon learned that the group shooting it out with police near the Desire Housing Project was the Black Panther Party. The nine men who were arrested came to OPP, and the three women—Catherine ("Top Cat") Bournes, age nineteen; Leah Bernadette Hodges, age eighteen; and Elaine (E-Baby) Young, age twenty-two—to the detention center next door. The youngest one, the one who wanted his mama, was a juvenile, so he was not held with the others.

Panthers at first were separated from other prisoners, but they all, nevertheless, found a way of communicating. According to King, "It was through this prison communication system that I met the firebrand of a sister, Top Cat, as she was called . . . a source of inspiration to many of the prisoners, and she was my greatest inspiration. In her letters to me she uttered the Party's Doctrine . . . as if she had written it herself."[3]

Ron Ailsworth also figured prominently in King's introduction to the Black Panther Party. After the bank robbery on Jefferson, he was housed with the escapees rather than the Panthers. "It was [Ron's] knowledge and revelation about the Party which ultimately tied me to the Party's Concept . . . It was from Ron that I was introduced to the Party's teaching and Platform. We began to hold political discussions, and it was through these discussions that I grasped the historical plight of Blacks and other poor people in America. I also learned the art of collectiveness, and the means and method of struggle."[4]

After the two groups of troublemakers had been separated for a time, prison officials came up with another idea. In 2002, Panther Malik Rahim remembered the encounter this way: "The guards said, 'Y'all think you some bad niggers. We're gonna send down some real bad niggers and they gonna kill you and have sex with all y'all.'"[5]

The guards planned to put the two groups together and let them kill each other. That's how OPP escapees Herman "Hooks" Wallace, Albert Woodfox, and King met the Panthers.

"Send 'em on down," Malik Rahim (then Donald Guyton) told the guards. "We know how to deal with them." When Woodfox arrived, Malik remembered, it was "real tense at first." Woodfox raised his fist. "Power to the People," he hollered, expressing solidarity instead of the violence the guards had anticipated. "They sent [Herman] Hooks [Wallace] down," Malik recalled. "He had no shoes." Malik insisted on giving Hooks his shoes when Hooks went to court. And that began their friendship.

King recalled that he immediately felt "awe and respect" for Malik and the other Panthers. "They would hold political education classes. I wasn't an official member at that time, but when they spoke, they spoke for me. I was just as eager as anyone to see conditions change."[6] There was a prisoners' rights movement sweeping the country, and the Black Panthers, according to King, brought that movement into OPP. "Guys who were eager to effect change weren't necessarily party sympathizers or members of the Black Panthers. But they knew that they were being treated badly. For me, Black Panther Party members helped articulate issues, lent a sort of legitimacy to my feelings."[7]

In his autobiography, King describes the horrible prison conditions they faced. "Tiers originally built to house only 48 prisoners were holding twice as many. Toilets ran all night, and water infested with feces would at times run into the hallways where prisoners had to sleep . . . Huge rats coming up from the sewer challenged prisoners for their food, rearing up at prisoners who attempted to eliminate them. The food was inadequate, poor in quality and quantity, having no nutritional value and prepared in an unsanitary manner."[8]

The one bright spot was when Marion, Mary, and Linda (who

were Tulane students, some of the very few black ones), Shirley, and Althea came to visit.[9] The women, three of whom would become Panthers, visited regularly. King especially looked forward to seeing Marion. He called her the "Tulane Babe."[10]

Another shuffle at OPP brought King into contact with Panthers Charles Scott and Harold Holmes (Poison). Scott submitted King's name to the Oakland Central Office, allowing him to become an official member of the Black Panther Party. Malik was pleased about that. He had known King since he was nine (and King was a few years older) in Algiers, where their backyards touched. While Wallace was known for his brilliance and Woodfox was a youngster with a "real big heart," King had the reputation of being "a real man." Malik knew he would be an asset to the party.

"While we were in there (OPP)," Malik told me, "we were writing Panther Papers. We had to write articles. We had an outreach to all brothers about how we were living, that there were rapes down here."

Their activism also took the form of a hunger strike. In January of 1971 the Panthers and the escapees organized a strike involving seven hundred inmates. The *Louisiana Weekly* reported: "Warden A. J. Falkenstein said that even though the strike originated in an area dominated by black militants both black and white inmates have been taking part in the strike."[11]

All of the Panthers arrested in and near Desire except Ailsworth stayed in OPP almost a year awaiting trial. Wallace, Woodfox, and Ailsworth were sent to Angola in 1971, before King. "They began teaching unity amongst the inmates, establishing the only prison chapter of the Black Panther Party in the nation."[12] That precipitated a palpable change at Angola.

In late April of 1972, when King was escorted back to Angola from OPP by the national guard, he was immediately put in solitary confinement. "My record traveled with me, so they knew of my Black Panther involvement."[13] Although King's human contact was now severely limited, he noted that "human communication always went on." He says in his autobiography, "I felt as if I had entered a different Angola than the one I had entered years before, where prisoners were totally subservient. Absent was the submissive, sycophantic behavior of by-gone years. In its place, I witnessed a quiet defiance among many of the prison's population. And I knew this was due mainly to the presence of Albert [Woodfox], Herman [Wallace], and Ron [Ailsworth]."[14]

A few weeks before King returned to Angola, a guard, Brent Miller, had been murdered, and prison officials were cracking down on prisoners they deemed "political." Woodfox and Wallace would ultimately be charged with that murder.

In 2003 Wallace wrote to the Coalition to Free the Angola Three from solitary confinement: "[Miller's] death had a radical impact on every prisoner at Angola . . . Men all over the prison who held any form of 'militant' view were all placed in administrative segregation [solitary confinement]. It is a dungeon," he wrote,

> a six-by-nine foot cage where physical and mental torture is meted out systematically and intentionally. The treatment is designed to destroy sanity and any thought of freedom or independence. I honestly don't think I could have survived these many years in solitary had it not been for the structure of the Black Panther Party's Ten Point Program. You have to have a belief structure to survive and the strength and truth of the Ten Point Program has kept Albert, Robert and myself strong enough to withstand the unremitting torture of 32 years in solitary for a crime we did not commit.[15]

When people ask King how he stayed sane, he says, "I was scared to go insane. The worst thing you can do in prison is go crazy."[16] He watched others go crazy, and each time it strengthened his resolve not to succumb to their fate.

Angola was its own kind of horror. King's autobiography describes the brutality in shocking detail. He credits Woodfox, Wallace, and Ailsworth with "bringing some order to this disorder." They reduced the incidence of inmate rape. They held political education classes. The food got a little better. Finding dormitories and eating facilities segregated, they brought the races together under an all-white prison administration; and they schooled themselves in the law. As a result of their efforts, King believes, Ailsworth was discharged to a federal facility and Woodfox and Wallace were placed in solitary confinement.

King did lots of things to survive his time in solitary confinement. In addition to practicing the Panther principles, he read, he wrote, he studied, he thought things out, he exercised, and he made candy. He became a jailhouse entrepreneur of sorts. During his first stint at Angola in 1962 King had pulled kitchen duty with fellow inmate Cap Pistol. Cap knew how to make pralines, a popular southern confection made with sugar, butter, milk and pecans; but he wasn't sharing his candy secrets with King.

King, however, was a good observer. He watched Cap cook when Cap didn't know he was looking. "I saw that candy change before my very eyes. I saw it go from liquid to almost solid." And so with smuggled ingredients, a stove made from aluminum cans, and a fire stoked with toilet paper, King created the candy he calls Freelines. The smooth-as-butter candy afforded him privileges in prison. "I didn't have too much problem getting what I needed," he told me. "I perfected the recipe."

By 1974, in addition to the thirty-five years at hard labor "for an armed robbery which I hadn't committed" and the eight years added on by the jailbreak "for the aggravation that I had caused my keepers," King was accused of having participated in the death of another prisoner and handed a life sentence without the possibility of parole, probation, or the suspension of sentence.

In 1987 two inmates who had testified against him in the stabbing death of that prisoner admitted to a judge that they had not witnessed the crime and professed King's innocence. For fourteen years King tried fruitlessly to clear his name. When it looked like there was nothing he could do about the life sentence, "the idea to write was born. If an epitaph was to be written of me, I wanted it written by me."[17] So he began writing his autobiography, "A Cry from the Bottom."

In it, King tells the seminal stories of his early years with his grandparents, which shaped the beliefs and consciousness of this curious, thoughtful, rebellious, precocious child. He describes the moral development of his teenage years, during which he was often on the wrong side of the law, and his adult years in Angola.

One story involves going with his grandmother to visit a cousin who was a janitor at the jail:

In the far corner was another Black Man. The man was behind what I then described as a "lot of skinny iron." From behind this iron, the man watched us all, somber-like. And looking into the man's face, I immediately felt some kinship with him . . . I asked Mama [as King called his grandmother] what was that other man doing at our cousin's house and why was he behind all that skinny iron? She told me that it wasn't our cousin's house but a jailhouse . . . and she told me that the man behind the bars must have done something bad to be there. She described the man as . . . a "cornvick." "Cornvick," my mind repeated. I was only about four years old . . . and my small mind went to work . . . My erroneous and errant mind told me that since there were many cornfields around, the man whom I saw behind the skinny iron bars lived in cornfields and was considered by some to be a "bad" man for doing so. And as a result, he was captured and forced to live in a small area, behind iron, in a place called jail and was obviously known as a cornvick. Of course years later I was to learn what convictism was all about.[18]

What King learned during his more than three decades in prison was that the explanation of why he was locked up was less logical than the deductions of that four-year-old.

Malik had tried to keep in touch with King, Woodfox, and Wallace over the years because he had promised them when he left OPP that he would do everything he could to help them. But each time he tried to send a message through another Angola prisoner, he was told that the message could not be delivered. It was too dangerous. In 1998 he spearheaded a grassroots effort to free King, Woodfox, and Wallace. Marion Brown and Althea Francois came on board, and in short order the effort became the National Coalition to Free the Angola Three, attracting national and international attention.

In the course of the next few years, the coalition would raise money for a top-notch legal team and mount an effective civil and criminal defense. But in the beginning, Malik had direct action in mind to free the Angola Three. He was planning another jailbreak.

He was also paying close attention to the situation in Iraq. In April of 1998 he accompanied a group organized by the International

Action Center to bring medical relief to Baghdad and other cities. Malik's assignment was to provide security for Marina Drummer, a foundation director and activist on behalf of Native Americans and prisoners. He was not looking forward to shadowing this "dizzy white girl" who lost her expensive sunglasses before they even got off the ground for New York. And Marina was annoyed that "he wouldn't shut up about the Angola Three" while just outside their window in Baghdad was extreme and immediate suffering.

But during the course of the trip the two formed a friendship, and when Marina got back to Berkeley, she sought out more information. She became what King calls "the navigator," an effective fundraiser writing to anyone she thought she could interest or influence to get involved. She went periodically to Angola to visit.

In May of 1999 the Angola Three—King, Woodfox, and Wallace—were disciplined for inciting a hunger strike. They were moved for nine months to an even more punitive area in Angola called Camp J, where, King says, "You're not allowed a sweatshirt or jacket in the winter—only the white prison-issue jumpsuit, a few pairs of boxer shorts, a couple of T-shirts. You have no television and no contact visits—only visitors behind a heavy screen."[19]

In March of 2000, the Angola Three filed a federal lawsuit against prison officials claiming that the conditions of their confinement were cruel and unusual punishment. When the case began successfully working its way through legal channels, Warden Burl Cain told the *Times-Picayune*, "They chose a life of crime . . . They're crybabies crying about it."[20]

Unimaginable as it may have seemed from Camp J, King would soon be free. He got another day in court on February 8, 2001. When he was sworn in and told to raise his right hand, he raised his left hand in defiance of the lie he knew he would have to tell.

The state agreed to release him if he pleaded guilty to conspiracy to commit murder. He refused at first because it wasn't true, but at the urging of Woodfox, Wallace, and his lawyers, who thought King could accomplish more for the Angola Three on the outside, he reluctantly entered a guilty plea and was released for time served.

At 4:12 p.m. on February 8, 2001, he walked out of Angola. The world he knew had disappeared, the Black Panther Party long dissolved, and its legacy all but whitewashed from history. When he walked out, he said, "I may be free of Angola, but Angola will never be free of me. I will always be a thorn in its side."[21]

"It is now July 2001," King writes in the preface to his autobiography,

> and I am into my fifth month of having been released from the confines of prison, though it was determined by reactionary forces that I would die there. In this respect, much has changed for me, in that I am no more saddled with time limits or other constraints which are inherent in the prison culture. Nevertheless, what hasn't changed for me is the desire to make my odyssey known—to write my own epitaph, and most of all, what will never change while I remain on this plane, is my total commitment to the struggle, and the driving desire to expose the reactionary force that held me in its grasp for three decades."[22]

In June of 2003, back at Angola, the mailroom denied Herman Wallace a package. The late Dame Anita Roddick, former owner of the London-based Body Shop and founder of Anita Roddick Publications, had sent him a copy of her new book *A Revolution in Kindness* . The book, about using the power of kindness to make the world a better place, included essays by Woodfox and Wallace. "My staff and I felt that their essays were among the best in the book," Roddick wrote to Angola's Warden Burl Cain in protest of his mailroom censure, and posted the letter on her Web site.[23]

Cain wrote back to agree that the world should be more kind, but he stuck by his ban on the grounds that Ms. Roddick's book "constitutes a threat to the internal security of the institution." He got that right. The internal security of Angola is based on a brutality that the courts are likely to find cruel and unusual.[24] A revolution in kindness most surely would have threatened that.

20 "The Mayor" Goes to Prison

> Here in Louisiana, particularly, every woman, whether young or old, lives in constant fear that her man or her brother or her father or son will be arrested and fed into the man-consuming gates of Angola State Penitentiary. This fear is real; this fear is justified. It is the same fear that has haunted our Black women since we were brought to this country in chains, 400 years ago. It is the knowledge that if her son shows the spirit and will to resist slavery, then his death by the hands of the racist ruling class is inevitable. Today in Louisiana everyone has a relative, a friend, a lover that has been in or is in this slave labor camp. Some of them returning crippled in mind and body; some of them never to be seen or heard of again. This evil inhumane system of forced labor of Black men is one of the many clear-cut contradictions that exist between the ruling class, the fascists, and the poor oppressed masses in the Deep South that is a daily reminder that Black people are still slaves.[1]

This article appeared in 1971 in the *Black Panther Newspaper* soon after King, Woodfox, Wallace, and Ailsworth had been shipped off to Angola. Another player in the Panther drama would join them there in four years—none other than the venerable "Mayor of Desire," Henry Faggen.

"They (police) did a big raid, a big drug bust down there in Desire. They swept up everything that was black," Bob Tucker recalled in a 2003 interview.[2] Faggen, the Desire resident who had helped the city administration avert a bloodbath during the Panther confrontation, got swept up, too.

The police had not left the Desire standoff in a good mood. Residents feared they would come back seeking revenge. "I wasn't dealin,'" Faggen said. "I had a good job." He was the coordinator of the Mobile Answer Desk, an extension of the Human Relations program based at City Hall. He had even saved up a little money and bought a 260Z sports car.

Faggen figures he was a marked man after the "Panther thing." And he counts his purchase of the sports car as a huge mistake. It attracted too much attention. In 1975 the police picked up Faggen for conspiracy to possess and distribute narcotics. He had run both a methadone clinic and a boys' club. He was a civic leader in Desire. He knew Mayor Landrieu and Police Chief Giarrusso personally. He had put Bob Tucker up in his house while Tucker conducted his study of Desire. He had been able to help broker the peace between the police and the Panthers, at great peril to his own safety, during the showdown because he was trusted by both sides. And still they picked him up and sent him to Angola, without cause.

Faggen recalled that there was a big machine gun on the back seat of the police car that nabbed him. Handcuffed, he picked up the gun, banged on the wire cage, and told the officers, "Here's your machine gun. I ain't got no use for this."

Faggen received a sixty-year sentence. Eddie Sapir and Johnny Jackson Sr., who were on the state pardon board, helped him acquire a good lawyer—Sonny Garcia. Eventually, his sentence was reduced to twenty-five years, then to eight, then six. He ended up serving two years, two months, and twelve days. His wife, Cecilia Price Faggen, now deceased, "put everything together to secure my freedom."

"They played with me," said Faggen. "Never, anywhere, had I seen anything like the physical and psychological brutality at Angola." But Faggen managed to garner respect even there—from inmates and from the Chief of Agriculture for whom he worked, a man named Carmouche.

When he got out of Angola, he went back to Desire to live. Faggen never wanted to live anywhere else. He remained in close contact with Don Hubbard and Charles Elloie, and he always knew that Tucker was there if he needed him. Faggen lived in Desire until plans were in the works to tear it down in the late 1980s.

The *Black Panther Newspaper* described Angola in the 1970s as a "slave labor camp" resembling a huge plantation, bordered on one side by swamp and the river and on the other three sides by woods and hills.

The guards at that time were "Black, boot-licking trustees" with long sentences to serve. They were armed with shotguns and rifles:

> They will get one year off their sentence for every "nigger" that they kill. If a prisoner steps out of the chow line, or is too slow cutting cane, or runs across a snake in the cotton fields and jumps out of the row to keep from getting bitten, he will be shot. In the fields there is a White man (the captain) on a white horse, overseeing the work. If a prisoner gets too close to this pig, he will be shot without warning. If a prisoner falls or is pushed off the back of one of the trucks or trailers, he will be shot.[3]

And then there was "Nigger." "The pigs of Angola had one huge dog named 'Nigger.' Every time he killed a brother the pigs would cap one of his teeth with gold. He had a mouth full of gold teeth to show how effectively he served his masters."[4]

In 2003, at the time of the interview I conducted at the Hubbard Mansion, Faggen's enormous family knew nothing of the part he had played in the Panther story. He never brought it up, because the Angola part was a carefully guarded secret. He was afraid his family wouldn't understand. It would not be until the fall of that year at a Panther reunion and public forum that this master storyteller would tell his story and be honored by the current mayor. His wife, his children, grandchildren, and great grandchildren were there. Faggen felt a huge sense of relief at no longer having to keep the secret that he had planned to carry to his grave. In his characteristic cadence of amused amazement, he added, "Damned if it didn't take a white girl to tell the whole thing!"

He told me later, "You put me on the map. You gave me a legacy to leave my grandchildren."

21

Geronimo ji Jaga

Geronimo ji Jaga (formerly Elmer Pratt), a Morgan City, Louisiana, native, was a Los Angeles Panther who successfully led underground military campaigns. By 1970 Pratt had risen to become the party's Deputy Minister of Defense.[1] Ji Jaga, like Malik Rahim, is a Vietnam veteran. He helped train Green Beret Special Forces in reconnaissance tactics. While serving as a paratrooper, he participated in a series of highly classified missions and received eighteen combat decorations. Despite his military heroics, ji Jaga became disenchanted with the nature of the war, the military system, and the social order that spawned them. In 1968, disillusioned with the United States' intervention in Vietnam, he returned to his native Louisiana.

But he didn't stay home long. That same year, he left the South to attend UCLA, where he encountered and joined the Black Panther Party. His work in the Southern California chapter contributed to the party's early popularity and helped win it community respect. He later went on to work at the national and international level as a member of the "First Cadre" of the Central Committee. In that capacity, he interacted with each and every legitimate Panther chapter.[2]

Though the Central Committee doubted the viability of a proposed New Orleans chapter, ji Jaga pushed for its establishment, citing the militant history in Louisiana of groups like the Deacons for Defense in Bogalousa and Jonesboro, Louisiana, who had armed themselves to thwart the Ku Klux Klan. So in 1970, the Central Committee agreed to let ji Jaga send Steve Green, Harold Holmes, and George Lloyd to help get the New Orleans chapter started. After the Piety Street shootout, he asked Jane Fonda to come to New Orleans to publicize the Panther cause and to transport the Panthers to a convention in Washington D.C.[3]

A year earlier in 1969, in an eerie foreshadowing of the showdown in Desire, Panthers in the Los Angeles Central Headquarters had engaged in a five-hour standoff with the Los Angeles Police Department. Eighteen Panthers, including ji Jaga, were subsequently arrested in three simultaneous predawn raids of their offices in South Central Los Angeles.

Kathleen Cleaver, who was the party's communication secretary at the time, says of Geronimo ji Jaga Pratt:

> Dedicating himself to the liberation of blacks within America, Pratt rose quickly in the Party leadership. He used his experience in guerrilla warfare to train the Los Angeles Panthers in revolutionary struggle. His skill as a leader enabled him to maintain discipline more effectively in Los Angeles than was the case in many other chapters, and luck helped him to survive several attempts on his life. When the Panthers found out that no one had been killed during the 1969 SWAT attack on the Los Angeles Panther office, Pratt was credited with the one "victory" in the sustained nationwide assault police were waging against the Black Panthers. He was revered as a hero, and *The Black Panther* praised him as representing "the essence of a revolutionary."[4]

In a fairly typical Panther arrest scenario, when one set of charges didn't stick, the enforcement authorities manufactured others. After being acquitted of the 1969 police raid charges, ji Jaga was charged and convicted in 1972 with the murder of a white school teacher. A number of FBI surveillance documents that supported ji Jaga's alibi mysteriously disappeared.

In 1994 he was denied parole for the twelfth time by the California State Board of Prison Terms. Ji Jaga claimed that if he had really committed the murder, he would have been released sooner. The average term served for murder in California in 1994 was less than ten years. [5]

Like the Angola Three, ji Jaga languished in prison for decades for a murder he did not commit. His case received more attention from Panther defenders than King's, Woodfox's, and Wallace's because ji Jaga had held a high-profile position with the Central Office and also because the Angola Three were not considered political prisoners until Malik Rahim, in 1998, made that case.

In 1997 a California judge ruled that a witness's testimony in ji Jaga's 1972 case was secretly biased. The witness was an FBI informant who had infiltrated the Black Panther Party, a fact that the witness denied under oath at the trial. The judge also ruled that evidence was suppressed by the prosecutors, thus freeing ji Jaga and ending a staggering twenty-seven years of incarceration.

The Panther scholar Ollie A. Johnson III notes, "Ji Jaga's true crime seems to have been that as a rank-and-file member and then Deputy Minister of Defense, he was a tremendously effective Panther . . . Ji Jaga taught other Panthers the basics of self-defense, military strategy and tactics, and political organizing," making his "crime" sound much like that of the Angola Three.[6]

When ji Jaga was released, most of the Black Panther Party activists had forgotten about the Angola Three. Marion Brown, who had moved to California in the meantime, assumed they had been freed years before. But ji Jaga, who had been privy to the struggles of many of the local chapters, hadn't forgotten. A month after his release, he was pressing for support for their freedom.

In 2001 those efforts came to fruition. On February 8, King walked free after thirty-one years in Angola. Soon after, King and ji Jaga cemented what would become a close friendship as they worked for the release of Woodfox and Wallace, the remaining two of the Angola Three.

Ji Jaga's link to King and Malik aroused his interest in our proposed Panther forum in 2003. Just as he had decades earlier, he contacted Steve Green and Jane Fonda and asked them to come to New Orleans. Fonda was unable to come but sent well wishes. Green actually showed up with Malik at a forum planning meeting—to the amazement of all of us who were present.

Ji Jaga himself came to several of those meetings, once with his wife Joju and their small son Kayoda. Joju is the daughter of legendary Panthers Eldridge and Kathleen Cleaver. In one of those moments when past and present swirl unexpectedly together, Malik and King both remarked that little Kayoda looks just like Eldridge.

Ji Jaga also used his new platform to establish the Kuji Foundation, which provides medical supplies and other assistance to East and West Africa, where he resides.

PART IV

Making Sense of It

22

Where Have All the Panthers Gone?

After Lolis Elie got Malik Rahim out of Orleans Parish Prison for the last time, Malik needed a "safe house." He knew that all freed Panthers could become police targets at any moment. Knowing that Marion Brown and her roommates lived in the Newcomb dorms, Malik thought, "What better safe house than a women's dormitory at an exclusive college?" In those days, dorms were strictly segregated by sex. It was the last place anybody would think to look for him. He had a maintenance man uniform in case anyone ever asked any questions, but no one did. Students and faculty got used to seeing him over the course of the next nine months. People assumed he was a student or that he worked there. So Malik came and went from those quiet stone halls unimpeded, sometimes with a companion. His fourth child was conceived in the Newcomb dorm.[1]

Later that year (1971), Marion joined the Party, dropped out of Tulane, and, with nine other New Orleans Panthers answered the call from the Central Office in Oakland to come there to work on Bobby Seale's mayoral campaign. Her parents were not happy. The Oakland experience for most of the New Orleans Panthers was a shock and a disappointment. They did not see the same discipline and commitment that they had established in New Orleans. Several felt that when they decided to leave Oakland, they barely escaped with their lives.[2]

The New Orleans Panther women had a particularly difficult adjustment. The party's stated ideals concerning women were high. Panther Linda Greene described the "new phenomenon" of the revolutionary black woman in a 1968 edition of the *Black Panther*

Newspaper. "She is a worker. She is a mother. She is a companion; intellectual, spiritual, mental, and physical . . . She is the strength of the struggle . . . She is militant, revolutionary, committed, strong, and warm, feminine, loving, and kind. These qualities are not the antithesis of each other; they must all be in her simultaneously."[3]

Point seven of the party's Eight Points of Attention states, "Do not take liberties with women." But the party struggled constantly with disparities between party rhetoric and the realities of daily life, according to women party members. Some claimed that it was sexual open season, with men demanding their right to the "revolutionary fuck."[4]

As is so often the case, New Orleans was different. New Orleans Panther Leah Hodges, the one who bit the jail guard when she was eighteen, addressed a gathering at the Community Book Center, a Black Panther Party photo exhibit in honor of the Angola Three. Thirty-three years later, she was still quite glamorous as she pursued her singing career. Recalling the discipline of working for the people from sunup until bedtime, she remembered the New Orleans brothers as respectful. "We were way too tired to be hot."[5]

To this, Marion Brown added that the Panthers attracted misfits, the "white sheep" of the family. "*We* were like a family, the odd ones, who finally found a place that made us feel at home. People could see the principles we were living day by day. Everybody was expected to pull their weight, male or female. It was not a sexist thing. We were ahead of our time."[6]

But in Oakland, Marion and Betty Powell, who had taken the buckshot in the final arrest, were "stuck in the child care center" taking care of Panther children "twenty-four/seven," which wasn't why they had come to Oakland. Both were eventually reassigned to positions in the field. But after a series of severe health problems, Marion left Oakland in October of 1972. Because she was shrewd, outspoken and feisty, and careful to put her complaints in writing, she was the last to be allowed to go "without a hassle."

Althea Francois had to leave on the sly. She called Central to say that she would not be opening up at the Lamppost, the Panther coffee house, that evening. She felt bad about not doing what she had said she would do. When I spoke to her in 2005, she remembered riding stony-faced past headquarters on a bus with her young daughter Olga on her lap, seeing party leaders going in and out. She recalled thinking that if they saw her, they surely would kill her.

Tyrone Edwards had a hard time leaving also. He was beaten as he tried to leave for some alleged infraction of party rules.

Althea got on the train and went to Kansas to stay with her sister for a year in a lovely, well-appointed house on a hill. She and Olga healed during that time and "life got back to normal." Over the next few years, she formed a close relationship with Ronald Ailsworth and wrote and visited him during his incarcerations in East Baton Rouge, Oklahoma, Tallahassee, and back at Angola. Her children became close to Ron. She took granddaughter Garielle to Angola to visit.[7]

Althea keeps in touch with seven of the New Orleans female Panthers. All but one attended her mother's funeral in 2003. In 2005 Althea attended a national Panther women's retreat held on St. Helena Island in South Carolina for about thirty women, a third of whom she knew. It was such a healing experience for her that she wants other New Orleans women to attend future retreats.

Kathleen Cleaver, a nationally renowned Panther and retreat organizer, now a professor at Emory Law School in Atlanta, told *Essence* magazine,

> To really start healing, you have to go to the root of it all, where your trauma and anxiety come from. I've helped put together healing retreats for women who had been in the Black Panther Party, women who had been living underground, who had been tortured, who had been exiled. We had meetings at places near the sea, and we talked about everything that happened to us— and all the people we lost to death or prison. I think it was very helpful for all of us. Still, if you're suffering from being caught up in a failed revolution, it's an ongoing issue. You can't ever say that you're fully healed. I'm just glad I can say I'm not crazy.[8]

Some did go crazy. One New Orleans Panther noted that after leaving New Orleans, William Cloud couldn't see the obvious shortcomings of the party in Oakland in the days of its decline. The party was his life. "Dogmatic Cloud—by the book. He lived and breathed the Party. It destroyed his mind. He believed so whole-heartedly in the

Party that reality was too much for him. He walked around babbling. He drowned in a canal in New Orleans."[9] The same source says Poison (Harold Holmes) lost his mind too, and did some time in San Quentin. There was just a remnant of the party left, headquartered on South Rochablave, when Marion got back to New Orleans from Oakland in 1972.

In 1981 several Panther deaths prompted a New Orleans Panther reunion of the survivors. In attendance were Tyrone Edwards and his brother Alton (Ed), both of whom had been arrested at the Piety Street headquarters. Tyrone took the pictures, and ten years later, when Marion started a Panther scrapbook, the film was still in his camera. But somehow the pictures survived.[10]

In 2005 Tyrone (or T. as he is called by his friends) was a paralegal, preacher, photographer, family man, and resource trainer for the People's Institute for Survival and Beyond. In a 1995 interview, he told the *Times-Picayune* that September 15, 1970, was the "day I should have died."[11] His mother, Dorothy Stone, cried when he joined the Black Panther Party in the summer of 1969—his other two brothers had joined the party also—and told him, "Just stay out of the graveyard and you will see a change."

"Our thing was about changing the conditions that black people were subjected to," Edwards told the *Times-Picayune*. He saw the Black Panthers as having had the right goals and accomplishing the hugely important task of "teaching me to love myself, to analyze situations and stand up for what I believe." Today he believes that violence should not be used to achieve social justice. He has long since outgrown his old conviction "that the highest form of solving any contradiction was war."

Plaquemines Parish, long a segregationist stronghold, where Edwards has lived most of his life, has changed, he said, because of people like himself who attend government meetings and organize to advance social causes. "I have a relationship with elected officials in Plaquemines. When things are wrong I can go and talk to them without talking about going down with a gun."

Edwards said he has been aided on his crusades to improve living conditions by both black and white people. He often reminds his son, Sadei, now a young adult, to focus on issues and not the group to which a person belongs.

"If I died at 18, people wouldn't have understood what I died for. I would have died for a cause people didn't even understand."

"After all the funerals, you try to reconstruct a life that won't put you in harm's way," Kathleen Cleaver told *Essence*. "You move to a new town, go back to school, reconnect with friends that you had left behind when you were in this revolutionary movement that scared the shit out of them. You try to make your life look like something that approaches normal. But that's all it is. Something that looks normal."[12]

In 2004 Herman Bell, the Panther arrested by Larry Preston Williams, wrote a statement from prison for the *Panther News*. The statement was part of the parole process; he was being considered for parole. It read:

> The Party's cultural and social programs were aimed at promoting a sense of self-awareness and cultural empowerment in Blacks to offset the oppressive practices perpetuated through Jim Crowism and other racist policies. My involvement resulted in my being falsely accused of the murder of NYPD officers Jones and Piagentini. I did not commit this offense . . . I am continuing to evolve as a member of the human family. I have received a bachelor's degree from SUNY–New Paltz and a master's degree in sociology from SUNY. I have participated in all the therapeutic and anti-aggression programs available within the correctional system, either as a participant or as a facilitator. I have designed Black Studies and academic programs that are still being modeled today and I continue to mentor and tutor young men who have returned to their respective communities to lead productive lives.[13]

He was not released.

In *Power to the People: The Rise and Fall of the Black Panther Party,* Jim Naskins sees the legacy of the party as primarily symbolic. And yet symbols are powerful. The image of defiant black men and women facing down racist law-enforcement authorities resonates in the souls of inner-city African Americans, and many other African Americans, as strongly now as it did thirty years ago, he believes. "It is a romantic image for the very reason that it is a doomed image." Of the Black

Panther Party, he writes, "Its time in the sun was so short; but the shadow it has cast is long."[14]

The story of the Black Panthers in New Orleans and their thirty-five-year shadow is a love story both doomed and romantic. It was love between the oppressed community and the Panthers, set appropriately in a place called Desire. It spawned at least one love story of the regular kind. After hours and hours of sitting on the plush brown couch in the home of Marion Brown and Robert King Wilkerson while they patiently talked into my tape recorder, I asked, "So, you two fell in love?" I was hoping for more than a yes or no answer.[15]

There was a small silence and a smattering of laughter as they thought back over a thirty-year sequence of events. King decided he'd better let Marion tell the story. He said he might tell it differently. He knew, too, that it was a sweet story. And behind his dark skin and many tattoos, I thought I saw a blush.

King got up and excused himself to go to the kitchen to wrap the candy he calls Freelines. But not long after Marion started to talk, King eased back into the room and into the conversation.

In 1970 Marion had been profoundly affected by the confrontation between the police and the Panthers in Desire. After the arrests, she had gone every day to observe the standing-room-only trials. She also frequented the Panther office, wanting to be helpful. When the Panthers at headquarters suggested that she and her roommates visit the Panthers locked up and awaiting trial in Orleans Parish Prison, they did.

The Panthers were locked up with so many other prisoners that Marion couldn't specifically remember King. He was part of the cadre of recaptured escapees. King, however, remembered each and every one of Marion's visits. He remembered calling her the Tulane Babe.

Three decades could hardly have taken the two farther in different directions, though the Panther principles had left a deep impression on both of them. Marion left the party, married, moved back to San Francisco and raised a son. King served out sentence after sentence at Angola for crimes he says he didn't commit. He saw people defeated by their prison experience. He felt for them. He saw them withdraw, little by little, retreat irrevocably into their shells. He told me he consumed their plights as if he were a vampire, using the "blood" of their bitterness to inoculate himself against a similar fate.

In 2000, Marion, who had maintained a love-hate relationship with New Orleans, decided she needed to come home to be closer to family. Malik Rahim had also been living in San Francisco for many years, working on securing rights for prisoners. When he learned that Marion was returning to New Orleans, he asked her help in trying to gain the release of the Angola Three. Marion had assumed that they were long since free and was shocked to learn that they were still sitting in solitary confinement at Angola.

When Malik asked Marion to work on behalf of the Angola Three, she jumped at the chance even though she had her responsibilities—a career, a child in college, and a network of friends. She hadn't been able to completely shake her past. The FBI still visited her on most of her jobs, but they didn't bother her much because they assumed she was "reasonable." King, on the other hand, was stuck in solitary confinement with nothing to bargain with except his wits and his candy.

About the time Marion decided to move to New Orleans, King felt his destiny change. He says he is spiritual, but not "religious in the sense of getting down on your knees." Still, he sensed a clear and present intervention of the Divine.

In 2000, Marion went again to visit the Panthers in prison—this time in Angola—thirty years after her first visit. It wasn't hard to keep track of them now because there were only three. Her meetings were limited to Woodfox and Wallace. King's visitor privileges had been curtailed, and he couldn't put Marion on his list.

She did more than visit. She wrote letters to Wallace as well. After two or three trips to Angola, she finally got to talk to King— through glass. Each had a hard time looking the other in the eye. When King looks a person in the eye, he sees right into the soul. Marion wasn't sure she was ready for that.

When King looked at Marion, though, he was looking for the face of the Tulane Babe who had come to check on him thirty years ago. It was solace to again discern that girlish smile.

During the interview in 2003 after King got back from the kitchen with his Freelines, he steered the conversation to the philosophical talks that he and Marion had. He particularly remembered the one about existentialism. But Marion couldn't recall it.

King told me he wasn't much of a letter-writer, but when he saw a thoughtful letter that Marion had written to Herman Wallace, he figured he could outdo Herman in a response. And he did.

About this time (early 2001), the judge in charge of King's case unexpectedly decided to revisit the question of King's guilt, setting in motion findings that would lead to King's release on February 8, 2001, after thirty-one years of incarceration, twenty-nine of them in solitary.

As events unfolded, according to King, Marion pursued him. According to Marion, that was all in his mind. "But, hey, I was very pursuable," King said with a twinkle in his eye. "And it's my blessing anyway." Then he winked, or did she wink? I wasn't sure. "You, know," said King, "you can't get that wink on your tape recorder."

23

Grits, Not Guns
The Panther Legacy

The war against the Panthers in New Orleans coincided with the war against the Panthers nationally. "The assault against us was an unrelenting campaign. Hoover wanted to shut us down by 1969. That didn't happen. But by 1971 we had been virtually destroyed, and almost 30 of us had been killed," Kathleen Cleaver told *Essence Magazine* in 2004 in an article discussing the Patriot Act and the effects of governmental oppression. Cleaver, the widow of Panther legend Eldridge Cleaver and communications secretary for the Black Panther Party in the 1960s, is a fifty-eight-year-old grandmother of six who teaches law at Emory and Yale Universities.[1]

What provoked the huge governmental response that Robert King Wilkerson refers to as the abortion of the revolutionary baby? New Orleanians Ernest Jones, Stephanie Moore, and Johnny Jackson see the Panther survival programs as the real legacy of the Black Panther Party, as well as the biggest threat to the establishment. Ironically, the survival programs may have ultimately cost the revolution its right to life (to borrow a phrase from a group not usually associated with revolution).

When I sat down to talk with him in 2003, Ernest Jones, the attorney for the Panthers, who is currently Lolis Elie's law partner, provided me with his thoughts on the history and legacy of the Black Panther Party nationally.[2] He noted that the party's first activity, with the dual purpose of fundraising and education, was publishing the *Black*

Panther Newspaper. Even though the rhetoric in the newspaper was powerfully revolutionary, Jones said that the authorities didn't take much notice of it. It wasn't until the Panthers started implementing community services, most notably the free breakfast program, that the establishment got upset.

"You had a bunch of folks with no particular resources, not even jobs in the traditional sense. They weren't participants in the economy, but they dared to say, 'There are people in our community who are hungry and we will feed them. They don't have to go to the welfare office. They don't have to go to any of the central institutions that America has set up. *We* will feed these hungry people.'

"I really believe that the intellectuals and theoreticians who understand political structure said that this is something that could not be permitted. It just can't happen. You can't do that. And that was the beginning of the war against the Black Panther Party. And it did turn out to be a *war*—here, Oakland, Seattle, New York, everywhere. There was a war against this organization. Most people think it was because the Black Panther Party used the slogan 'off the pigs.' It wasn't that. It was about the survival programs.

"I don't mean to say that there weren't people in the party who only related to the armed struggle business—the guns and the black berets—just like people join the Catholic Church because they like the mystery and the rituals and the smoke. But it was the second program, the free breakfast program, that caused people to really take notice."

Stephanie Moore was a child in the Lafitte Housing Project near downtown New Orleans in 1970 when the Panthers fed and taught her. She remembers having breakfast before school—not just cereal, but grits and eggs, and toast and milk. The Panthers also provided pep talks, arts and crafts, modern dance lessons, and booster shots. These offerings made a lasting impression on her.

Moore says she thinks it was the grits—a peculiarly southern food staple—not the guns, that really threatened the government, because with the grits came pride and self worth. "We were well on our way to becoming self sufficient, but they [the establishment] had a different plan for us. That's the reason the Panther story was suppressed."[3]

Kathleen Cleaver said this to *Essence* about the Panther programs: "The Black Panther Party represented concrete action against racism and domination. We fed people, provided them with medical care and took families to visit loved ones in prison. These were activities that people could identify with. You didn't have to be a radical to support a breakfast program."[4]

Jones, speaking of the Panthers both in New Orleans and nationally, says: "Many of those survival programs— free food for poor children, health clinics, clothing and shoe giveaways— today have been institutionalized by government and churches. The story kind of illustrates how human beings move social institutions, in fits and false starts, bits and pieces. Many times people do not have a full understanding of the effect of what they are doing on the larger community and on the world. A bunch of young kids who knew that they wanted to do something, weren't real sure how to go about it, had some guidance, and gave it their best effort—that was the Panthers. Moon and Giarrusso— they too moved in ways that they didn't expect, didn't fully understand or comprehend. None of us can understand until we look back."

Johnny Jackson Jr. lived in Desire during the party's heyday and managed the Desire Community Center. He went on to become a state representative and a city council member. In a 1995 interview on the anniversary of the Piety Street shootout, he told the *Times-Picayune* that the free breakfast program and the after-school tutorial program have been incorporated into the public school system. He also attributed the birth of the Urban Squad to the Panthers. It was New Orleans' first attempt at community policing.[5]

Jones concluded: "We let the movement drift away from us, but I'll bet you have found in your research that most of those folks are still in some fashion working for some kind of social change. They've never stopped."

My research does, indeed, bear that out.

Kathleen Cleaver described the Black Power Movement as incredible because it was an "exuberant, creative burst of imagination. It spread across everything in our culture—from literature to education to politics. Nothing was unaffected. It was like an earthquake."[6]

Unlike the civil rights movement, the Black Panther Party made no claim to pacifist piety and did not care whether displays of aggression would alienate white supporters. It didn't turn the other cheek but instead employed direct defiance of authority, shocking young people out of political fatalism by demonstrating that black salvation lay in black people themselves and not in laws or white largesse. It was markedly secular. Instead of nonviolence, it preached and practiced the human right of self-defense.

Curtis Austin sums it up well in his insightful book *Up Against the Wall: Violence in the Making and the Unmaking of the Black Panther Party:*

> That they lost this fight is not proof that their efforts were in vain. That they displayed the courage and audacity to fight and teach themselves the rudiments of self-reliance inside a nation they knew could brutally crush their movement at the first sign of success is a testament not just to the Panthers, but to the seminal idea of freedom by any means necessary. In reality, their goal was not to overthrow the government, but to infect the masses with the revolutionary zeal to do it themselves, since it was this group that suffered the most from racism, the most damaging by-product of capitalism."[7]

"The Black Panther Party made (white) America feel many things," said the former Panther, journalist, and political prisoner Mumia Abu-Jamal, "but safe wasn't one of them."[8]

The New Orleans Panthers evoked sympathy and admiration, but they garnered little political support. The Tulane historian Lance Hill sees the Panthers as primarily political theater, which often backfired when massive overreaction to trivial threats reflected a white mood of near paranoia. Former NOPD intelligence officer Larry Preston Williams made that point repeatedly in his stories about Landrieu and Giarrusso.

To a good number of the ten thousand residents of Desire, the Panthers were heroes, and many other blacks bitterly resented the way authorities harassed and persecuted the Panthers. The final arrest involving police disguised as Catholic priests evoked considerable anger. And yet there was relatively little political fallout for Landrieu, and black leadership, on the whole, shunned the Panthers.

The Panthers missed the mark with their supposition that a revolutionary situation existed in New Orleans. Despite the enormous needs in Desire and the courage and leadership of its residents, the anatomy of New Orleans did not include a revolutionary womb. Jones pointed out to me that New Orleans doesn't have a history of confrontational change. Its citizens don't want to think that some group might alter that, even a group that "scared the bejesus out of everybody in City Hall, the police department, everybody. People were scared of their own children," as Jones put it.

By 1970 blacks in New Orleans were more committed to electoral politics than ever. Landrieu had placed blacks in charge of city departments, selected a black executive assistant, appointed a black chief administrative officer, and ensured that black allies received patronage jobs and "sweetheart deals."

Leaders of both races had a profound desire to avoid the kind of racial violence that had wracked other cities. As members of the oldest urban black community in America, people of color in New Orleans had a sense of belonging. This helps to explain why, even with all of the elements that predicted catastrophe, the massacre didn't occur.

"The Panthers were not a racist organization," Jones told me. "They had many white allies. They were not just interested in black power, but all power to all the people. Despite the diversity of its base, though, things started coming apart for the Panthers, both locally and nationally, after the trial of the New Orleans Panthers." The revolutionary baby was aborted. New Orleans and the nation never got to test Robert King Wilkerson's thesis about the future woes that might have been avoided had the revolutionary baby had been allowed to gestate to term.

In 2003, when Cecil Carter, Don Hubbard, Bob Tucker, and Henry Faggen gathered for an interview at the Hubbard Mansion, an opulent bed and breakfast on St. Charles Avenue, New Orleans' grandest street, they offered perceptive comments about those present and future woes.[9] The Mansion, built by Don and Rose Hubbard in 1998, is a large red-brick two-story house—constructed to look like the other antebellum homes, as if it had been on St. Charles for decades. Its veranda and balcony supported by white pillars feature a row of comfortable white wicker rockers inviting guests to rest, sit, and take in the view. The gardens are enclosed by a traditional wrought-iron fence.

"This beautiful edifice," said Tucker to the assembled group, "that Don has put in place on St. Charles Avenue—after he went through all the trials and tribulations of getting it placed here, he wasn't the most welcome person on the Avenue. There's only one other person of color on the Avenue."

It was strange—vividly recreating a collective memory of the Panthers from a venue that in New Orleans represents the very essence of privilege.

For Tucker, the Hubbard Mansion, with its implicit contradictions, is a symbol of race relations in New Orleans. As he spoke, I could feel the presence of the original New Orleans Panthers in the room. Here in New Orleans, we live with our ghosts. We even make friends with them. Past and present merge. "The white community never could accept blacks on an economic parity," Tucker said. "Everything is just below the surface. There's just a hum. I won't call it racism because it defies exact definition. We've dialogued to death. We've talked to the business community . . . How do we create jobs and economic development? How do we move our city forward beyond just having a good Mardi Gras, Jazz Fest, and Essence Festival?"

"Thirty-three years later and you are *still* asking those questions!" I heard an imaginary chorus of Panthers retort, with a flash of anger and more than a hint of comic irony.

Tucker told me that he viewed the political structure as proactive, historically. He had been a significant part of it. But, he added, the business community in New Orleans has always been reactive. He knows the business community from the inside; he is a successful businessman himself. "The action was always on the political side, the reaction on the business side. New Orleans is probably the ultimate city of cultural diversity. But there's no economic diversity in this city."

His view is backed up by "A Haunted City? The Social and

Economic Status of African Americans and Whites in New Orleans," a report released on May 3, 2003, by the research analyst Dr. Silas Lee. According to the report, with median family income for whites almost twice what it is for blacks, "racial exclusion undermines the opportunities and mobility for many in this community."

Lee describes race relations in New Orleans as a simmering volcano that never quite erupts. He states, "Our celebratory culture and accepting nature conceals a city with a troubled soul."

"Never quite erupts," fumed the chorus of imaginary Panthers hovering close to the polished walls. "But we brought it damn close."

Nestled into a red chair and oblivious of the Panther chorus, Cecil Carter is remembering July of 1959. He had just come back home to New Orleans from the army. He was twenty-one years old. "One of the first things I wanted to do was register to vote," he told me. "I had two years of college and an honorable discharge from Uncle Sam's army. But according to the clerks in the voter registration office, I was totally incapable of completing the voter registration form."

He tried to register half a dozen times before he got a lawyer to go with him to the voter registration office and "raise hell." "That's what was going on back then," he said. "I don't think I've missed but one or two elections since 1959. I wish I could transfer that sense of struggle to my son."

Carter was one of the founding members of the group Community Organization for Urban Politics (COUP). He came into the Landrieu administration as a "piece of their patronage. My appointment to the Human Relations Committee was due to the recommendation of COUP with the blessing of SOUL. I had to get all of that before I got that job. I stayed five years. It was good. I liked it . . . I hope I was worth it."

The interview at the Hubbard Mansion was punctuated, every ten minutes or so, by the sound of the streetcar gliding by the big house on the Avenue. Hubbard carefully pulled a plank out of a drawer of an ornate antique armoire. It was a polished wood slat that used to fit in pegs on all of the city's streetcars. Black letters etched into the wood like a brand read: "For Colored Patrons Only." Glancing down from his pillared balcony onto the majesty of the great oaks on St. Charles Avenue, Hubbard said he keeps the sign as a reminder.

The clank and hum of the streetcar faded slowly into the moist evening air. The Panther chorus got loud. "Power to the People! *Always* remember," it insisted.

The measure of a social movement is not how long it endures, Lance Hill reminds us. "Like a bee with a stinger you lose your stinger, but you only have to sting once," he told me.[10]

Perhaps the only reason to study history is to change the future. Mumia ends his book by saying, "The Black Panther Party may indeed be history, but the forces that gave rise to it are not.

"They wait, for the proper season, to arise again."[11]

In New Orleans we think of hurricane season as anything but proper. And yet the 2005 hurricane season, when Katrina blew in and the levees failed, exposed in shocking ways that the potent forces that once gave rise to the Black Panther Party—racism, classism and the myriad forms of fear, brutality, and vengeance that they beget—are still very much alive.

How then, did the characters in this story fare after Katrina?

24
And Then Came Katrina

Before the deluge, I left town hastily, a split-second change of mind early Sunday morning, a day ahead of Katrina. I wasn't planning to stay away long. Like so many others, I didn't think beyond a few changes of summer clothes. Malik Rahim remained at home in Algiers because he had only thirty dollars in his pocket and no transportation. Marion Brown evacuated with the old people from the nursing home where she worked, but King stayed in their midcity home with his dog Kenya. Royce Osborn, chronicler of the Panther story on film, and his wife Dama rode out the hurricane at the Fairmont Hotel, where he was employed as a doorman. Four days later, they hitched up with some German tourists, hoisted their belongings and a carrier with their cat in it over their heads, and waded through chest-deep water to the Superdome. They took one look and decided not to stay.

Father Jerome LeDoux wasn't too worried about the storm. He's not the worrying kind. He had enough raw vegetables (his diet staple) and candles to ride out the storm in the rectory of St. Augustine Church in Tremé, just blocks from the relatively high ground in the French Quarter. He knew he could give aid and comfort to many of his flock who had no transportation and little money and were unable or unwilling to leave. Playing the piano helped him calm his mind so he could write another chapter of his historical novel about the church. He stayed put, carrying out the remnants of his pastoral routines until the National Guard made him leave a week after the storm.

Royce and Dama broke with the ragtag Fairmont group, procured a ride in a jeep with someone who recognized Royce, and miraculously squeezed onto a bus headed for Houston, still carrying their cat. Royce had a wad of cash in his pocket, so from that point it wasn't hard to book a flight to Los Angeles where his mother lived. Ten days after Royce had trudged through treacherous waters, fearing for his life, he found himself in California on the Tavis Smiley Show describing the horrors he had experienced. His local celebrity status as a cultural documentarian was suddenly elevated to national attention.

During these strange times there were many sudden and dramatic ironies. Bob Tucker had put his house, nestled beside the fashionable Bayou St. John, on the market two months before the storm for an asking price of over a million dollars, figuring that it was a good time to sell. Two weeks after Katrina hit, I reached Bob on his cell phone in the food-stamp line in Florida. His insurance company had informed him that his home, now under three feet of water, was not covered for floods. As the line snaked slowly toward its humble destination, Bob's mind was whirling, as it generally is. He was trying to figure out how he would take care of his business, his house, his wife's business, and a large contingent of relatives.

When Katrina churned into the Gulf, Malik Rahim and his partner Sharon Johnson decided to hunker down in the Algiers bungalow that had once belonged to Ms. Lubertha, Malik's mother, that fiercely determined "mother of the revolution." Sharon and Malik had always ridden out hurricanes. And as a former deputy of security in the Black Panther Party, Malik knew quite a lot about making preparations for just about anything.

Three days after the storm, a techno-miracle occurred. Mary Ratcliff, editor of the *San Francisco Bay View,* reached Malik on his land line. He was incensed. "This is criminal," he told her. "There are gangs of white vigilantes near here, riding around in pick-up trucks, all of them armed . . . People whose homes and families were not destroyed went into the city right away with boats to bring survivors out, but law enforcement told them they weren't needed. I'm in the Algiers neighborhood. The water is good. Our parks and schools could easily hold forty thousand people, and they're not using any of it . . . This is criminal." Ratcliff typed like crazy as he talked.[1]

Meanwhile, Scott Crow and Brandon Darby, white activists from

Austin who had worked with Malik to publicize the plight of the Angola Three, felt drawn to New Orleans to help. Scott and Brandon brought Malik some supplies and then went to look for King in the flooded midcity in New Orleans proper. But they were turned away by the authorities.

I posted a notice about King on Vincent Sylvain's *Alternative Newsletter* in the missing persons category. Davia Nelson of National Public Radio's Kitchen Sisters read it with alarm. She remembered the voice mail I had left on her machine two years earlier when she was collecting stories about hidden kitchens describing the way King had made his Freelines in a solitary cell in Angola State Penitentiary. She hadn't used the story in her radio series, but she had contacted me before the storm to get permission to use my voice message in a book. When Davia saw the missing persons announcement, she emailed me conveying her concern about King.

Scott and Brandon returned to Austin for more supplies and this time vowed to swim to King's house if they had to. Brandon talked some rescue workers into going to look for King. When they got to King's house, there he was, ensconced on his second floor, carrying out his postflood daily routine of animal rescue. The rescue workers agreed to take King's dog, so he got into the boat and met Brandon on higher ground. Brandon and King headed for Malik's. It had been a long two weeks for all of us, wondering if King was alive.

I was able to send an email back to Davia with the glorious news that King and Kenya had been ferried from their home and taken to Malik's house. I told Davia that King and Malik were embarking on a previously arranged trip to San Francisco and that she might want to interview them. She confided in me later that she had had some trepidation about that interview, but Davia and King established an instant camaraderie and they remain fast friends to this day.

Davia and her partner produced a piece on King that aired throughout the country on National Public Radio about his time in Angola, his hidden candy making, the days he spent with Kenya upstairs in his flooded home after the storm eating peanut butter, feeding hungry dogs in the neighborhood, wiping oil from the wings of disabled birds, and refusing offers of rescue that didn't include Kenya. He spoke of his wish to help his comrades who were still locked up.

The story moved so many people deeply that King was able to launch his candy business in a big way and bring additional attention to the plight of the Angola Three.[2]

Malik was interviewed as well, almost daily. He told Amy Goodman of the radio program *Democracy Now*, "While we [he and King] was together, we—every evening, we used to have these dialectical discussions, and one of our main discussions was on why progressive movements have always started with such a bang and then end in such a frizzle. And we kept coming up with that we allowed our petty differences to stop us from working together . . . King said that the thing that we need to find is the common ground, and so with that, we took that name . . . and Common Ground was founded. Sharon Johnson, my partner, she put up $30. I put up $20. And with that $50, we founded Common Ground."[3]

Before the storm, Sharon had had no community-organizing experience, and she and Malik were a newly established couple. But she chose to stay. And with enormous grace and spiritual radiance, she took on critical organizing roles and held together an odd, ever-expanding commune of people determined to help.

I tell the story of the birth of the Common Ground Health Clinic here because it is just one example of the Panther Ten Point Program in action. Malik and his organization, Common Ground, became a conduit for the twenty-first-century version of the Ten Point Program.

Ratcliff had emailed her group the "This is Criminal" missive, and they forwarded it around the country. A few days later, activists began arriving in Algiers—Jamie "Bork" Laughner, an advocate for the homeless from Washington D.C.; street medics Roger Benham from Connecticut, Noah Morris from Rhode Island, and twenty-year-old Scott Mechanic from Philadelphia (we called him Boy Scott to distinguish him from the two other Scotts). Two weeks later, Mo, a registered nurse and herbalist from Dillon, Montana, came. She and Bork had conceived the idea of an anarchist clinic in New Orleans before they met Malik.

When the self-identified white anarchists knocked on Malik Rahim's door, he directed them to the mosque he once attended, Masjid Bilal, where they emptied the refrigerator, put tarps on the floor in deference to the sacred Muslim space, and set out supplies.

This was September 9, 2005, eleven days after the storm. Bork spray-painted "Solidarity, not Charity," "First Aid," and "No Weapons, including Police and Military" on plywood outside of the mosque. Then the group began to think about how to get patients.

Their first ambassador was a local woman, Mama Souma, and her daughters, who took them around the neighborhood knocking on doors. Malik was as interested in easing the racial tensions as he was in building a patient base. New Orleanians fleeing the flood had been turned away at gunpoint by authorities as they tried to walk across the Mississippi River Bridge to higher ground. The governor had issued a "shoot to kill" order, affirmed by New Orleans' mayor and police chief, on looters, many of whom were only securing survival rations. Algiers had been invaded by soldiers, federal police officers, and private paramilitary personnel—creating an atmosphere of tension and trepidation. Bodies were left to bloat on the streets of Algiers, covered by pieces of corrugated tin and ignored by guardsmen passing by. Malik points out one of the bodies in the documentary *Welcome to New Orleans*.[4] But the film could well be "Welcome to Anywhere, USA"—anywhere that disaster pulls the usual covers off of profound systemic racism.

The newly arrived young white medics fanned out on bicycles, asking people if they needed water and telling them about the clinic. Malik knew that white skin had its privilege and its uses. He could see the real possibility of the whole African American community in Algiers being slaughtered.

When people asked the medics if they were Red Cross or FEMA, neither of which had made an appearance in Algiers, they said no, they were just volunteers who had come without authorization. They took blood pressure, offered first aid, and checked for diabetes, anxiety, and depression. "It was the street medics who really stopped this city from exploding into a race war, because they were white and serving the black community at a time when blacks were fed up. They are the real heroes of this thing," Malik said.[5]

Boy Scott limited his conversation with guardsmen to health care. But Bork saw fit to reveal her anarchist political context, causing one incredulous soldier to ask, "So you're the anarchists in the mosque brought in by the ex-Black Panther giving free health care?"

"Yeah. And we're environmentalists, too," Bork replied. The next day, the soldier, having done some research, addressed her by her real name.[6]

The medics were followed a few days later by a caravan of doctors, nurses, grief counselors, acupuncturists, and herbalists from San Francisco. On September 11 a French relief organization, Secours Populaire, arrived. When the French physicians accompanied Roger on house calls, they were amazed at people's poor health. "Chronic illnesses, old untreated injuries, and results of neglect had only been exacerbated by Katrina, not created by it," Roger wrote in *What Lies Beneath: Katrina, Race, and the State of the Nation*.[7] In this regard, New Orleans is merely a microcosm of a health-care disaster that is happening nationwide.

Word spread, and almost overnight, health practitioners and political activists arrived in droves. On September 22, with Hurricane Rita threatening to make landfall who knew where, my son Jonathan Arend called me from New York where he was doing a community medicine residency. He was aching for his home town. He said FEMA and the Red Cross had not been responsive to his offers to help and did I know of anything? I called Malik and he told me about the first-aid station. But he recommended that volunteers not come until we knew where Rita was going.

Jonathan, who only had a week off, pondered the situation into the wee hours and then hopped on a plane, figuring the worst that could happen would be that he'd evacuate with me and his stepfather from our rented house in Luling where we were living until the authorities would let us back into the city. The next morning, I crossed the Mississippi River and picked him up at the New Orleans airport. It wasn't hard to find him. As far as I could see, we were the only people there.

Malik wanted rain gear. When we found ponchos at a Dollar Store, we felt like we had won the lottery. We made our way to the mosque, bullying through all the checkpoints and defying the mandatory evacuation order. The guards with guns made me nervous, but Jonathan's stethoscope worked like a charm—that and the fact that we were white. I left him at the mosque and headed back to Luling wondering to what great vortex of weather and social chaos I had just sacrificed my first-born son.

Jonathan was able to make some of the initial crucial contacts with the local medical community, including Ravi Vadlamudi, who became the clinic's first and much-loved medical director. My daughter Rebecca Arend came down a couple of months later to donate her skills as a medical student. Her contribution of love and hard work, like that of so many others, helped build the clinic. Every day that I sat outside the mosque back then, I'd see lovely young women in green scrubs or jeans trailing suitcases—Latina, black, Asian, and white—laughing with each other, appearing out of nowhere on the trashed and ruined streets of Algiers like a glorious mirage in a thirsty dessert. "Where did you *come* from?" I would insist. "San Francisco. I can only stay a couple of days and I'm going to set up your pharmacy." Thank you. Thank you to each and every one.

Jed Horne notes in his excellent book *Breach of Faith,* "Six days after the clinic opened, some forty out-of-state activists were camped out in and around Rahim's home. By year's end, a total of one hundred seventy volunteers would have rotated through the clinic, including three dozen locals . . . Common Ground's first aid station had become a full-service medical clinic, still a cash-free operation dependent on in-kind donations and volunteers."[8] In addition to traditional medicine, it offered herbalism, massage therapy, and acupuncture.

By early October, the clinic was treating over a hundred drop-ins per day. It also spawned the Latino Health Outreach Project to help migrant workers with health and legal issues. They even made house calls for workers injured on the job.

Scott Weinstein, a tall, slender RN from Quebec who arrived soon after the clinic opened, quickly made strategic linkages with what was left of the New Orleans medical community. He says that the clinic reshaped the way he thinks about politics. "Most people think of direct action as taking a street during a demonstration," he says, "but big deal, so you got a street. This is not about taking the streets; it's about taking health care."[9] "Solidarity, not charity" became the clinic's motto.

During the week that Jonathan was there, the clinic never closed, and volunteers slept wall-to-wall on the floor. Intake was thorough and records were meticulously kept. The list of projects and tasks on the wall that needed volunteers included "critical incident debriefing;

medical legal support—or covering our heinies; and infusing all we do with anti-oppression intentions."[10]

Jonathan told Michelle Garcia of the *Washington Post* that locals such as Swamp Rat Jack, who lives across the street from the clinic, stayed away from the medical facilities with soldiers stationed out front. He preferred to have his asthma checked at home, where he could show off photos of the gators he had shot down in the bayou.[11]

The Common Ground Health Clinic has since spun off from Common Ground Collective. It is a fully independent free clinic as of November 2, 2005, and it now has a talented executive director and a board of directors well connected with the local medical and organizing community. Antor Ndep Ola, the clinic's director, says that the Common Ground Health Clinic is here to stay and to provide free primary health care for all who walk through the door. "We remain true to the model that we are here in solidarity. We are not charity. We are in solidarity with the community," she says. Even though there is no blueprint out there, Antor acknowledges, she sees the clinic as a catalyst for change. "Yes, we are providing quality primary health care. But we are taking it a step further and that further step is recognizing that racism does exist and it does influence health. We recognize that there are people out there who are hard working people and still cannot afford health care and should be receiving health care."[12]

Antor points out that the clinic was founded by volunteers entrenched in community building and community involvement, committed to creating the right environment for people to be able to break free from oppressive institutions, to find their voice, and to take ownership of their medical care. At the clinic's second-year anniversary, neighbors turned out. "It was their party, not the clinic's party," says Antor. "And that is something I appreciate being a part of."

In the weeks after Katrina, most of us thought the clinic was something that would serve a short-term, emergency need. We had no time to give thought to long-term planning. Volunteers from all over the world worked night and day unloading trucks, sorting supplies, cooking food, and building sheds and workspaces. They slept in tents in Malik's yard.

What was once a spontaneous relief center was exploding into a giant survival program called Common Ground. In the weeks after the storm, hundreds of volunteers arrived from forty states and nine foreign countries to tarp roofs, cut down and remove trees and debris, treat patients, dispense legal aid, and create a brain trust for future action. They included doctors, nurses, lawyers, engineers, environmental scientists, filmmakers, and an array of holistic healers. At a breakfast meeting in early 2008, Malik told the group that Common Ground volunteers had served over 180,000 in direct services to anyone who walked through the door. Malik remembers a vigilante who had bragged on film about it being "open season on niggers" coming into the clinic for medication for his mother. He couldn't look Malik in the eye.

Common Grounders have gutted three thousand houses in New Orleans alone. Malik pointed out that since the end of Reconstruction, this is the first time that blacks have seen a large group of whites coming into the black community "for anything other than oppression or exploitation."[13]

Nevertheless, the military and police response after the storm had clear parallels with the military and police response to the Panthers in 1970. Major Frank Emanuel of the Louisiana National Guard sent his lieutenant to raid Malik's house because it had been reported to him that armed blacks were robbing the community and selling the spoils in Malik's yard. When the officer arrived and instead found seventy white kids, he thought he had gotten the wrong house. The rap morphed from armed black criminals to "nigger-lovin' outsiders."[14]

In fact, Malik caught hell from all sides. He was accused of being a sell-out to whites, and was portrayed in the black community as being senile, illiterate, ignorant, crazy, and an Uncle Tom. Common Ground volunteers worked twenty hours a day to clean 90 percent of the storm drains in Algiers before Hurricane Rita hit, ensuring that Algiers stayed dry. But the organization was never given any recognition or practical help by city government. Indeed, police harassment of volunteers continued.[15]

While Royce was educating the nation about the seemingly drowned New Orleans culture, Dama was mucking out their partially flooded house in Gentilly. Dama and I made contact somehow soon after I moved back to New Orleans after the storm. All I remember is a reunion on the street, both of us in our overalls, clutching each other and crying. When Dama's signals of distress and Royce's wish to film the cultural resurgence of our ruined city brought him home—after what seemed like an eternity to Dama—they stayed for a few weeks at my relatively unscathed uptown house with a constant stream of my homeless friends and Common Ground volunteers. King was a housemate as well, having stepped away from his celebrity status in San Francisco to come to New Orleans to sort through and store his cooking pots, books, and a few clothes. Even his dog Kenya had achieved fame in *Bark Magazine*.[16]

King lives in Austin now but still considers New Orleans his home. The prospects for the Angola Three have never looked better, with both civil and criminal trials for them approaching. Malik still is masterfully managing an enormous relief enterprise that works from a conscious perspective of social justice. Royce has filmed that endeavor as well as the many other grassroots witnesses to the resilience of the people of New Orleans.

Father LeDoux came back to New Orleans as soon as the National Guard let him. He knew that the church home would be as important to many of his parishioners as their own private, often-ruined abodes. The church itself had sustained little damage. But after only two masses, the Archdiocese of New Orleans decided to close the historic and culturally significant parish, claiming that hurricane expenses made it financially unfeasible to keep it open. St. Augustine parishioners, revolutionaries who had come to New Orleans to work with Common Ground, and supporters in high places took exception. Common Grounders assisted parishioners in seizing and occupying the rectory for twenty days, barricading themselves inside and creating a national media stir.[17]

Parishioners and protesters were there in the church on the day the new priest came to take Father LeDoux's place. He was escorted by ten plainclothes guards with guns hidden in their pockets. Protesters marched behind the interloping celebrant carrying hand-painted signs that read "I say unto them that thou art Peter and upon this rock I will build my church and the gates of HELL shall not prevail against it" and "You can't erase our history." The congregation burst into song, "Shake, Shake, Shake, Shake the Devil Off" and "We Shall Not Be Moved." The new priest and his assistant left the church in the middle of the mass, claiming they feared for their lives. The archbishop closed the church as well as the parish and declared the altar defiled.

Royce as well as the Swedish documentarian Peter Entell filmed it all.[18] In the end, Ted Quant mediated between the parish and the archdiocese to settle the dispute and keep the parish open. But for reasons some linked to racism, after Father LeDoux's fifteen years of establishing St. Augustine as the black cultural hub of New Orleans, the Archbishop retired LeDoux. The superiors in his order sent him away to serve a parish in Fort Worth, Texas.

Supporters and activists in and around the St. Augustine rectory who held court, ate, sang, danced, and sent out press releases and pleas for help read the Panther booklet in which Father LeDoux played a starring role. They learned that from the time of his involvement with the Panthers as a mediator in 1970 until the present day, Father LeDoux's stand against racism had not changed. In fact, there were some eerie parallels. In 2006, when the priests entered St. Augustine Church with police officers dressed like parishioners except for the fact that they had guns in their pockets, it was reminiscent of the final arrest of the Panthers in Desire when police had disguised themselves as priests and postal workers. Both exhibited an unnecessary and deceitful show of force, using religion as a ruse, in the first instance invading the Panthers' home as they prepared for Thanksgiving, and in the second, invading our church as we prepared for the Lord's resurrection.

The Panther booklet that sparked the forum for reconciliation between Panthers and city officials thirty-three years after the shootout went into its second printing. The legions of Common Grounders from all around the country, now working in the Lower Ninth Ward, a stone's throw from Piety and Desire, all wanted the book. They cared about our history.

The Ninth Ward has seen a lot of changes since the days of the Panthers. The most dramatic, of course, was its near total destruction as a result of the levees' failure and flood following Katrina. In 2007 the actor Brad Pitt's beautiful pink solar-lit structures blossomed next to the Common Ground headquarters. Malik Rahim is a partner in this project, which is raising money to build affordable, energy-efficient houses for New Orleans residents who want to return. On a fall evening about the time the pink structures appeared, only blocks away, over a thousand people sat raptly attentive as a New York theater company performed *Waiting for Godot* on the place where a house used to be. Yoga instructors give free classes in a Buddhist tent/temple in the Common Ground compound. It was set up by a passerby suffering from a fatal disease. Egrets have made their nests on adjacent slabs.

Just before Christmas 2007, I examined a fish embedded in the plaster about nine feet above ground level of a house renovated by Common Ground that had survived the levy breach. The force of the water created a new-age fossil. The fish evoked my wonder at the strange circumstances that had brought the Ninth Ward, Piety, and Desire world attention and pulled so many of us down here for twilight encounters.

But there is still a thread of continuity in the Lower Nine from the heyday of the Panthers to the present. Hilderbrand, Crow, and Fithian note that the philosophy and grassroots organizing tradition of the Black Panther Party, specifically the survival programs, seemed well-suited to use in the political vacuum of post-Katrina New Orleans.[19] Incoming volunteers in the early days were heavily influenced by the party's theories and organizing strategies. The party's survival programs included medical clinics, free breakfast for children, food giveaways, free clothing, political education, and prisoner support, all of which Common Ground was providing. Then and now, young people, fearless and full of hope for the future, seized buildings to take a righteous stand. Then and now, young people handed out food and medical supplies to provide aid where the government failed. The lessons of the Panthers, self-determination and political activism, rediscovered in their basic form as if they had been evolving in some counterculture time capsule, are again being applied.

But after thirty-five years, the elder Panthers have incorporated spirituality and built a broader base of support. In New Orleans today, the new revolutionaries tend to have college degrees, socially privileged families, and use of the Internet. Many of them are white.

It's too early to say what the effect the destruction, attention, and energy for renewal unleashed by Katrina will have on New Orleans. But it is clear that the Panthers will have a role in that legacy. It's hard to decide when to stop writing a book about the Panthers. The story never ends.

EPILOGUE

The more interviews I collected, the more questions I fielded from my sources about what I had learned from the interviews of others. Perhaps I listened more as a mediator (my primary calling) and a psychotherapist than as a journalist. While I slowly pieced together the New Orleans Panther events in my own mind, I developed an intense wish for my disparate sources to hear the powerful narrative from each other's point of view. But when I broached the subject of bringing them together in a forum/reunion, they all thought it was an unrealistic idea, considering that some of them *had* been shooting at each other—all except Bob Tucker. He advised putting together a booklet from columns of my interviews published in the *Louisiana Weekly,* finding a place, inviting people to participate, and then "just see[ing] what happens."

Bob and I asked Ted Quant, director of the Twomey Center for Peace through Justice at Loyola University, to be the forum moderator because we knew of no person more skilled in the art of facilitation, especially when the subject matter is charged. We were also thinking of the advantages of the credibility of a university setting for the forum, should Ted be able to acquire that for us.

Ted was immediately receptive to our proposal. To our amazement, we learned that he had moved to New Orleans in 1970 and that one of his first acts in establishing his ties with his new city was to stand between the police and the Panthers during the showdown.

Inspired by Bob's enthusiasm, others got on board. In late summer of 2003 a forum planning committee began meeting weekly at the Ashe Cultural Arts Center, a creative exhibition space and Afrocentric cultural center in what is known as the Central City neighborhood of New Orleans. The planning committee consisted of Bob Tucker, Malik Rahim, Robert King Wilkerson, Ted Quant, Royce Osborn, and myself.

Ultimately, the Panther forum/reunion idea was too threatening for Loyola—both the university and the law school—even though it would feature several Loyola Law School graduates. Ted agreed to moderate, however, and we realized that the Ashe Center was actually the more appropriate venue because of its history, its accessibility, and its location on Oretha Castle Haley Boulevard, formerly known as Dryades. Oretha Castle Haley was a courageous young civil rights organizer in New Orleans. In Greek mythology the dryads were female spirits of nature who presided over groves and forests. If a tree perished, a dryad would die, and if a mortal was responsible, he would be punished. I like to think that the spirits of Oretha and the dryads still watch over the boulevard, hoping that modern-day humans will wake up to their task of accountability, or at least stop killing each other in Central City.

After the planning group decided on a location for the forum, we hastily assembled a booklet of my Panther columns from the *Louisiana Weekly* called *Showdown in Desire* and printed it at the Twomey Center print shop in July of 2003. Bob Tucker and Don Hubbard offered to put up some money to defray costs for the booklet and forum. Others followed their example, and soon we had about seven thousand dollars. We hired Lili LeGardeur, a journalist who had edited the columns originally, to be our media liaison. Douglas Redd, the artistic director of Ashe, created a program describing all of the panelists.

The booklet, which was informally distributed by planning group members, found its way to some unexpected places. A professor in Iowa requested eighty copies to use as a text for her folklore class over two semesters. A posh clothing store in Lower Manhattan had copies for sale on its wall. My nephew who is serving time in a California prison pointed out to me that an anarchist press in the Bay Area was selling pirated copies through its catalogue. I received many e-mails from strangers thanking me for the booklet and requesting more information. Local bookstores agreed to carry it. Students at a public high school made video shorts based on what they had learned from the booklet.

THE FORUM AND REUNION

Meanwhile, the forum idea developed a momentum of its own. The writer and director Chakula cha Jua scripted a docudrama with the local newscaster Norman Robinson reporting the news about the show-down. In real time, Robinson was reporting the news about the forum for WDSU TV channel 6. Mayor Ray Nagin agreed to honor the participants. Panther scholars Charles Jones and Curtis Austin from Georgia State University and Jackson State University, respectively, decided to attend the forum as a result of reading the booklet. Marina Drummer, the "navigator" for the Angola Three, came from California. The filmmakers Shana Griffin and Brice White offered film clips from news reports from 1970, which were a part of their evolving Panther documentary *It's about Time*. And twelve people who were directly involved in the Panther incidents, including former Mayor Moon Landrieu, agreed to be panelists.

The Panther forum/reunion was held on September 17, 2003, almost thirty-three years to the day after the Piety Street shootout. The panelists were Bob Tucker, Landrieu's special assistant in 1970; Malik Rahim and Althea Francois, both former Panthers; William Barnwell, an Episcopal priest mediator between the Panthers and the police; Ted Quant, who stood with Desire residents to protect the Panthers; Cecil Carter, deputy director of the Human Relations Committee in 1970; Robert Glass and Ernest Jones, attorneys for the Panthers; Moon Landrieu, mayor in 1970; Henry Faggen, Desire resident in 1970; and Don Hubbard and Charles Elloie, who directed federal and city programs in Desire. The panelists saw the forum as an opportunity for truth-telling and healing, a chance to find answers to lingering questions and to reinsert a lost page (Bob Tucker wondered if the page had been torn out) of New Orleans history, and an occasion to laugh and see old friends.

In anticipation of the forum, former Panthers had a range of reactions. One Panther who had been arrested on Piety Street refused to be interviewed or to participate on the panel. We had known each other and worked together amicably through the People's Institute for Survival and Beyond, an antiracist training organization, for about ten years. A few days before the presentation, he told me he was working on picket signs to carry in protest of the event with fifteen of his friends. He said he didn't like the way I told the story. The protest never materialized.

Another former Panther, Steve Green, appeared in New Orleans only weeks before the forum. He came with Malik Rahim to a planning meeting after having been estranged from the New Orleans group since before the shootout. At first, he agreed to be part of the panel. He later changed his mind.

As the forum approached, no one felt qualified to predict the results. A few days before the gathering Moon Landrieu asked me, "Are the Panthers still revolutionary, or have they mellowed?"

"Both," I told him.

Former Panthers Marion Brown and Robert King Wilkerson declined to be speakers. But both felt an irresistible urge to be there, as did many others who were part of the Desire drama. The forum attracted a crowd that spilled onto the sidewalk outside of the Ashe Cultural Arts Center. Traffic was backed up for blocks in all directions. Many had to be turned away. Don Hubbard told the audience that he had been one of the naysayers. He thought no one really cared about this story. Clearly moved by the size and enthusiasm of the crowd, he admitted that he had been wrong.

On the morning of the forum, the *Times-Picayune* ran an article announcing the forum under a 1970 picture of the infamous "war wagon."[1] In the image accompanying the article, Tucker, Faggen, Elloie, and Sherman Copelin (who would go on to serve in the state legislature) were striding alongside the war wagon, which has become an enduring symbol of both the drama and the absurdity of the drama.

The atmosphere was congenial as people queued up for red beans and rice at Ashe before the event started. Royce Osborn had set up an interview room with cameras upstairs to record people's stories, and several took the opportunity to reminisce. There was a table of thank-you Freelines for contributors to the event wrapped in ribbons of Panther baby blue. Chairs in rows facing the long table of panelists quickly filled as people ate and talked. The crowd swelled to approximately 250, all ages, and about three-fourths black. A few people came intending to disrupt. But the mounting interest and curiosity in the audience, combined with Ted's facilitation skills, kept the proceedings respectful, with no more interruption than occasional background muttering.

Edna Silvester was one of the early arrivals. She had lived across the street from the Desire complex in November of 1970. With her three children and hundreds of Desire public housing residents, she had resisted the equal number of New Orleans police officers who had come to evict the Panthers. On the night of the forum, the memories came rushing back.

"We were going to have victory," Silvester told a *Times-Picayune* reporter, "and had we died, we wouldn't have died in vain."[2]

"This [forum] represents that we're coming together to reflect on our past to build a future for the young people," she continued. "We can no longer allow oppression to divide us."[3]

Between the docudrama and the panel presentation, Mayor Nagin's representative awarded certificates of appreciation for "Heroism in Race Relations" to all the panelists as well as to Clarence Giarrusso, Father Jerome LeDoux, Lubertha Johnson, Marion Brown, and Robert King Wilkerson. After the forum, Steve Green asked me to save his certificate for him because his children might want it. He never picked it up.

The night of the forum, Landrieu was on the hot seat, but one would never have known it from his gracious demeanor. "God bless them," he said of the Panthers. "They drove me crazy at times. I had a grudging respect for them, though I thought, and still think, that the path they took was incorrect."

After the forum, Landrieu told a reporter that, looking back, he believes the path the city chose also was incorrect. "I think we should not have gone into the project with such massive force. It seemed to be reasonable at the time, but in retrospect we could have found a better way to do that. It was a contentious period. It was an unfortunate period. Hopefully it will never happen again."[4]

Malik Rahim commended Landrieu for having the courage to "sit and reflect" with the Panthers at the forum. "This was a very historic occasion," Rahim said that evening during the event. "Maybe, just maybe, if we had been able to do this then [in 1970], those shootouts would have been avoided."

He then reached out and shook Landrieu's hand. "My hat goes off to you," he said as their eyes connected.

Marion Brown had a different reaction to Landrieu. She had to step outside when he spoke because she felt like she might throw up. Thirty-three years hadn't much tempered her disdain for him.

The following day, the *Times-Picayune* featured the forum on the front page with a picture from 1970 showing a sea of Desire residents, unarmed, facing police in riot gear. The large headline reads, "A Day to Remember." Also on the front page was a picture of Malik Rahim and Bob Tucker in a bear hug. Another picture shows a young man, handcuffed, being escorted back to the Piety street house by two policemen. "An arrest," the caption reads. Malik took one look at the picture and said, "That's me." The *Times-Picayune* editors hadn't realized that Malik appeared in both pictures in the article, thirty-three years apart—in one as a captive, and in the other as a gracious host and panelist.

The *Times-Picayune* noted that thirty-three years after the incident, it was easy for both sides to look back with less animosity. I take issue with that analysis. The Panthers worked very hard to support each other in attending the forum. Althea almost couldn't do it. It was only after reading a message from Herman Wallace, still locked up in solitary at the time, that she could transcend her emotions in order to speak. There were others, like Betty Powell, who wanted to be there but at the last moment found that they just couldn't. The act of looking back, a true gift to the community, was far from easy.

At the time of the forum, Malik's mother, Mrs. Lubertha Johnson, was suffering from a variety of terminal health problems. She couldn't speak or feed herself. When she heard about the forum, however, she miraculously recovered temporarily and even went out and bought a new dress for the occasion. She passed away a year later on September 22, 2004.

The event reportedly was cathartic for many; but there was also criticism. Some detractors thought that it glorified the Panthers, while others insisted that it unduly credited the city administration. I saw many heroes in the story. I admired everyone I interviewed in depth. The one point of agreement among the diverse audience, including me, was that the real heroes of the story were the long-suffering and courageous residents of Desire.

The years I spent absorbing this story caused me to examine my own belief system and my ability or inability to adhere to actions consistent with it. Philosophically, the Panthers and I diverge. I am a committed pacifist. "By any means necessary," seems Machiavellian to me. Although I grew up in a secular family, I am a practicing, church-going Christian. And yet I can't say for sure that I have principles that I would die for.

The Panthers I interviewed and came to know well have internalized the party principles, the Ten Point Program. I noticed that these principles provide them with an anchor of strength and commitment, a protection against the enormous assaults designed to silence or kill them, an anchor that endures as they age. Everybody lives out the principles they truly believe in. In the case of these Panthers, the fruits of their beliefs are effective organizing, an enjoyment of life, strong, healthy bodies, beautiful homes, and nourishing relationships. Even after Katrina, they continue to thrive.

How has this affected me? In some unexpected ways. I have been surprised to find my commitment to my own, somewhat different, beliefs fortified by the Panther example of action and fearlessness. I even got a taste of the sickening betrayal that the Panthers repeatedly bore—comrade against comrade—when Brandon Darby, the white activist from Austin who rescued King and helped found Common Ground, revealed in early 2009 that he had been working undercover for the FBI. At this point there are more questions than answers about Brandon's motives and tactics, as well as the repercusions for himself and others of his monumental decision.

I am still amazed that I have been granted entrance as an observer and storyteller into a world and a reality that is so foreign to me—and yet in some ways so strangely familiar. Perhaps many of us, myself included, harbor a secret wish, in another context, and under different circumstances, to be Panthers.

ACKNOWLEDGMENTS

These are some of the people who stepped, or were hauled, into the creative circle with me to make this labor of love possible:

My editors, Beverly Rainbolt, Lili LeGardeur, Edmund Lewis, and Renette Dejois-Hall, and the *Louisiana Weekly,* where many of the interviews were first printed; John Kemp and the Louisiana Endowment for the Humanities; and Larry Malley at the University of Arkansas Press and Beth Ina, the freelance copyeditor hired by the press. Thanks also to Lynn Cunningham at the *Times-Picayune* for help with photographs, and to the New Orleans police historian Ruth Asher.

Robert King Wilkerson, Malik Rahim and his mother Ms. Lubertha Burnett Guyton-Johnson, Bob Tucker, Royce Osborn, Don and Rose Hubbard, Lolis Elie, Ernest Jones, Marion Brown, Henry Faggen, Moon Landrieu, Clarence Giarrusso, Ted Quant, Geronimo ji Jaga, and Father Jerome LeDoux, who trusted me with their stories and so much more.

Scholars and friends Martha Ward, Chris Wiltz, Lance Hill, Charles Jones, Curtis Austin, David Madsen, Evelyn Seelinger, Julie Gustafson, Keith Medley, Oliver and Lisa Houck, Jed Horne, Jane Wholey, William and Corinne Barnwell, Ron Chisom, Mary LaCoste, my Gurdjeiff group, Marina Drummer, Beverly McKenna, Carol Bebelle, Douglas Redd, Rhoda Faust, Kathy Engleman, Stephanie Mendlow, Leighton Brown, Vivian and Richard Cahn, Jane Eyrich, Jean Ann Tonka, and Mike Osborne.

Photographers Nijme Rinaldi Nun, Alan Pogue, Pat Jolly, Ann Harkness, and Fred Plunkett.

My father, Bob Eckhardt, who taught me to embrace the truth and a good story, and my mother, Orissa, who comes to me in dreams.

My sisters, Rosalind Sanford and Sarah Eckhardt, who are strong and fearless.

My daughter Rebecca Arend, son Jonathan Arend, and daughter-in-law Jaime Hanaway, who are constant sources of inspiration and support.

Amy Saxer, Michael Saxer, and Ham Saxer, who have brought me into their family.

My steadfast and loving husband Richard Saxer, who will go anywhere with me, and without whose wisdom, patience, and constant encouragement none of this would have been possible.

APPENDIX A

Cast of Characters

Ronald Ailsworth—Panther arrested on Piety Street. Serving a life sentence in Angola State Penitentiary.

Bernard J. Bagert—Judge of Criminal District Court in 1970. Owner of the building where the Panthers first established their headquarters at 2353 St. Thomas Street.

William Barnwell—White Episcopal priest who tried to mediate between the Panthers and police in 1970. Teaches and works in outreach in New Orleans.

Kenneth Borden—Young black man shot and killed by police on Sept. 15, 1970, outside of Clarence Broussard's grocery store. He was twenty-one.

Clarence (Gus) Broussard—Owner of the Piety Street Panther house and a grocery store nearby.

Marion Brown—Tulane student who joined the Black Panther Party in New Orleans in 1970. Worked with the Party in Oakland.

Cecil Carter—Director of the city's Division of Youth Services in 1970. Retired from advocacy work. Lives in New Orleans.

Lolis Elie—Black attorney who represented the Deacons for Defense and Justice and the Black Panthers.

Charles Elloie—Director of the city's Division of Youth Services in 1970. Later served as a criminal court judge in New Orleans.

Henry Faggen—Desire resident, activist, and organizer. Moved to Desire in 1956.

Israel Fields—Undercover policeman exposed on Piety Street. Died November 11, 2007, at the age of fifty-nine.

Jane Fonda—Actress/activist.

Althea Francois—New Orleans Panther who organized free breakfast and sickle-cell testing programs in 1970. Works with the National Coalition to Free the Angola Three.

Clarence Giarrusso—Police chief appointed by Mayor Landrieu on August 25, 1970. Died November 2, 2007, at the age of eighty-six.

Robert Glass—White attorney for the Panthers in 1970. Defense attorney in New Orleans.

Joseph Giarrusso—Police chief just before the Piety Street shootout. Clarence's brother.

Steve Green—Founder of the Louisiana chapter of the Black Panther Party. Given name: Green Stevens Jr.

Donald Guyton—a.k.a. Malik Rahim. Panther arrested on Piety Street.

Harold Holms—a.k.a. Poison. Panther from Des Moines who came to New Orleans to help organize the chapter.

Melvin Howard—Undercover policeman exposed on Piety Street. Works for the New Orleans police force.

Don Hubbard—Director of the community center in Desire in 1970. Owns the Hubbard Mansion Bed and Breakfast.

Johnny Jackson Jr.—Director of the Desire Community Center. Later served in the state legislature and on the New Orleans City Council.

Lubertha Johnson—Malik Rahim's mother. Died September 22, 2004.

Ernest Jones—Black attorney for the Panthers in 1970. Partner in Elie, Jones, and Associates.

Moon Landrieu—Mayor of New Orleans, 1970–78.

Jerome LeDoux—Black Catholic priest who tried to mediate between the police and Panthers in 1970. Served St. Augustine's Catholic Church in Tremé (New Orleans) until 2006.

John Pecoul—Head of the New Orleans Human Relations Committee in 1970. Retired from city employment and from Xavier University.

Betty Powell—New Orleans Panther shot by policemen disguised as priests on Thanksgiving early morning, 1970. Was Huey Newton's bodyguard in Oakland, California in 1971. Has a ministry in New Orleans.

Joe Putnam—Pastor of St. Francis De Sales Church in 1970. Organized the mediation effort between the Panthers and police. Died March 30, 1993.

Ted Quant—Stood with the community between the Panthers and the police in 1970. Moderated the Panther reunion/forum in 2003. Directs Loyola University's Twomey Center for Peace through Justice.

Malik Rahim—Panther in charge of security during the Piety Street shootout. Activist for prison reform and housing. Given name: Donald Guyton.

Raymond Reed—Black policeman assigned to patrol Desire in 1970.

Walter Rogers—Construction worker who helped build Desire. Community activist in Desire in 1970.

Bill Rouselle—Deputy director of the New Orleans Human Relations Committee in 1970. Works in media and public relations.

Charles Scott—Nineteen-year-old New York Black Panther sent in 1970 to help organize the New Orleans chapter.

Louis J. Sirgo—Deputy police chief under Clarence Giarrusso. Killed in New Orleans in the Mark Essex sniper attack in 1973.

Robert H. Tucker—Special assistant to Mayor Moon Landrieu in 1970. A New Orleans businessman.

Robert King Wilkerson—Encountered the Panthers in New Orleans Central Lockup in 1971. Served thirty-one years in Angola State Penitentiary. Along with Herman Wallace and Albert Woodfox, started the first chapter of the Black Panther Party behind bars in Louisiana. These men are known as the Angola Three. King travels worldwide to advocate for prisoners. Given name: Robert H. King.

Larry Preston Williams—Former NOPD police officer. In 1970 he was part of the NOPD Intelligence Division in charge of managing the infiltration of the Black Panther Party, the Republic of New Africa, the Ku Klux Klan, and the American Nazi Party. In 2005 he was a private detective.

APPENDIX B

October 1966 Black Panther Party
Platform and Program

What We Want
What We Believe

1. *We want freedom. We want power to determine the destiny of our Black Community.*

   We believe that black people will not be free until we are able to determine our destiny.

2. *We want full employment for our people.*

   We believe that the federal government is responsible and obligated to give every man employment or a guaranteed income. We believe that if the white American businessmen will not give full employment, then the means of production should be taken from the businessmen and placed in the community so that the people of the community can organize and employ all of its people and give a high standard of living.

3. *We want an end to the robbery by the CAPITALIST man of our Black Community.*

   We believe that this racist government has robbed us and now we are demanding the overdue debt of forty acres and two mules. Forty acres and two mules was promised 100 years ago as restitution for slave labor and mass murder of black people. We will accept the payment in currency which will be distributed to our many communities. The Germans are now aiding the Jews in Israel for the genocide of the Jewish people. The Germans murdered six million Jews. The American racist has taken part in the slaughter of over fifty million black people; therefore, we feel that this is a modest demand that we make.

4. *We want decent housing fit for shelter of human beings.*

We believe that if the white landlords will not give decent housing to our black community, then the housing and the land should be made into cooperatives so that our community, with government aid, can build and make decent housing for its people.

5. *We want education for our people that exposes the true nature of this decadent American society. We want education that teaches us our true history and our role in the present-day society.*

We believe in an educational system that will give to our people a knowledge of self. If a man does not have knowledge of himself and his position in society and the world, then he has little chance to relate to anything else.

6. *We want all black men to be exempt from military service.*

We believe that Black people should not be forced to fight in the military service to defend a racist government that does not protect us. We will not fight and kill other people of color in the world who, like black people, are being victimized by the white racist government of America. We will protect ourselves from the force and violence of the racist police and the racist military, by whatever means necessary.

7. *We want an immediate end to POLICE BRUTALITY and MURDER of black people.*

We believe we can end police brutality in our black community by organizing black self-defense groups that are dedicated to defending our black community from racist police oppression and brutality. The Second Amendment to the Constitution of the United States gives a right to bear arms. We therefore believe that all black people should arm themselves for self-defense.

8. *We want freedom for all black men held in federal, state, county and city prisons and jails.*

We believe that all black people should be released from the many jails and prisons because they have not received a fair and impartial trial.

9. *We want all black people when brought to trial to be tried in court by a jury of their peer group or people from their black communities, as defined by the Constitution of the United States.*

We believe that the courts should follow the United States Constitution so that black people will receive fair trials. The 14th Amendment of the U. S. Constitution gives a man a right to be tried by his peer group. A peer is a person from a similar economic, social, religious, geographical, environmental, historical, and racial background. To do this the court will be forced to select a jury from the black community from which the black defendant came. We have been, and are being tried by all-white juries that have no understanding of the "average reasoning man" of the Black community.

10. *We want land, bread, housing, education, clothing, justice and peace. And as our major political objective, a United Nations–supervised plebiscite to be held throughout the black colony in which only black colonial subjects will be allowed to participate, for the purpose of determining the will of black people as to their national destiny.*

When, in the course of human events, it becomes necessary for one people to dissolve the political bands which have connected them with another, and to assume, among the powers of the earth, the separate and equal station to which the laws of nature and nature's God entitle them, a decent respect to the opinions of mankind requires that they should declare the causes which impel them to the separation.

We hold these truths to be self-evident, that all men are created equal; that they are endowed by their Creator with certain unalienable rights; that among these are life, liberty, and the pursuit of happiness. *That, to secure these rights, governments are instituted among men, deriving their just powers from*

the consent of the governed; that, whenever any form of govern-
ment becomes destructive to these ends, it is the right of the
people to alter or to abolish it, and to institute a new govern-
ment, laying its foundation on such principles, and organizing its
powers in such form, as to them shall seem most likely to effect
their safety and happiness. Prudence, indeed, will dictate that
governments long established should not be changed for light
and transient causes; and, accordingly, all experience hath
shown, that mankind are more disposed to suffer, while evils
are sufferable, than to right themselves by abolishing the
forms to which they are accustomed. *But, when a long train of*
abuses and usurpations, pursuing invariably the same object,
evinces a design to reduce them under absolute despotism, it is
their right, it is their duty, to throw off such government, and to
provide new guards for their future security.

From the *Black Panther Newspaper,* August 9, 1969, 26.

APPENDIX C

Eight Points of Attention

1. Speak politely.
2. Pay fairly for what you buy.
3. Return everything you borrow.
4. Pay for anything you damage.
5. Do not hit or swear at people.
6. Do not damage property or crops of the poor, oppressed masses.
7. Do not take liberties with women.
8. If we ever have to take captives do not ill-treat them.

From the *Black Panther Newspaper,* August 9, 1969, 27.

APPENDIX D

Three Main Rules of Discipline

1. Obey orders in all your actions.
2. Do not take a single needle or piece of thread from the poor and oppressed masses.
3. Turn in everything captured from the attacking enemy.

From the *Black Panther Newspaper,* August 9, 1969, 27.

CHRONOLOGY

May 21, 1956

The Desire Housing Development opens.

1956

Henry Faggen moves to Desire.

September 15, 1963

Four little black girls die in the bombing of a Birmingham church.

September 9, 1965

Hurricane Betsy hits New Orleans. The levees near Desire are breached.

1967

The New Orleans City Council creates the Human Relations Committee under Mayor Victor Schiro on the day Martin Luther King dies.

Late May 1970

The Human Relations Committee says it gets a call from "Steve from the West Coast" announcing that he is setting up a Black Panther headquarters in New Orleans.

Mid-June 1970

The Panthers are served with eviction papers by Criminal District Court judge Bernard Bagert, owner of the St. Thomas Street building, which was the first Panther headquarters in New Orleans.

August 25, 1970

Mayor Landrieu appoints Clarence Giarrusso police chief.

August 29, 1970

Newly elected mayor Moon Landrieu calls a "summit meeting" of city officials, including the new police chief Clarence Giarrusso, to decide how to deal with the Panthers. Clarence Broussard, owner of a grocery store and the Piety house where the Panthers live, moves to evict the Panthers.

September 14, 1970

Undercover policemen Israel Fields and Melvin Howard are exposed and thrown out of the Panther headquarters on Piety Street.

September 15, 1970

The Piety Street shootout. Fourteen are arrested. Kenneth Borden, a twenty-one-year-old who was not a Panther, is killed by police outside of Clarence Broussard's grocery store.

September 21, 1970

Twelve Panthers are charged with five murder attempts.

October 25, 1970

The Panthers move into Desire Project House #3315.

November 19, 1970

The Panthers and the police face each other in an all-day standoff in Desire.

November 24, 1970

The actress Jane Fonda leads a protest to challenge the Housing Authority of New Orleans' refusal to rent the Desire apartment to Panther Harold Holmes.

November 25, 1970

Twenty-five people are arrested as they try to leave New Orleans in four cars rented for them by Jane Fonda en route to the People's Revolutionary Constitutional Convention in Washington D.C.

Thursday, November 26, 1970, 1:30 a.m., Thanksgiving

Police disguised as priests and postal workers raid the Panther Desire headquarters. Betty Powell is shot. Six

Panthers are arrested and charged with attempted murder and violation of the Federal Firearms Act.

January 11, 1971

Both Panther headquarters, 3315 Desire, apartment A, and 3542 Piety Street, as well as two other nearby buildings, burn to the ground as firefighters try to conquer the blaze amid rock throwing and Panther chants.

August 7, 1971

A jury of ten blacks and two whites returns a unanimous verdict of not guilty for the Panthers arrested on Piety Street, in the Fonda cars, and in Desire. They deliberate thirty-one minutes.

1971

Ten New Orleans Panthers go to Oakland, California, to help with Panther Bobby Seale's mayoral campaign.

1972

Marion Brown leaves the Black Panther Party and moves back to New Orleans.

April 1972

Robert King Wilkerson is escorted back to Angola from Orleans Parish Prison and placed in solitary confinement.

1974

Robert King Wilkerson, accused of participating in the death of another prisoner, is handed a life sentence without possibility of parole, probation, or suspension of sentence.

1987

Robert King Wilkerson begins writing his autobiography, *A Cry from the Bottom*.

1998

Malik Rahim spearheads a grassroots effort to free the Angola Three, which becomes the National Coalition to Free the Angola Three.

February 8, 2001
Robert King Wilkerson is freed from Angola State Penitentiary.

September 17, 2003
The Black Panther Reunion and Forum is held at the Ashe Cultural Arts Center.

August 29, 2005
Hurricane Katrina hits the Gulf Coast of the United States.

ABBREVIATIONS

BPP—Black Panther Party

CORE—Congress of Racial Equality

COUP—Community Organization for Urban Politics

HANO—Housing Authority of New Orleans

HOPE VI—Housing Opportunities for People Everywhere, a federal housing initiative

HRC—Human Relations Committee

HUD—Housing and Urban Development

NCCF—National Committee to Combat Fascism, an organizing bureau of the Black Panther Party

NOLAC—New Orleans Legal Assistance Corporation

OPP—Orleans Parish Prison

SOUL—Southern Organization for Unified Leadership

NOTES

FOREWORD

1. Clayborne Carson, foreword to *The Black Panthers Speak,* by Philip S. Foner (New York: Da Cap Press, 1995), ix.

2. Judson L. Jeffries, *Huey P. Newton: The Radical Theorist* (Jackson: University Press of Mississippi, 2002); Jeffery Ogbar, *Black Power: Radical Politics and African American Identity* (Baltimore: Johns Hopkins University Press, 2005); Curtis Austin, *Up Against the Wall: Violence in the Making and Unmaking of the Black Panthers* (Fayetteville: University of Arkansas Press, 2006); and Andrew Witt, *The Black Panthers in the Midwest* (New York: Routledge, 2007).

3. Mumia Abu-Jamal, *We Want Freedom: A Life in the Black Panther Party* (Cambridge, MA: South End Press, 2004); Jasmine Guy, *Afeni Shakur: Evolution of a Revolutionary* (New York: Simon and Schuster, 2005); Evans D. Hopkins, *Life after Life: A Story of Rage and Redemption* (New York: Free Press, 2005); Florence Forbes, *Will You Die with Me? My Life and the Black Panther Party* (New York: Simon and Schuster, 2006); Elbert "Big Man" Howard, *Panther on the Prowl* (Published by the author, 2008); Charles E. Jones, "Recovering the Legacy of the Black Panther through the Photographs of Stephen," in *The Black Panther Photographs*, by Stephen Shames, 138–45 (New York: Aperture, 2006). Edited collections include David Hilliard and David Weise, eds., *The Huey P. Newton Reader* (New York: Seven Stories Press, 2002); Sam Durant, ed., *Black Panther: The Revolutionary Art of Emory Douglas* (New York: Rizzoli International, 2007); and Kathleen Cleaver, ed., *Target Zero: A Life in Writing Eldridge Cleaver* (New York: Palgrave Macmillan, 2007).

4. Michael Newton, *Bitter Grain: The Black Panther Story* (Los Angeles: Holloway House, 1980).

5. Adam Fairclough, *Race and Democracy: The Civil Rights Struggle in Louisiana, 1915–1972* (Athens: University of Georgia Press, 1995), 427.

6. Earl Anthony, *Picking up the Gun: A Report on the Black Panthers* (New York: Dial Press, 1970).

PREFACE

1. Robert King Wilkerson, interview with the author, tape recording, New Orleans, December 2002. Unless otherwise noted, subsequent Wilkerson quotes in the preface are from this interview.

2. See appendix B.

3. Brett Anderson, "Sweet Freedom," *Times-Picayune,* 5 March 2002.

4. Marion Brown, interview with the author, tape recording, New Orleans, Dec. 2002.

5. Malik Rahim, interview with author, tape recording, New Orleans, Dec. 2002.

CHAPTER 1

1. Malik Rahim, interview with author, tape recording, New Orleans, Dec. 2002.

2. *Times-Picayune,* 19 June, 1989.

3. Quoted in the *Times-Picayune,* 19 June 1989.

4. *Times-Picayune,* 19 June 1989.

5. *Times-Picayune,* 16 Sept. 1970.

6. Quoted in Gene Bourg, "Desire Project Incubator for Crime, Report Says," *States-Item,* 15 Sept. 1970.

7. Ibid.

8. Ibid.

9. *Times-Picayune,* Sept. 1970.

10. Walter Rogers, "To the People of Desire," flier distributed in Desire, 30 Sept. 1970, Mayor Moon Landrieu Records, 1970–78, Special Collections, Louisiana Division, New Orleans Public Library.

11. Ibid. This was a common misconception after Hurricane Betsy and after Hurricane Katrina; it arose in part because the levees had indeed been intentionally breached during the Mississippi River flood of 1927. See John M. Barry, *Rising Tide: The Great Mississippi Flood of 1927 and How It Changed America* (New York: Simon and Schuster, 1997).

12. Rogers flier.

13. Rogers flier.

14. "Death in Desire," *Time Magazine,* 28 Sept. 1970.

15. *States-Item,* 16 Sept. 1970

16. Superintendent Joseph I. Giarrusso, Department of Police, confidential interoffice correspondence, 17 July and 20 Aug. 1970, Mayor Moon Landrieu Records, 1970–78, Special Collections, Louisiana Division, New Orleans Public Library.

17. Ibid.

18. "The Press and the Panthers," *NOLA Express,* [early Sept. 1970], clippings file, Special Collections, Louisiana Division, Howard-Tilton Memorial Library, Tulane University, New Orleans.

19. *Times-Picayune,* 17 Sept. 1970. The bulldozing of the St. Thomas Housing Development occurred in 2002. Judge Bagert's grandson Brod Bagert Jr. details the wrongheadedness of the endeavor and the injustice to residents in his PhD dissertation, "Hope VI and St. Thomas: Smoke, Mirrors, and Urban Mercantilism" (PhD diss., London School of Economics, August 2002).

20. Joseph Giarrusso, memo to Moon Landrieu, 30 July 1970, Mayor Moon Landrieu Records, 1970–78, Special Collections, Louisiana Division, New Orleans Public Library.

21. Barbara Guyton, flier distributed in Desire, now in Mayor Moon Landrieu Records, 1970–78, Special Collections, Louisiana Division, New Orleans Public Library.

22. Joseph Giarrusso, memo to Moon Landrieu, 20 Aug. 1970, Mayor Moon Landrieu Records, 1970–78, Special Collections, Louisiana Division, New Orleans Public Library.

23. *Times-Picayune,* 16 Sept. 1970.

24. *Black Panther Newspaper,* 14 Nov. 1970. The police, in turn, would try to reclaim the word *pig* by saying that it stood for pride, integrity, and guts (pers. comm., Beverly Rainbolt).

25. Joseph Giarrusso, memo to Moon Landrieu, 5 Aug. 1970, Mayor Moon Landrieu Records, 1970–78, Special Collections, Louisiana Division, New Orleans Public Library.

26. As noted in Joe Putnam's sermon "Statement to the Mayor, the Police, and the Panthers," delivered at St. Frances De Sales Church, New Orleans, 20 Sept. 1970, Mayor Moon Landrieu Records, 1970–78, Special Collections, Louisiana Division, New Orleans Public Library.

CHAPTER 2

1. Malik Rahim, interview with author, tape recording, New Orleans, Dec. 2002. Unless otherwise noted, all subsequent quotes from Rahim in this chapter are from this interview.

2. Henry Faggen, Bob Tucker, Cecil Carter, and Don Hubbard, interviews with the author, tape recordings, Hubbard Mansion Bed and Breakfast, New Orleans, Apr. 2003. All subsequent quotes from them in this chapter are from this interview.

CHAPTER 4

1. Larry Preston Williams, interview with the author, tape recording, New Orleans, 19 Apr. 2005. All Williams quotes in this chapter hereafter are from this interview.

CHAPTER 5

1. Kim Lacy Rogers, *Righteous Lives: Narratives of the New Orleans Civil Rights Movement* (New York: New York University Press, 1993).

2. The 1880 ward boundaries—established for voter registration purposes—are the original source of the use of ward names for neighborhood names. In New Orleans, African American communities have come to use ward names as social identification.

3. Rogers, *Righteous Lives.*

4. Moon Landrieu, interview with the author, tape recording, New Orleans, Feb. 2003. Unless otherwise noted, all additional Landrieu quotes in this chapter are from this interview.

5. *Times-Picayune*, 22 Nov. 1970.

6. The quotes from Giarusso's colleagues are from ibid.

7. Clarence Giarrusso, interview with the author, tape recording, New Orleans, Mar. 2003. Unless otherwise noted, all additional Giarrusso quotes in this chapter are from this interview.

8. Clarence Giarrusso died on 2 Nov. 2007.

9. Quoted in Allen Johnson, "The Heroes of Howard Johnson's," *Gambit Weekly*, 7 Jan. 2003. The quotes from Sirgo that follow are from this article.

10. There is a rumor that Sirgo's own men, and not Essex, killed him, because of his progressive views.

11. Quoted in Rogers, *Righteous Lives*, 59.

12. Ibid., 60.

13. Ibid., 108.

14. *Times-Picayune*, 17 Sept. 1970.

15. Larry Preston Williams, interview with the author, tape recording, New Orleans, 19 Apr. 2005. Unless otherwise noted, all additional quotes from Williams in this chapter are from this interview.

CHAPTER 6

1. Malik Rahim, interview with author, tape recording, New Orleans, Dec. 2002. Unless otherwise noted, all subsequent quotes from Rahim in this chapter are from this interview.

2. *Black Panther Newspaper*, 12. Sept. 1970.

3. Ibid.

4. Ibid.

5. *Times-Picayune,* 17 Sept. 1970.

CHAPTER 7

1. Henry Faggen, interview with the author, tape recording, Hubbard Mansion Bed and Breakfast, New Orleans, Apr. 2003.

2. Cecil Carter (April 2003 and June 2003) and Linda Francis (June 2003), interviews with the author, tape recording, New Orleans. Unless otherwise noted, additional quotes from Carter and Francis in this chapter are from these interviews.

CHAPTER 8

1. *Times-Picayune,* 24 Sept. 1970.

2. Ibid.

3. Ibid.

4. *Times-Picayune,* 25 Sept. 1970.

5. Malik Rahim, interview with author, tape recording, New Orleans, Dec. 2002. Unless otherwise noted, all subsequent Rahim quotes in this chapter are from this interview.

6. *Times-Picayune,* 25 Sept. 1970.

7. Robert Glass, interview with the author, tape recording, New Orleans, Aug. 2003. Unless otherwise noted, all subsequent Glass quotes in this chapter are from this interview.

8. *States-Item*, 25 Sept. 1970.

9. When Glass reported to Orleans Parish Prison to do his time, A. J.

Falkenstein, the warden, and Sheriff Louis Heyd were not there. They left "an old leathery ex-marine named Captain Johnny" in charge. "He took it upon himself to give me two-for-one credit, so I wound up doing two and a half days on five," Glass said. "They were concerned about whether I had enemies in Parish Prison and how I would be treated. . . . So I ended up sleeping in Warden Falkenstein's weight-lifting room, on his weight-lifting table, which was about two feet wide."

10. Ernest Jones, interview with the author, tape recording, New Orleans, Aug. 2003. Unless otherwise indicated, all subsequent Jones quotes in this chapter are from this interview.

11. Darlene Fife, *Portraits from Memory: New Orleans in the Sixties* (New Orleans: Surrengional Press, 2000), back cover.

12. Darlene Fife, editorial, *NOLA Express,* 16 Sept. 1970.

13. *NOLA Express,* 14 Sept. 1970.

14. Ibid.

15. *States-Item,* 15 Sept. 1970.

16. Israel Fields, phone interview with the author, New Orleans, 31 May 2005. Unless otherwise noted, all subsequent Fields quotes in this chapter are from this interview.

17. Rahim interview.

18. Althea Francois, phone interviews with the author, 24 May 2005, 31 May 2005. Unless otherwise noted, all subsequent Francois quotes in this chapter are from this interview.

19. *States-Item,* 15 Sept. 1970.

20. *New York Times,* 19 Sept. 1970. I tried to interview Howard, who was still on the police force in 2002, but he told me he didn't want to rehash the past.

21. *States-Item,* 16 Sept. 1970.

22. *NOLA Express,* Sept. 1970.

23. *States-Item,* 16 Sept. 1970.

24. Francois interview.

CHAPTER 9

1. Roy Reed, *New York Times*, 15 Sept. 1970.

2. *Times-Picayune,* 15 Sept. 1970.

3. Malik Rahim, interview with author, tape recording, New Orleans, Dec. 2002. Unless otherwise indicated, all subsequent Rahim quotes in this chapter come from this interview.

4. Marion Brown, interview with the author, tape recording, New Orleans, December 2002.

5. "Death in Desire," *Time Magazine,* 28 Sept. 1970, 13.

6. *States-Item*, 16 Sept. 1970.

7. Larry Preston Williams, interview with the author, tape recording, New Orleans, 19 Apr. 2005. Unless otherwise indicated, all subsequent Williams quotes in this chapter are from this interview.

8. Althea Francois, phone interviews with the author, 24 May 2005, 31 May 2005.

9. Clarence Giarrusso and Moon Landrieu, transcript of press conference, 15 Sept. 1970, Mayor Moon Landrieu Records, 1970–78, Special Collections, Louisiana Division, New Orleans Public Library.

10. *New York Times,* 15 Sept. 1970.

11. Paul Atkinson, "Desire Area Residents Nervous after Shootings," *Times-Picayune,* 16 Sept. 1970.

12. *New York Times,* 15 Sept. 1970.

13. *New York Times,* 17 Sept. 1970.

14. *States-Item*, 21 Sept. 1970.

15. Darlene Fife, editorial, *NOLA Express*, 16 Sept. 1970.

16. *New York Times,* 19 Sept. 1970.

17. Steve Green (Green Stevens Jr.), statements made at an Anti-Violence Coordinating Committee meeting, Ashe Cultural Arts Center, New Orleans, Aug. 2003.

18. Quoted in the *States-Item*, 15 Sept. 1970.

19. *States-Item,* 16 Sept. 1970.

CHAPTER 10

1. *States-Item,* 17 Sept. 1970. The quotes in the opening paragraphs and from the group's statement appear in this article.

2. Ibid.

3. "Death in Desire," *Time Magazine,* 28 Sept. 1970.

4. *States-Item,* 16 Sept. 1970. The Jefferson McCormick quote that follows is also from this article.

5. *Times-Picayune,* 22 Sept. 1970.

6. Moon Landrieu, interview with the author, tape recording, New Orleans, Feb. 2003. Unless otherwise indicated, subsequent Landrieu quotes in this chapter are from this interview.

7. This and the following quotes are from the text of Joe Putnam's sermon "Statement to the Mayor, the Police, and the Panthers," delivered at St. Frances De Sales Church, New Orleans, 20 Sept. 1970, Mayor Moon Landrieu Records, 1970–78, Special Collections, Louisiana Division, New Orleans Public Library.

8. Letter from the National Council of Jewish Women to Moon Landrieu, 20 Sept. 1970, Mayor Moon Landrieu Records, 1970–78, Special Collections, Louisiana Division, New Orleans Public Library.

9. *States-Item,* 17 Sept. 1970. The quotes from John Pecoul that follow are also from this article.

10. *States-Item,* 16 Sept. 1970.

11. WWL editorial transcript, Mayor Moon Landrieu Records, 1970–78, Special Collections, Louisiana Division, New Orleans Public Library.

12. Ibid.

13. Michael H. Kulka, letter to the editor, *States-Item,* 30 Sept. 1970.

14. *New York Times,* 20 Sept. 1970.

15. Clarence Giarrusso, interview with the author, tape recording, Mar. 2003, New Orleans.

CHAPTER 11

1. Althea Francois, phone interviews with the author, Atlanta, 24 May 2005, 31 May 2005.
2. Moon Landrieu, interview with the author, tape recording, New Orleans, Feb. 2003.
3. Larry Preston Williams, interview with the author, tape recording, New Orleans, 19 Apr. 2005.
4. *Black Panther Newspaper,* 12 June 1971, quoted in "Why Twenty-Four Panthers Are Political Prisoners in Louisiana," 20 Nov. 2002, http://www.angola3.org.
5. *NOLA Express.*
6. "More than a Foothold," *NOLA Express.*
7. *Times-Picayune,* 18 Nov. 1970.
8. Panther flier, clippings file, Special Collections, Louisiana Division, Howard-Tilton Memorial Library, Tulane University, New Orleans.
9. Bulletin from Tulane University Student Senate News Service, clippings file, Special Collections, Louisiana Division, Howard-Tilton Memorial Library, Tulane University, New Orleans.
10. *New York Times,* 19 Nov. 1970.

CHAPTER 12

1. William Barnwell, unpublished memoir.
2. Jerome LeDoux, interview with the author, tape recording, New Orleans, Dec. 2002. Unless otherwise indicated, subsequent LeDoux quotes in this chapter are from this interview.
3. *Louisiana Weekly*, weekly column of Father LeDoux, 2002.
4. Cecil Carter, Henry Faggen, Don Hubbard, and Bob Tucker, interviews with the author, tape recordings, Hubbard Mansion Bed and Breakfast, New Orleans, Apr. 2003. All subsequent quotes from Carter, Faggen, Hubbard, and Tucker in this chapter are from these interviews.
5. Ibid.

CHAPTER 13

1. Article from the clippings file, Special Collections, Louisiana Division, Howard-Tilton Memorial Library, Tulane University, New Orleans.
2. *Times-Picayune,* 18 Nov. 1970.
3. Clarence Doucet, in an unidentified local newspaper, 22 Nov. 1970, clippings file, Special Collections, Louisiana Division, Howard-Tilton Memorial Library, Tulane University, New Orleans.
4. Quoted in ibid.
5. Ibid.
6. Ibid.
7. *Daily Iberian*, 20 Nov. 1970.
8. Quoted in Doucet article.

9. Larry Preston Williams, interview with the author, tape recording, New Orleans, 19 Apr. 2005.

10. Doucet article.

11. Jerome LeDoux, interview with the author, tape recording, New Orleans, Dec. 2002. Unless otherwise mentioned, subsequent LeDoux quotes in this chapter are from this interview.

12. Quoted in Doucet article.

13. Robert Tucker, interview with the author, tape recording, New Orleans, Apr. 2003. Unless otherwise indicated, all subsequent Tucker quotes in this chapter are from this interview.

14. Doucet article.

15. Henry Faggen, interview with the author, tape recording, Hubbard Mansion Bed and Breakfast, New Orleans, Apr. 2003. Unless otherwise indicated, subsequent Faggen quotes in this chapter are from this interview.

16. Moon Landrieu, interview with the author, tape recording, New Orleans, Feb. 2003. Unless otherwise indicated, subsequent Landrieu quotes in this chapter are from this interview.

17. Roy Reed, "A Police-Panther Confrontation Ends Peacefully in New Orleans," *New York Times,* 19 Nov. 1970.

18. *Black Panther Newspaper,* 12 June 1971, quoted in "Why Twenty-Four Panthers Are Political Prisoners in Louisiana," 20 Nov. 2002, http://www.angola3.org.

19. *Louisiana Weekly,* 28 Nov. 1970.

20. New Orleans Human Relations Committee statement, Mayor Moon Landrieu Records, 1970–78, Special Collections, Louisiana Division, New Orleans Public Library.

21. Marion Brown, interview with the author, tape recording, New Orleans, Dec. 2002.

22. *Louisiana Weekly,* 28 Nov. 1970.

CHAPTER 14

1. Don Hubbard, interview with the author, tape recording, Hubbard Mansion Bed and Breakfast, New Orleans, Apr. 2003. Unless otherwise indicated, subsequent Hubbard quotes in this chapter are from this interview.

2. Henry Faggen, interview with the author, tape recording, New Orleans, Apr. 2003. Unless otherwise indicated, subsequent Faggen quotes in this chapter are from this interview.

3. *Louisiana Weekly,* 28 Nov. 1970.

4. Letter from Carl Jones to Moon Landrieu, 19 Nov. 1970. Mayor Moon Landrieu Records, 1970–78, Special Collections, Louisiana Division, New Orleans Public Library.

5. Telegram from C. M. Rhodes to Moon Landrieu, Nov. 1970. Mayor Moon Landrieu Records, 1970–78, Special Collections, Louisiana Division, New Orleans Public Library.

6. Robert Tucker, interview with the author, tape recording, New Orleans, Apr. 2003. Unless otherwise indicated, subsequent Tucker quotes in this chapter are from this interview.

7. Ibid.

8. Moon Landrieu, interview with the author, tape recording, New Orleans, Feb. 2003. His later words appear at the end of chapter 8. Unless otherwise indicated, subsequent Landrieu quotes in the present chapter are from this interview.

9. Charles Elloie, interview with the author, tape recording, New Orleans, May 2003. Unless otherwise indicated, subsequent Elloie quotes in this chapter are from this interview.

10. Cecil Carter, interview with the author, tape recording, Hubbard Mansion Bed and Breakfast, New Orleans, April 2003 and June 2003. Unless otherwise indicated, subsequent Carter quotes in this chapter are from this interview.

CHAPTER 15

1. "The Revolutionary Peoples Constitutional Convention," 1970, flier, Mayor Moon Landrieu Records, 1970–78, Special Collections, Louisiana Division, New Orleans Public Library.

2. *States-Item,* 24 Nov. 1970.

3. George L. Bott, memo to HANO, 1970, Mayor Moon Landrieu Records, 1970–78, Special Collections, Louisiana Division, New Orleans Public Library.

4. *States-Item,* 24 Nov. 1970.

5. *NOLA Express,* 1 Dec. 1970.

6. Larry Preston Williams, interview with the author, tape recording, New Orleans, 19 Apr. 2005. Unless otherwise noted, subsequent Williams quotes in this chapter are from this interview.

7. *Louisiana Weekly,* 5 Dec. 1970.

8. *NOLA Express,* 1 Dec. 1970.

9. Johnny Jackson Jr., open letter to "All Black People and Concerned People," *NOLA Express,* 1 Dec. 1970.

10. *Louisiana Weekly,* 5 Dec. 1970.

11. *NOLA Express,* 1 Dec. 1970.

12. *NOLA Express,* 1 Dec. 1970.

13. *Black Panther Newspaper,* 12 June 1971, quoted in "Why Twenty-Four Panthers Are Political Prisoners in Louisiana," 20 Nov. 2002, http://www.angola3.org.

14. From an NOPD internal newsletter in the files of Ruth Asher, the official police historian for the NOPD.

15. Ibid.

16. Moon Landrieu, interview with the author, tape recording, New Orleans, Feb. 2003.

17. Henry Faggen, Bob Tucker, Cecil Carter, and Don Hubbard, interviews with the author, tape recordings, Hubbard Mansion Bed and Breakfast, New Orleans, Apr. 2003.

18. Malik Rahim, interview with author, tape recording, New Orleans, Dec. 2002.

19. Jerome LeDoux, interview with the author, tape recording, New Orleans, Dec. 2002.

20. *Louisiana Weekly,* 12 Dec. 1970.

21. Ibid.

22. Letter from F. Winter Trapolin, president of the Catholic Human Relations Commission, to Clarence Giarrusso, 1 Dec. 1970, Mayor Moon Landrieu Records, 1970–78, Special Collections, Louisiana Division, New Orleans Public Library.

23. Letter from Sister M. Harriet Waldo, R.S.M., to Moon Landrieu, Human Relations Committee File, box 4, Special Collections, New Orleans Public Library.

24. Clarence Giarrusso, interview with the author, tape recording, New Orleans, March 2003.

CHAPTER 16

1. Henry Faggen, Bob Tucker, Cecil Carter, and Don Hubbard, interviews with the author, tape recordings, Hubbard Mansion Bed and Breakfast, New Orleans, Apr. 2003. Unless otherwise noted, all subsequent quotes from them in this chapter are from this interview.

2. Quoted in *Times-Picayune,* 13 Jan. 1971.

3. *Times-Picayune,* 14 Jan. 1971.

4. Warren Brown, "Desire, Has It Changed?" *States-Item,* 15 Sept. 1971.

5. Ibid.

6. Ibid.

7. Quoted in *States Item,* 12 Jan. 1971.

8. *States Item,* 12 Jan. 1971.

9. Ferrel Guillory, *States-Item,* 15 Sept. 1971.

10. Jonathan Eig, "A Project Named Desire, " *Times-Picayune,* 19 June 1989.

11. "Desire Development Neighborhood Snapshot," Greater New Orleans Community Data Center, http://www.gnocdc.org/orleans/7/16/snapshot.html.

CHAPTER 17

1. *Times-Picayune,* 30 Sept. 1970.

2. *States-Item,* 22 Sept. 1970.

3. Ibid. Rouselle would go on to become head of a public relations firm in New Orleans.

4. *Times-Picayune,* 25 Sept. 1970.

5. *States-Item,* 26 Sept. 1970.

6. Lolis Elie, interview with the author, tape recording, New Orleans, Mar. 2003. Unless otherwise indicated, subsequent Elie quotes in this chapter are from this interview.

7. *Times-Picayune,* 25 Sept. 1970.

8. *States-Item,* 22 Sept. 1970.

9. *Times-Picayune,* 25 Sept. 1970.

10. Larry Preston Williams, interview with the author, tape recording, New Orleans, 19 Apr. 2005. Unless otherwise indicated, subsequent Williams quotes in this chapter are from this interview.

11. Robert King Wilkerson, interview with the author, tape recording, New Orleans, Dec. 2002.

12. Malik Rahim, interview with author, tape recording, New Orleans, Dec. 2002. Unless otherwise indicated, subsequent Rahim quotes in this chapter are from this interview.

13. "Do not be alarmed, but do be informed," flier, clippings file, Special Collections, Louisiana Division, Howard-Tilton Memorial Library, Tulane University, New Orleans.

14. Althea Francois, phone interviews with the author, Atlanta, 24 May 2005, 31 May 2005.

15. Lubertha Johnson, interview with the author, tape recording, New Orleans, Dec. 2002. Unless otherwise noted, all subsequent Johnson quotes in this chapter are from this interview.

16. *Times-Picayune*, 7 Aug. 1971. All of the quotes in the concluding section of this chapter come from this article.

CHAPTER 18

1. Malik Rahim, interview with author, tape recording, New Orleans, Dec. 2002.

2. Lolis Elie, interview with the author, tape recording, New Orleans, Mar. 2003.

CHAPTER 19

1. Robert King Wilkerson, "31 Years as a Political Prisoner," talk given to Students Organized against Racism, Tulane University, October 2004.

2. Wilkerson, "A Cry from the Bottom" (unpublished manuscript), 1

3. Ibid., 5.

4. Ibid., 7.

5. Malik Rahim, interview with author, tape recording, New Orleans, Dec. 2002. Unless otherwise indicated, subsequent quotes from Rahim in this chapter are from this interview.

6. Quoted in Katy Reckdahl, "Panther Sprung," *Gambit Weekly,* 6 Mar. 2001.

7. Ibid.

8. Wilkerson, "A Cry from the Bottom," 7.

9. First names have been used to protect anonymity.

10. Wilkerson, "A Cry from the Bottom"; Robert King Wilkerson, interview with the author, tape recording, New Orleans, Dec. 2002.

11. *Louisiana Weekly,* 16 Jan. 1971.

12. Wilkerson, "A Cry from the Bottom," 9.

13. Quoted in Reckdahl, "Panther Sprung."

14. Ibid., 9.

15. Letter from Herman Wallace to the Coalition to Free the Angola Three, written in 2003, from Angola's CCR.

16. Robert King Wilkerson, "31 Years As a Political Prisoner," talk given to Students Organized against Racism, Tulane University, October 2004.

17. Wilkerson, "A Cry from the Bottom," i.

18. Ibid., 57 and 58.

19. Quoted in Reckdahl, "Panther Sprung."

20. *Times-Picayune,* 2 May 2002.

21. Quoted in Richard A. Webster, "Free at Last," *New Orleans City Life,* Jan. 2005.

22. Wilkerson, "A Cry from the Bottom," ii.

23. http://AnitaRoddick.com. The quote from Cain's letter mentioned in the next paragraph is also from this Web site.

24. In 2008 Woodfox and Wallace were moved from solitary confinement to general population after the advocacy efforts of the Coalition to Free the Angola Three were stepped up.

CHAPTER 20

1. *The Black Panther Newspaper,* 13 March 1971.

2. Henry Faggen, Bob Tucker, Cecil Carter, and Don Hubbard, interviews with the author, tape recordings, Hubbard Mansion Bed and Breakfast, New Orleans, Apr. 2003. All subsequent quotes from them in this chapter are from this interview.

3. *The Black Panther,* 13 March 1971.

4. Ibid.

CHAPTER 21

1. Peniel E. Joseph, *Waiting 'till the Midnight Hour: A Narrative History of Black Power in America* (New York: Henry Holt, 2006), 261–62.

2. Charles Jones, *The Black Panther Party [Reconsidered]* (Baltimore: Black Classic Press, 1998).

3. Geronimo ji Jaga, statements made at an Anti-Violence Coordinating Committee meeting, Ashe Cultural Arts Center, New Orleans, August 2003.

4. Quoted in Jones, *Black Panther Party.*

5. Ibid.

6. Ollie A. Johnson III, assistant professor of Government and Politics and Afro-American Studies at the University of Maryland, qtd. in Jones, *Black Panther Party,* 397.

CHAPTER 22

1. Malik Rahim, interview with author, tape recording, New Orleans, Dec. 2002.

2. Althea Francois, phone interviews with the author, Atlanta, 24 May 2005, 31 May 2005.

3. Quote from the *Black Panther Newspaper,* Sept. 1968, in Jones, *The Black Panther Party [Reconsidered]* (Baltimore: Black Classic Press, 1998), 287.

4. Ibid.

5. Leah Hodges, untitled talk about the photo exhibit *It's about Time,* 3 Apr. 2003, Community Book Center, New Orleans.

6. Marion Brown, interview with the author, tape recording, New Orleans, Dec. 2002. Unless otherwise indicated, subsequent Brown quotes in this chapter are from this interview.

7. Only first names have been used here to protect privacy.

8. "Celebrating Our Heritage—Kathleen Cleaver Said Interviewed by Asha Bandele," *Essence*, Feb. 2004.

9. Anonymous Panther source.

10. Brown interview.

11. Leslie Williams, "Ex-Panther Thankful He Survived," *Times-Picayune*, 15 Sept., 1995. The Edwards quotes in this and the next few paragraphs are all from this article.

12. Kathleen Cleaver interview, *Essence*, Feb. 2004.

13. Statement from Herman Bell, special issue of *Panther News* 1.1 (Spring 2004): 4, www.itsabouttimebpp.com.

14. Jim Naskins, *Power to the People: The Rise and Fall of the Black Panther Party* (New York: Simon & Schuster Books for Young Readers, 1997).

15. Brown interview; Robert King Wilkerson, interview with the author, tape recording, New Orleans, Dec. 2002. All of the Brown and Wilkerson quotes that follow are from this interview.

CHAPTER 23

1. "Celebrating Our Heritage—Kathleen Cleaver Said Interviewed by Asha Bandele," *Essence*, Feb. 2004.

2. Ernest Jones, interview with the author, tape recording, New Orleans, Aug. 2003. Unless otherwise indicated, subsequent Jones quotes in this chapter are from this interview.

3. Stephanie Moore, Anti-Violence Coordinating Committee Meeting, Ashe Cultural Arts Center, New Orleans, Aug. 2003.

4. Kathleen Cleaver interview, *Essence*, Feb. 2004.

5. *Times-Picayune,* 15 Sept. 1995.

6. Kathleen Cleaver interview, *Essence*, Feb. 2004.

7. Curtis J. Austin, *Up Against the Wall: Violence in the Making and Unmaking of the Black Panther Party.* (Fayetteville: University of Arkansas Press, 2006), 347.

8. Mumia Abu-Jamal, *We Want Freedom: A Life in the Black Panther Party* (Cambridge, MA: South End Press, 2004), 7.

9. Cecil Carter, Don Hubbard, Bob Tucker, and Henry Faggen, interviews with author, tape recordings, Hubbard Mansion Bed and Breakfast, New Orleans, 2003. Subsequent quotes from these men in this chapter are from this interview.

10. Lance Hill, conversation with the author, 1 Nov. 2004.

11. Abu-Jamal, *We Want Freedom,* 250.

CHAPTER 24

1. Quoted in Jed Horne, *Breach of Faith: Hurricane Katrina and the Near Death of a Great American City* (New York: Random House, 2006), 222.

2. Davia Nelson, Hidden Kitchens series, *Morning Edition,* National Public Radio, 4 Nov. 2005.

3. Amy Goodman, interview with Malik Rahim, *Democracy Now* (radio program), 28 Aug. 2006. Transcript at http://www.democracynow.org.

4. Rasmus Holm, *Welcome to New Orleans,* DVD (Friothjol Film, 2006).

5. Quoted in Tim Shorrock, "The Street Samaritans," *Mother Jones Magazine,* March/April 2006.

6. Orissa Arend, "Birth of the Common Ground Health Clinic," *New Orleans Tribune,* October/November 2007.

7. South End Press Collective, eds., *What Lies Beneath; Katrina, Race, and the State of the Nation* (Cambridge, Massachusetts: South End Press, 2007).

8. Horne, *Breach of Faith,* 230.

9. Scott Weinstein, conversation with the author, New Orleans, 15 Jan. 2006.

10. Shorrock, "Street Samaritans."

11. Michelle Garcia, "For a Former Panther, Solidarity after the Storm," *Washington Post,* 4 Dec. 2005.

12. Quoted in Arend, "Birth of the Common Ground Health Clinic."

13. Malik Rahim, "Common Ground Update," talk given at the Gillespie Community Breakfast, Unitarian/Universalist Church, New Orleans, 12 Jan. 2008.

14. Ibid.

15. Ibid.

16. "Life Is Sweet," *Bark Magazine,* May/June 2006.

17. Bruce Nolan, "Tremé Churgh Fights for Survival," *Times-Picayune,* 14 Feb. 2006.

18. *Shake the Devil Off,* dir. Peter Entell. DVD. (Fournex, Switzerland: Show and Tell Films, 2006).

19. South End Press Collective, eds., *What Lies Beneath,* 88.

EPILOGUE

1. *Times-Picayune,* 17 Sept. 2003.

2. *Times-Picayune,* 18 Sept. 2003.

3. Ibid.

4. Ibid. Landrieu's comment in the previous paragraph was made during the forum itself.

SUGGESTED READING AND VIEWING

The Panther-police confrontation in New Orleans was, at its heart, the massacre that did not occur. Everyone I interviewed had expected a massacre after the negotiations broke down, and they all had theories, ranging from the mystical to the practical, about why that did not happen. My own theory is that while luck and divine intervention probably played a part, the unique history and culture of New Orleans brought together circumstances and people that defied the American racial narrative that the United States had tried to impose since it bought the city as part of the Louisiana Purchase in 1803. That narrative in 1970 said that police and Panthers were supposed to kill each other.

A racial narrative is simply a collectively agreed-upon story that people tell themselves about what we call "race" to justify, explain, and predict our thoughts, feelings, behaviors, and political and social acts. Narratives are both personal and collective. They govern all aspects of our thinking, giving us a sense of continuity and control. They evolve. For instance, a personal narrative about romance that emerged from one's childhood could be based on something as ephemeral as a favorite fairy tale. We adjust that narrative (sometimes) as life experiences accrue.

Racial narratives evolve to deal with changing laws, perceptions, and social conditions. The New Orleans narrative about race seems to me to be less cut-and-dried than the larger American narrative, more given to loopholes, caveats, and time-outs. Because people who live in New Orleans tenaciously remember history and the traditions of place and belonging, they tend to be more connected, even across race lines. European, African, and Native American bloodlines mingled early on in this city. The New Orleans narrative is, above all, creative in its ability to circumvent the absurdities that racism presents at any given moment in time.

The American racial narrative asserted itself particularly forcefully

243

during the Civil War, the first Reconstruction (1866–77), the Jim Crow era at the end of the nineteenth and the first half of the twentieth century, the second reconstruction when legal segregation ended (1956–66), and the third New Orleans reconstruction that is now happening post-Katrina. But the American racial narrative, to this day, never quite sticks. New Orleanians have always had their own parallel and competing narrative that is far more fluid and complex than the nation as a whole wants or is able to understand. And yet because of its "otherness," this narrative can inform and perhaps eventually transform the larger racial narrative into a story of healing.

The Panther scholars Charles Jones and Curtis Austin have been my mentors and have anchored the New Orleans story in their foreword and introduction to the larger Panther history and literature. Curtis Austin's bibliographic essay in *Up Against the Wall: Violence in the Making and the Unmaking of the Black Panther Party* provides a complete review of current Panther literature. I will therefore limit this essay to the sources that have informed my understanding of the New Orleans racial narrative and some aspects of the city's history that framed the Panther confrontation.

Gwendolyn Midlo Hall's *Africans in Colonial Louisiana: The Development of Afro-Creole Culture in the Eighteenth Century* describes how Africans from Senegambia shaped the culture and society of colonial Louisiana. In the eighteenth and nineteenth century "Creole" meant indigenous to Louisiana or New Orleans. For a discussion of the free black, or *libre,* society in colonial New Orleans, 1769–1803, the era of Spanish rule, see Kimberly S. Hanger's *Bounded Lives, Bounded Places.* During this period, free people of African descent in New Orleans advanced their legal rights and privileges, their vocation, and their social standing as well as increasing their numbers. They inhabited two psychological worlds—free and nonwhite. Hanger's book explores the origins of antebellum New Orleans' free black population, unique in the South because of its size and influence, and its ambiguous status in what has remained until today an intricate and stratified society.

Martha Ward brings nineteenth-century New Orleans vividly to life in *Voodoo Queen: The Spirited Lives of Marie Laveau,* her study of the two Voodoo priestesses the Marie Laveaus, who were mother and daughter, free women of color, and prominent French-speaking Catholic Creoles. Their lives spanned the time when Creole racial flexibility gave way to Anglo-American apartheid in New Orleans, but they nevertheless used their Voodoo powers to shift the course of love, luck, and the law against slavery and its forces.

Walter Johnson's *Soul by Soul* takes us inside North America's largest slave market, where 100,000 men, women, and children passed through New Orleans' slave pens and into showrooms where they were displayed, questioned, and examined. The interdependencies among the enslaved person, the slave trader, and the slaveholder are chronicled in story after heartbreaking story in which chattel bondage and the master's fantasies of power, control, pleasure, and even his or her own perceived benevolence conspire to create a gruesome rationale for the institution of slavery.

An Absolute Massacre: The New Orleans Race Riot of July 30, 1866, by James G. Hollandsworth Jr., reminds me that a massacre could have occurred in New Orleans in 1970 and in fact did occur soon after the Civil War in this city so closely knit that racial memory is long. On July 30, 1866, the issue before the Constitutional Convention was that blacks be allowed to vote and that former Confederates relinquish that right. A procession of black suffrage supporters were attacked by an angry throng of whites as they tried to make their way to the convention. "It was no riot," General Philip H. Sheridan, the military commander of Louisiana and Texas wrote to President U. S. Grant on August 2, 1866. "It was an absolute massacre." Hollandsworth shows that no other "riot" in American history had a more profound or lasting effect on the country's political and social fabric. The disturbance set in motion a chain of events that unified the South politically.

On June 7, 1892, Homer Plessy, a Creole so light-skinned that he could pass for white, boarded a train to challenge the Separate Car Act, one of the many Jim Crow laws that threatened the freedoms gained by blacks in New Orleans after the Civil War. Homer Plessy, born a free man of color, was baptized at St. Augustine Church and had probably brushed shoulders with one or both of the Marie Laveaus. He enjoyed relative equality while growing up in Reconstruction-era New Orleans. Yet his arrest on the train that day led to the Supreme Court case *Plessy v. Ferguson,* which established the separate-but-equal doctrine that prevailed in America until the *Brown v. Board of Education* decision in 1954. Keith Weldon Medley, a New Orleans native, brings all of the characters in this complex drama to life in *We as Freemen; Plessy v. Ferguson* while documenting the civil rights triumphs of Reconstruction-era New Orleans. Medley is featured in the scholarly and riveting 2007 documentary *Faubourg Treme: The Untold Story of Black New Orleans,* directed by Dawn Logston (the daughter of the New Orleans historian Joe Logston) and written and narrated by Lolis Eric Elie (the son of civil rights legend and Panther lawyer Lolis Elie). For more information about the film, see http://www.treme-doc.com.

Creole New Orleans: Race and Americanization, edited by Arnold R. Hirsch and Joseph Logston, is a collection of six original essays that explore the ethnic composition and history of New Orleans and how its people navigated a multiethnic environment. The collection explores the Franco-American protest tradition in New Orleans and how it collides with the Anglo-America mindset that enforced a stark racial dualism. In New Orleans, racial totalitarianism never quite managed to obliterate ethnicity, so that a strain of assertive, independent Creole radicalism emerged to challenge Jim Crow.

Moving to the field of twentieth-century history, John Barry's *Rising Tide: The Great Mississippi Flood of 1927 and How It Changed America* puts many current themes in context, discussing the misuse of engineering as a result of political trade-offs, incompetence, and greed, and the way a natural disaster can disclose a society's fragile workings. It raises the possibility that these calamities can also serve as a catalyst for changes in the established order of race, class, power, politics, and social structure. Adam Fairclough's *Race and Democracy: The Civil Rights Struggle in Louisiana, 1915–1972,* traces the fight for political, economic, and social rights for African Americans in "the most diverse and unique southern state" from the final years of Huey Long to the 1972 election of Governor Edwin Edwards. He sees black protest between the late 1930s and the mid-1950s as not just a "mere prelude to the drama proper," but "the first act of a two-act play." Likewise, Liva Baker, in *The Second Battle of New Orleans: The Hundred-Year Struggle to Integrate the Schools,* takes the long view that the "pre-movement" movement, including the NAACP, the Legal

Defense Fund, and many other nearly forgotten organizations and heroes, made their mark with remarkable perseverance.

Harry Haywood's *Black Bolshevik: Autobiography of an Afro-American Communist* helped me understand the evolution of black revolutionary thinking. His narrative describes his slave grandparents, his participation in both world wars, his studies in Russia, his radical labor organizing, and his analysis in 1978 of Black Power. He was married to the historian Gwendolyn Midlo Hall.

Kim Lacy Rogers's *Righteous Lives: Narratives of the New Orleans Civil Rights Movement* tells the story of black and white civil rights activists who worked to end racial segregation and discrimination in New Orleans in the 1950s and 1960s. Perceptions of the possibilities for African American liberation and how it might be achieved were homegrown, Rogers contends, flowering from miscegenation and less intimate forms of race mixing. The book contains autobiographical accounts that illustrate the personal consequences of political activism and provides insights into issues of collective and individual memory. It also examines how issues of caste, class, gender, and generation played out in the civil rights movement in New Orleans. For the personal perspective of a black New Orleans civil rights activist, see Tom Dent's memoir *Southern Journey: A Return to the Civil Rights Movement*.

Nonviolence defined the black freedom movement in New Orleans and throughout the country in the late 1950s and early 1960s. But that strategy had perilously underestimated racism and mistakenly placed confidence in the American conscience and democratic institutions. In 1964 a small group of African American men in Jonesboro, Louisiana, defied the mainstream civil rights movement and formed an armed self-defense organization—the Deacons for Defense and Justice—to protect movement workers from vigilante and police violence. Lance Hill's *The Deacons for Defense: Armed Resistance and the Civil Rights Movement* is the first detailed history of the Deacons, whose philosophy foreshadowed the Panthers in small Louisiana towns and elsewhere in the heart of Klan country.

Kent Germany's *New Orleans after the Promises: Poverty, Citizenship, and the Search for the Great Society* is an in-depth study of the transformation of New Orleans in the 1960s and 1970s as the demands for inclusion of the civil rights movement and the reality of the demise of legal segregation hit home. The economic opportunity legislation of the 1960s allowed black and white New Orleanians to cautiously partner with each other and with the federal government to expand liberalism in the South. Germany gives a detailed account of the political, civic, social, and governmental organizations that participated in the War on Poverty and Black Power in New Orleans from 1964 to 1974. He also provides the most in-depth description of the Panther activity in Desire that I have found in a book.

For a window into what life is like for a prisoner at Angola State Penitentiary—a window, quite frankly, that I had tried to avoid in my interviews with Robert King Wilkerson—see Jed Horne's *Desire Street: A True Story of Death and Deliverance in New Orleans.* Curtis Kyles, who had roots in the Desire Housing Project, spent fourteen years on Angola's death row before being freed. As Wilbert Rideau, founding editor of *The Angolite,* the inmate publication of the Louisiana State Penitentiary at Angola says of the book, it exposes "the horrific flesh-and-blood workings of the criminal justice system, where prejudice, politics, and chance shape what passes for justice today." One of the key players in the book, Herman Wallace, one of the Angola Three still in Angola State Penitentiary, provided key information at great personal cost that helped to free the protagonist Curtis Kyles. King and I both read the book when it first came out in 2005, and neither of us could go to sleep until we had finished it.

For a view of what Desire is and was like through the eyes of teenagers who lived there, see *Piety and Desire,* published by Sold Skull Press in Brooklyn, New York, in 2005 (just months before Hurricane Katrina) as part of John McDonogh Senior High School's Neighborhood Story Project. Sister and brother Arlet and Sam Wylie lived above a neighborhood store on St. Claude Avenue between Piety and Desire streets. They took pictures, interviewed their elders, and described both their external and internal terrains. In another book in the series, *Women: Stories from the Ninth Ward,* Waukesha Jackson interviews her mother, grandmother, and other women in the neighborhood, including Evella "Mr. Coochie" Pierre, whose mother lived in the Desire Housing Project. The interview includes her memories of the Panthers in Desire. Julie Gustafson's feature-length documentary called *Desire* takes viewers into the project itself as girls who live there film their lives and tell their stories and then share these stories with working-class and upper-class New Orleans girls. Over a period of five years, the girls film their circumstances, their fears, their fantasies, their triumphs, and their struggle with what it means to be a mother or what it means to reject that possibility. In a visceral way, the film takes the viewer back to those poignant choices made in adolescence.

For a heartbreaking and yet thoroughly charming account of Hurricane Betsy and the organizing in its aftermath in the Lower Ninth Ward in 1965, see "Riding the Nightmare Express," written by Elizabeth Cousins Rogers in 1965 and updated in 1975. She and her husband Walter Rogers (quoted in chapter 1 of this book) were radical labor organizers, two of just a handful of white people then living in the neighborhood. Though Betsy flooded Lower Nine houses to the roof, as did Katrina, there was no resulting diaspora. "Refugees" were housed in public shelters in the city. Ms. Rogers describes how they were "treated like animals" and sent home with a small broom and pail "to clean up your house with."

Rogers writes that whites "scurried out" of her neighborhood in the wake of school desegregation in 1954. She gives moving, personal accounts of her neighbors. She tells what it was like to wake up with water filling the house with no warning, what she and her neighbors lost, and how they made do and helped each other. Trash lay on the Ninth Ward streets for a year, neglected by the city, until it was finally picked up by out-of-state college volunteers. She and her husband helped organize a group of flood victims who were scoffed at or ignored by those in authority. Rogers subscribes to the widespread local belief that the levees were intentionally breached as they had been in the flood of 1927. She recounts the internal obstacles to organizing, such as the church leaders who charged rent for meeting space, said long prayers, and absconded with the group's meager funds. She laments the refusal of CORE or even the black media to take up the cause of victim assistance. All of this was very recent memory when, five years later, the Panthers came to town. Rogers's article can be accessed through the Hurricane Digital Memory Bank at http://hurricanearchive.org/object/26649.

Mardi Gras, our multifaceted pre-Lenten revelry, has long incorporated rituals that define social stratification, including assumptions about race and class. It also incorporates rituals that mock or defy this stratification. The rituals tend to be almost caricatures (in this late-comer's view), with the liberating cover of masks, alcohol, and drum-induced altered states, and a socially contracted period of time when anything goes. James Gill's *Lords of Misrule: Mardi Gras and the Politics of Race in New Orleans* lays out the history of Mardi Gras, its roots in the nineteenth century, and the purpose it serves for the city's busi-ness and social elite. It illuminates a tradition of formalized prejudice, as does Rebecca Snedeker's *By Invitation Only*. Snedeker decided to forgo the debutante tradition that had been the birthright of the women in her family to explore what it really means to be the queen of masked men. She keenly and bravely delineates the tensions she feels between family, social status, and her own convictions.

Royce Osborn's award-winning documentary *All on a Mardi Gras Day* traces Mardi Gras history from the black perspective—the Mardi Gras Indians, the Skeletons, the Baby Dolls, the Zulu parade, and ties to Africa and Haiti. He shows how these have always provided pow-erful resistance to white supremacy. Phoebe Ferguson, the grand-daughter of John Ferguson, the judge who first ruled against Homer Plessy, is completing a documentary film called *Member of the Club* about the Original Illinois Club's 2004 Mardi Gras and black Creole society. Keith Plessy, a relative of Homer Plessy is in the film. Ferguson explains that in this generation, instead of Plessy versus Ferguson it will be Plessy AND Ferguson, because they are starting a foundation together.

Peter Entell's film *Shake the Devil Off* begins with the first Mardi Gras after Hurricane Katrina. This was a Mardi Gras most of the coun-try thought New Orleans shouldn't have. But we really didn't care what most of the country thought. We had it for ourselves. The documen-tary takes us through Lent as the Catholic authorities try to shut down the historic St. Augustine Church, the first black Catholic parish in the nation, built in Tremé during slavery, with a biracial history and cul-ture that continues today. He shows distraught parishioners, civil dis-obedience by young activists, and spontaneous protest eruptions during mass by the mixed-race congregation—all set to New Orleans music with its melodious call to defiance and praise. Entell is a Swiss filmmaker, but he practically lived at St. Augustine the whole forty days of Lent, and he got its story of resurrection just right.

Welcome to New Orleans, by the Scandinavian director Rasmus Holm, is another full-length post-Katrina documentary of note. It follows Malik Rahim in the weeks after the storm as Common Ground comes into being and documents the horrific conditions that Malik so eloquently speaks about. Holm also interviews the Algiers vigilantes, who are brutally honest with him, assuming that because he is European, he shares their ideology.

Several post-Katrina books have aided my understanding of this our third reconstruction and our alternative New Orleans racial narrative. *What Lies Beneath: Katrina, Race, and the State of the Nation,* edited by the South End Press Collective, offers a radical analysis of the powers and the powerless in the aftermath of Katrina. Jed Horne's *Breach of Faith: Hurricane Katrina and the Near Death of a Great American City* includes a chapter on Malik Rahim and Common Ground. It's just one of the many stories of storm victims dealing with politicians, thieves, nurses, urban visionaries, and entrepreneurs with an eye for quick profit at public expense, stories that form the most complete and compelling Katrina analysis that I have found. Horne does not look away from the race and class tensions that are hampering the ongoing reconstruction efforts.

Unnatural Disaster: The Nation on Hurricane Katrina, edited by Betsy Reed, is a collection of articles and editorials published in *The Nation* in the months following the storm that expose the gross negligence of the Bush administration, the failures of neoliberalism, and the heroic efforts of community organizers and ordinary citizens to put New Orleans back together again. Malik Rahim appears in two essays in the collection: Christian Parenti's "The Big Easy Dies Hard" and Jon Elliston's "FEMA: Confederacy of Dunces."

On August 27, 2005, two days before Katrina made landfall, the last Amtrak train left the station in New Orleans with equipment, but without any passengers. In his essay "The Station," which appears in *After the Storm: Black Intellectuals Explore the Meaning of Hurricane Katrina,* edited by David Dante Troutt, Anthony Paul Farley uses the station as a metaphor for a place where African Americans wait for nothing. The rails were laid a long time ago—parallel tracks of class and race—and they lead inevitably to white power in a white-over-black Promised Land, Farley contends. He claims we have collectively forgotten the unbearable trauma of the original accumulation/original dispossession, slavery, which was no accident. Thus, subsequent traumas, including the failure of the levees, are not accidents but in fact play out in ways predetermined by that original one. New Orleans was a slave market, Farley reminds us, and Plessy could not board the train.

Francesco di Santis defied the mandatory evacuation order and arrived at the Common Ground Collective two weeks after the storm. In a period of thirteen months, he drew two thousand portraits, in charcoal, carbon, graphite, china marker and pastel, of anybody who was here and would sit still. Each subject wrote on his or her portrait in unscripted vernacular, their story, their observations, their memory, and/ or their current condition. Subjects who preferred to talk were taped, and with permission, their tapes were transcribed. Subjects who couldn't or wouldn't talk or write were given their portraits as a gift.

I first encountered these narratives of survival, renewal, and struggle as what looked like wallpaper in the Common Ground relief centers in the Ninth Ward where I stood transfixed and weeping, reading them for as long as I could take it all in. They have been collected into a beautiful, glossy coffee-table book published in 2007 by di Santis and Loulou Latta called *The Post-Katrina Portraits: Written and Narrated by Hundreds,* a media project of the Common Ground Collective. You can contact the artist at wanderer@riseup.net or www.postkatrinaportraits.org.

My own understanding of what racism and white-skin privilege are and how they operate in me and in the institutions I participate in has come primarily from the People's Institute for Survival and Beyond, which, through its Undoing Racism Workshops and community organizing initiatives, is building a broad-based movement for social change. For the past ten years I have participated in and helped to organize dozens of workshops. I never cease to be challenged and inspired by what I learn in a workshop. The relationships, the fights, the love, the cultural sharing, and the insights have sustained me over the years. The principles that inform the workshops are laid out in a book by Ronald Chisom and Michael Washington called *Undoing Racism: A Philosophy of International Social Change,* published by the People's Institute Press in 1997.

Racial narratives, both locally and nationally, are in a state of accelerated flux in 2008. A black man has been elected president. Latino workers are bringing their families to New Orleans as they help us reconstruct our city. And so the New Orleans narrative is no longer just about black and white and something in between. It is an important time for all of us to consciously acknowledge and examine the stories we tell ourselves about race, with an eye toward a happy ending. The stand the Black Panthers took in New Orleans in 1970 provides important lessons as our narratives evolve, lessons that perhaps are more useful than ever almost forty years after the fact.

BIBLIOGRAPHY

SPECIAL COLLECTIONS

Black Panthers, vertical files. Special collections, Louisiana Division, Howard-Tilton Memorial Library. Tulane University, New Orleans.

Major Moon Landrieu Records. 1970-78. Special collections, Louisiana Division, New Orleans Public Library.

BOOKS

Abu-Jamal, Mumia. *We Want Freedom: A Life in the Black Panther Party*. Cambridge, Massachusetts: South End Press, 2004.

Austin, Curtis J. *Up Against the Wall: Violence in the Making and Unmaking of the Black Panther Party*. Fayetteville: University of Arkansas Press, 2006.

Baker, Liva. *The Second Battle of New Orleans: The Hundred-Year Struggle to Integrate the Schools*. New York: HarperCollins, 1996.

Barry, John M. *Rising Tide: The Great Mississippi Flood of 1927 and How It Changed America*. New York: Simon and Schuster, 1997.

Brown, Elaine. *A Taste of Power: A Black Woman's Story*. New York: Anchor, 1992.

Chisom, Ronald, and Michael Washington. *Undoing Racism: A Philosophy of International Social Change*. New Orleans: People's Institute Press, 1997.

Dent, Tom. *Southern Journey: A Return to the Civil Rights Movement*. New York: W. Morrow, 1997.

Di Santis, Francesco. *The Post-Katrina Portraits: Written and Narrated by Hundreds*. A Media Project of the Common Ground Collective. Published by Francesco di Santis and Loulou Latta, 2007. http://www.postkatrina-portraits.org.

Fairclough, Adam. *Race and Democracy: The Civil Rights Struggle in Louisiana, 1915–1972*. Athens: University of Georgia Press, 1995.

Germany, Kent B. *New Orleans after the Promises: Poverty, Citizenship, and the Search for the Great Society*. Athens, Georgia: University of Georgia Press, 2007.

Gill, James. *Lords of Misrule: Mardi Gras and the Politics of Race*. Jackson, Mississippi: University of Mississippi Press, 1997.

Hall, Gwendolyn Midlo. *Africans in Colonial Louisiana: The Development of Afro-Creole Culture in the Eighteenth Century.* Baton Rouge: Louisiana State University Press, 1992.

Hanger, Kimberly S. *Bounded Lives, Bounded Places: Free Black Society in Colonial New Orleans, 1769–1803.* Durham: Duke University Press, 1997.

Haywood, Harry. *Black Bolshevik: Autobiography of an Afro-American Communist.* Chicago: Liberator Press, 1978.

Hill, Lance. *The Deacons for Defense: Armed Resistance and the Civil Rights Movement.* Chapel Hill: University of North Carolina Press, 2004.

Hirsch, Arnold R., and Joseph Logsdon, eds. *Creole New Orleans: Race and Americanization.* Baton Rouge: Louisiana State University Press, 1992.

Hollandsworth, James G., Jr. *An Absolute Massacre: The New Orleans Race Riot of July 30, 1866.* Baton Rouge: Louisiana State University Press, 2001.

Horne, Jed. *Breach of Faith: Hurricane Katrina and the Near Death of a Great American City.* New York: Random House, 2006.

———. *Desire Street: A True Story of Death and Deliverance in New Orleans.* New York: Farrar, Straus and Giroux, 2003.

Jackson, Waukesha. *What Would the World Be without Women: Stories from the Ninth Ward.* New Orleans: The Neighborhood Story Project. Brooklyn, New York: Soft Skull Press, 2005.

Johnson, Walter. *Soul by Soul: Life inside the Antebellum Slave Market.* Cambridge, Massachusetts: Harvard University Press, 1999.

Jones, Charles E., ed. *The Black Panther Party [Reconsidered].* Baltimore: Black Classic Press, 1998.

Joseph, Peniel E. *Waiting 'till the Midnight Hour: A Narrative History of Black Power in America.* New York: Henry Holt, 2006.

Medley, Keith Weldon. *We as Freemen:* Plessy v. Ferguson. Gretna, Louisiana: Pelican, 2003.

Naskins, Jim. *Power to the People: The Rise and Fall of the Black Panther Party.* New York: Simon & Schuster Books for Young Readers, 1997.

Reed, Betsy. *Unnatural Disaster: The Nation on Hurricane Katrina.* New York: Nation Books, 2006.

Roddick, Anita, ed. *A Revolution in Kindness.* Chelsea Green Publishing, 2003.

Rogers, Kim Lacy. *Righteous Lives: Narratives of the New Orleans Civil Rights Movement.* New York: New York University Press, 1993.

South End Press Collective, ed. *What Lies Beneath: Katrina, Race, and the State of the Nation.* Cambridge, Massachusetts: South End Press, 2007.

Sublette, Ned. *The World That Made New Orleans: From Spanish Silver to Congo Square.* Chicago: Lawrence Hill Books, 2008.

Troutt, David Dante, ed. *After the Storm: Black Intellectuals Explore the Meaning of Hurricane Katrina.* New York: The New Press, 2006.

Ward, Martha. *Voodoo Queen: The Spirited Lives of Marie Laveau*. Jackson: University Press of Mississippi, 2004.

Wylie, Arlet, and Sam Wylie. *Between Piety and Desire*. New Orleans: Neighborhood Story Project. Brooklyn, New York: Soft Skull Press, 2005.

NEWSPAPERS AND PERIODICALS

Black Panther Newspaper (Oakland). 1969–72.

Gambit Weekly (New Orleans).

Louisiana Weekly (New Orleans). 1970–71.

New Orleans Tribune. October/November 2007.

NOLA Express (New Orleans). 1970–71.

New York Times. 1970–71.

States-Item (New Orleans). 1970 and 1971.

Times-Picayune (New Orleans). 1970–2003.

DOCUMENTARY VIDEOS

All on a Mardi Gras Day. Written and produced by Royce Osborn. DVD. [New Orleans]: WYES Productions, 2003. http://www.spyboypics.com.

By Invitation Only. Produced, directed, and written by Rebecca Snedeker. Coproduced and cowritten by Tim Watson. DVD. [Harriman, New York]: New Day Films, 2006. http://www.byinvitationonlythefilm.com.

Desire. Directed by Julie Gustafson. DVD. New York: Women Make Movies, 2005, 2008. http://www.DesireDocumentary.com.

Faubourg Tremé: The Untold Story of Black New Orleans. Dawn Logston, Lolis Eric Elie, Lucie Faulknor, and JoNell Kennedy. DVD. San Francisco: [Distributed by] California Newsreel, 2008. http://www.tremedoc.com.

Member of the Club. Produced by Phoebe Ferguson. DVD. Scheduled for completion in 2008.

Shake the Devil Off. Produced by Peter Entell. DVD. Fournex, Switzerland: Show and Tell Films, 2006. http://www.shakethedeviloff.com.

Welcome to New Orleans. By Rasmus Holm. DVD. Denmark: Friothjol Film, 2006. http://www.commongroundrelief.org or http://www.welcome-toneworleans.dk.

UNPUBLISHED MANUSCRIPTS

Barnwell, William. Unpublished memoir. In author's archives. Quoted by permission from William Barnwell.

Lee, Silas. "A Haunted City?: The Social and Economic Status of African Americans and Whites in New Orleans. A Comparison of the 1983 and 2003 Census Data." Report issued 3 May 2003.

Rogers, Elizabeth Cousins. "Riding the Nightmare Express." Written in 1965; updated in 1975. Available through Hurricane Digital Memory Bank at hurricanearchive.org/object/26649.

Wilkerson, Robert King. "A Cry from the Bottom." Autobiography manuscript in author's archives. Quoted by permission from Robert King Wilkerson.

INTERVIEWS WITH THE AUTHOR

Barnwell, William. Tape recording. April 2003. New Orleans.

Brown, Marion. Tape recording. December 2002. New Orleans.

Carter, Cecil. Tape recording. April 2003 and June 2003. Hubbard Mansion Bed and Breakfast, New Orleans.

Elie, Lolis. Tape recording. March 2003. New Orleans.

Elloie, Charles. Tape recording. May 2003. New Orleans.

Faggen, Henry. Tape recording. April 2003. Hubbard Mansion Bed and Breakfast, New Orleans.

Fields, Israel. Phone interview. 31 May 2005. New Orleans.

Francis, Linda. Tape recording. June 2003. New Orleans.

Francois, Althea. Phone interviews. 24 May 2005, 31 May 2005. Atlanta.

Giarrusso, Clarence. Tape recording. March 2003. New Orleans.

Glass, Robert. Tape recording. August 2003. New Orleans.

Hubbard, Don. Tape recording. April 2003. Hubbard Mansion Bed and Breakfast, New Orleans.

Johnson, Lubertha. Tape recording. December 2002. New Orleans.

Jones, Ernest. Tape recording. August 2003. New Orleans.

Landrieu, Maurice (Moon). Tape recording. February 2003. New Orleans.

LeDoux, Jerome. Tape recording. December 2002. New Orleans.

Ola, Antor Ndep. Tape recording. August 2007. New Orleans.

Rahim, Malik (Donald Guyton). Tape recording. December 2002. New Orleans.

Tucker, Robert. Tape recording. April 2003. Hubbard Mansion Bed and Breakfast, New Orleans.

Wilkerson, Robert King (Robert King). Tape recording. December 2002. New Orleans.

Williams, Larry Preston. Tape recording. 19 April 2005. New Orleans.

INDEX

Nazis, 35. *See also* American Nazi Party

NCCF. *See* National Committee to Combat Fascism

Nelson, Davia, 193, 242

Newcomb College of Tulane, 111, 175

New Orleans Black Panthers, xv, xcii, xxiv; in Orleans Parish Prison, 158; women members, 26, 76, 139–40, 156, 175–77. *See also* Brown, Marion; *see also* Guyton, Barbara; *see also* Francois, Althea; *see also* Hodges, Leah; *see also* Powell, Betty; *see also* Bournes, Catherine "Top Cat"; *see also* Young, Elaine "E-Baby"; *see also* National Committee to Combat Fascism; *see* also Headquarters, Panther, New Orleans

New Orleans Legal Assistance Corporation (NOLAC), 57, 59, 227

New Orleans Police Department (NOPD), xiv, xxx, 11, 13, 29, 36, 41, 63, 64, 73, 74, 77, 80, 103, 120, 122, 124, 125, 126, 127, 144, 186, 216, 237. *See also* police, Giarrusso, Clarence; *see also* Giarrusso, Joseph; *see also* Fields, Isreal; *see also* Howard, Melvin; *see also* Williams, Larry Preston

Newton, Huey, xi, xii, xvii, xxviii, 15, 215, 229

Newton, Michael, xiii, 229

New York Times, 24, 61, 66, 69, 76, 77, 78, 85, 94, 110, 233, 234, 235, 257

Ninth Ward, 7, 156, 201, 202, 248, 249, 252, 256. *See also* Lower Ninth Ward

NOLAC. *See* New Orleans Legal Assistance Corporation

NOLA Express, 10, 24, 55, 60, 61, 66, 76, 93, 120, 122, 125, 230, 233, 234, 235, 237, 257

NOPD. *See* New Orleans Police Department

NPR. *See* National Public Radio

O

Ogbar, Jeffery, xii, 229

O'Neal, William, xiv, 20

O'Sullivan, Sgt. Fredrick, 31, 34

Oakland Panther Central Office. *See* Central Office

Ola, Antor Ndep, 198, 258

OPP. *See* Orleans Parish Prison

Orleans Parish Prison (OPP), xxvii, 26, 75, 91, 126, 137, 140–42, 143, 144, 147, 155–58, 161, 175, 180, 225, 227, 232, 232

Orticke, Joseph, 12, 66

Osborn, Royce, xxx, 29, 30, 191–92, 199, 200, 201, 203, 206, 211, 250, 257

P

Panther mythology, xiii

Panther on the Prowl (Howard), xii, 229

Panther Party chapter locations, viii, xxvii–xvii; Angola State Penitentiary, xxviii; Chicago, xiv, xx; Los Angeles, California, xix, xx, xxi, xxii, xxiii, 170; New York City, xxiii, 35, 184; Oakland, California, xix, xxvi, 176, 184, 213, 215, 225. *See also* New Orleans Black Panthers

Panther principles, xxviii, 4, 16, 64, 139, 143, 160, 176, 180, 209

Peace and Freedom Party, xxiv

Pecoul, John, 83, 215, 234

People's Institute for Survival and Beyond, 178, 205, 252, 255

People's Revolutionary Constitutional Convention, 26, 125, 224

Perez, Leander, 18, 100, 140

Picking up the Gun (Anthony), xiv, 229

Piety Street Shootout. *See* Shootout on Piety Street

Pitt, Brad, 201

Plaquemines Parish, 18, 178

Points of Attention. *See* Eight Points of Attention

ORISSA AREND is a mediator, freelance journalist, and psychotherapist in private practice in New Orleans. She has worked as a community organizer with the People's Institute for Survival and Beyond. She currently serves as a member of the Trinity Undoing Racism Network of Trinity Episcopal Church and is a founding member of Community Mediation Services, both located in New Orleans. Arend has written for the *Louisiana Weekly,* the *New Orleans Tribune,* and the *Times-Picayune* for a number of years. This book developed out of a series of columns she wrote for the *Louisiana Weekly* and a compilation of those columns published as *Showdown in Desire: People, Panthers, Piety, and Police: The Story of the Black Panthers in New Orleans*

CURTIS J. AUSTIN is associate professor of history and director of the Center for Black Studies at the University of Southern Mississippi. He is the author of *Up Against the Wall: Violence in the Making and Unmaking of the Black Panther Party* (University of Arkansas Press).

CHARLES E. JONES is associate professor and founding chair of the Department of African-American Studies at Georgia State University. He is the editor of *Black Panther Party Reconsidered* and the recipient of the National Council for Black Studies' Mary McLeod Bethune and Carter G. Woodson Award in 2005.